SEX, SEXUALITY, AND THE

ANTHROPOLOGIST

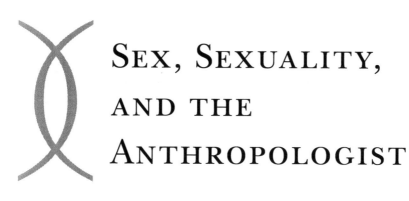

# Sex, Sexuality, and the Anthropologist

*Edited by*

Fran Markowitz and

Michael Ashkenazi

UNIVERSITY OF ILLINOIS PRESS

URBANA AND CHICAGO

Library of Congress Cataloging-in-Publication Data
Sex, sexuality, and the anthropologist / edited by
Fran Markowitz and Michael Ashkenazi.
p.   cm.
Includes bibliographical references.
ISBN 978-0-252-02437-5 (cloth : acid-free paper)
ISBN 978-0-252-06747-1 (pbk. : acid-free paper)
1. Ethnology—Field work.
2. Anthropologists—Sexual behavior.
3. Sex customs—Cross-cultural studies.
4. Sex role—Cross-cultural studies.
I. Markowitz, Fran.
II. Ashkenazi, Michael.
GN346.S48   1999
306.7—ddc21   98-19727
CIP

To Merav

CONTENTS

## ACKNOWLEDGMENTS

The editors wish to express their gratitude to William L. Leap for his insightful critique of the Introduction and helpful suggestions about the entire book. We are also appreciative of the comments offered by Walter Williams on an earlier draft. The volume never would have come to light, however, without the support of Elizabeth Dulany, associate director of the University of Illinois Press, who believed in the project from its inception and guided it over many hurdles. We wish to acknowledge, as well, the expert copyediting of Mary Giles. Most of all, we are grateful to Merav Shavit, who, as a beginning anthropology graduate student in 1993, brought to our attention the problem of "Sex, Sexuality, and the Anthropologist."

INTRODUCTION

# Sexuality and Prevarication in the Praxis of Anthropology

*Michael Ashkenazi and Fran Markowitz*

The genesis of this book occurred a few years ago when a distressed graduate student spoke to us about an unwelcome, unanticipated sexual advance foisted on her at the close of an ethnographic interview. After describing the interview setting, she recounted how, as she rose to leave, the interviewee turned her handshake into a passionate embrace. Then she looked up from her coffee, visibly shaken, and tearfully asked, "What did I do wrong?" "Nothing!" we declared. We explained that the closeness temporarily created during the course of a life history interview is open to interpretation and that a narrator may regard it as an invitation to more intimate contact. "Surely you know that," we added. "No," she replied, "how could I?"

How could she? How did we? Looking for published materials to bolster our words of support and advice led to a dead end. Not one of the field manuals we consulted had even an index listing for "sex" or "sexuality." Worse still, the few times that these subjects were raised in the text they were given short shrift or trivialized. Sexuality in the field was treated as a joke, brushed aside with funny anecdotes about how to avoid "romantic encounters" or embarrassment.

Where did this silence come from? Why were anthropologists, of all people, making light of sexuality—one of the most basic spheres of human interaction (Fisher 1983)? More directly to the point, Why are apprentice anthropologists sent into the field unprepared for sexual advances, to say nothing of boredom, repulsion, disgust, fear, even desire? What is the purpose of such secrecy? How are anthropological pursuits to be served by such a silence?

Sherlock Holmes once said that the fact that the dog did not bark in the night was highly significant. Linguists also recognize that silences, the pauses in speech, may often "say" more than the precise words that are uttered. Thus the silence enshrouding sex in the field must derive from axiomatic issues at the core of the culture that produced anthropology and from its foundations as a science.

Participant observation, the key methodological tool of anthropology, is based on the epistemology of positivist empiricism and assumes that (a) culture can be known by sensual experience. As a corollary to that axiom, anthropologists were to follow the centuries-long tradition of clergy and scholars and depersonalize themselves for fieldwork by emptying their heads and hearts of preconceived notions. Ashkenazi was told by his teachers to be as a fly on the wall; Markowitz was instructed to assume the pose of a little child. To do their job as ethnographers, anthropologists had to become instruments of culture absorption; like litmus paper and thermometers, they had to become passive vessels that were receptive and all-embracing. To that end, they were to rid themselves of enculturation, adult and gendered statuses, and desires, passions, comforts, and disgusts. Otherwise, so science dictated, they would be unable to meet the natives on their turf, to embrace, engulf, absorb, and ultimately know the other culture. Without ever saying so aloud, self-negation was the methodological prerequisite to quality fieldwork.

Two additional interrelated reasons may also help explain the demand for an asexual anthropologist. The first concerns the context in which anthropology arose on two continents. In the United States, after more than two hundred years of systematic pressures on Native Americans to abandon their land and lifeways and often to give up their very lives, the mandate for anthropology that arose under Franz Boas's tutelage was to salvage cultures on the verge of extinction. The creation of an ethnographic record was critical to document and record stories, provisioning and enculturation techniques, songs, dances, religious rites, and social relations before they disappeared. For that task, the anthropologists' preferences and predilections had no place. Each ethnographer had to be the equivalent of the other to ensure correct inscription of each culture in its own right.

In Europe, anthropology's birth from the uncomfortable merger of natural history with sociology and folklore accompanied colonialist expansion and the desire to know (so best to sell to and control) the natives. Self-negation not only followed from Malinowski's prescriptions for building anthropological science but also exempted ethnographers from taking moral stances as they encountered far-from-pristine natives grappling with the contradictions of colonialism. Boasian relativism and British functionalism subtly battled against racist-social evolutionary theories of progress and mankind, but anthropologists were often dupes of the colonialist enterprise. Taking the person out of the anthropologist allowed him (and only secondarily, her) to avoid political confrontations and moral dilemmas. An espousal of the value-neutral stance of science, or the notion of "benevolent universalism" that emphasizes the equivalence of all humans, supports the ethnographic stance of being an empty vessel waiting to be filled with the culture under investigation (Goldweisser 1937).

In this way, the passive anthropologist emerged to join the purposeful missionary, his Janus-faced twin, as capitalist Euro-America standardized its encounters with others. Fueled with the desire to know the other—in order to sell to him, dominate him, convert him, or even dream of alternatives to our own best of all possible worlds—universities, governments, industries, and even charitable organizations demanded gaining a picture of the other—the primitive and savage. The anthropologist was irrelevant to these projects save to capture them for the taxonomist, the administrator, the missionary, the merchant, and the reading public. Consideration of the poignantly personal in a field encounter would thus not only have negated the scientific objectivity of anthropology as a new social science but also interfered with the type of knowledge that other social institutions wished to derive from ethnographic reports—to say nothing of what kind of knowledge the anthropologist wished to transmit in the first place. Given these constraints, it is not surprising that sex, along with most other personal behaviors and desires, was never expressed in anthropological texts. On the rare occasions that it did emerge, sexual or other passions (such as the desire for a special food) were treated within the context of an amusing field anecdote, irrelevant to the "real" research in which the ethnographer was engaged.

Starting somewhere in the late 1960s under the joint influences of structuralism and Marxism as well as the rise of feminism and the rediscovery of hermeneutics, anthropology's discourse opened itself to challenge and contestation. So, too, did its silences, particularly its silent complicity with colonialism and its tacit privileging of heterosexual men and male culture. The 1980s witnessed a proliferation of experimental ethnographic genres and a call for inserting field experiences into the ethnography (Marcus and Cushman 1982). Yet the question of sex in the field remained outside even the most radical calls for disciplinary upheaval and self-critique (Clifford and Marcus, eds. 1986; Marcus and Fischer 1986).

In 1993, however, after witnessing the distress that the lack of attention to sex in fieldwork had brought to one of our most promising students, it took only a matter of moments for us to agree that instead of advancing anthropology as a social science all the silence did was add to anthropology's mystification. Instead of aiding researchers and readers in understanding the ethnographic encounter, it confused and confounded them. Mulling over the contusions and ecstasies of our field experiences and the sexual encounters we had never discussed, we concluded that this silence was antithetical to what we considered the primary aim of anthropology—making accessible and understandable the 'exotic' of other cultures and problematizing the 'naturalness' of our own. Because it obstructed this process and impeded the people attempting to do it, we resolved that the silence was unethical.

Putting theory into practice, we put together a session on "Sex, Sexuality, and the Anthropologist" at the 1994 meetings of the American Anthropological Association and then expanded that session into this volume. Our original aims were modest. We wished to alert anthropology students and seasoned field veterans to the theoretical, methodological, and personal consequences of sexual encounters in the field in order to mitigate against the agonizing, self-blaming experience of our student. The resulting book was to be a supplement to standard field manuals, which even in the 1990s remain stalwartly sex-free. It would move the causes and consequences of sex and sexuality in the field from the silenced peripheries into the contentious center of the discipline's discourse.

But on the way to publication the silence surrounding ethnographers' sexuality broke. Following earlier tentative efforts, most notably Whitehead and Conaway's *Self, Sex, and Gender in Cross-Cultural Fieldwork* (1986) and then Newton's controversial "My Best Informant's Dress" (1993), two pathbreaking collections, Kulick and Willson's *Taboo* (1995) and Lewin and Leap's *Out in the Field* (1996), burst onto the scene. Suddenly anthropologists who had a broad range of ethnographic interests and sexual orientations were publicly challenging the status quo by revealing a long-kept secret—like it or not they are sexed human beings who often cannot help having sexual or sexually tinged encounters as they conduct their research.

Sex and sexuality are not novel topics in anthropology, nor is a consideration of participant-observation as method and epistemology. What is new is linking these two themes in the person of the anthropologist. Our modest aim of breaking the silence has now been redirected into experimentation with a variety of intersections where sexuality and epistemology meet. This book is offered as a challenge to anthropologists to explore the theoretical and methodological results of the effects of sexuality on fieldwork.

## Ethnography and Sexual Positioning

On the first page of his introduction to *Taboo*, Don Kulick states that the volume "is a perhaps inevitable consequence of two events: the posthumous publication of Bronislaw Malinowski's *A Diary in the Strict Sense of the Word* in 1967 and the reflexive turn in the discipline that rose to prominence during the 1980s." We beg to differ and believe that this explanation is both overly simplistic—the "reflexive turn" encompasses a variety of approaches and developments—and internally contradictory. Although the publication of Malinowski's diary caused a self-critical stir in the discipline, its negative reception reinforced the taboo against revelations that would link anthropologists to lust, desires, and disgusts while in the field. What we suggest instead is that a number of intersecting developments have occurred since the mid-1970s that help explain the receptivity of the anthropological community to books on the topic of sex and sexuality linked to its methodology and practitioners.

If anything, the publication of Malinowski's diary in 1967 confirmed what many anthropologists knew: Better to let secrets—especially those enshrouded in sex—remain secret. Although America's youths were experimenting with a sexual revolution, their professors on the same campuses were not quite ready to embrace its spirit. In the wake of the *Diary*'s publication, Malinowski was soundly thrashed, and his ethnographic work almost discredited when his racist, misogynist, and lustful—albeit private—musings while conducting fieldwork were revealed. The *Diary* was an important vehicle for cracking the self-serving, self-confident objectivist stance in anthropology, but it would take several more years to advance the importance of sexuality and sexual positionings within the fieldwork enterprise.

In the following years a confluence of three developments in anthropology occurred that permitted thinking of bringing sex in the field out of the closet, breaking the silences, and proposing altered models that conjoin the ethnographer as person to the process of field research. The three developments were:

1. Twenty years of research moved women, sex roles, gender ideology, and sexuality from the peripheries—what Kulick calls the "sideshow"—of anthropology to its very center. Although Malinowski (1955) and Mead (1963) had made pioneering contributions to the cross-cultural study of sexuality and gender, it would take several more decades of concerted efforts, mainly from feminist and gay and lesbian scholars, to establish gender studies as a legitimate, even mandatory, field of inquiry within anthropology. From the mid-1980s on, courses such as "Culture, Sex and Gender" and "The Cross-Cultural Study of Sex" have become regular offerings in many anthropology departments. Moreover, consideration of gender asymmetry and the symbolic meanings and social roles of males, females, and other genders have become standard fare in most ethnographies. "Sex among the Others" has been a titillating entertainment in anthropology since Bourke (1891), but these representations were carefully sanitized and placed under the rubric of "exotic customs." Making an exploration of heterosexualities, bisexualities, homosexualities—and not exclusively among the others—something anthropologists can and must write about was a critical development that helps account for the acceptance of *Taboo, Out in the Field,* this volume, and others in the 1990s.

2. Inquiries into the cultural meanings and social consequences of sex contributed to the rise of another development in anthropology: de-essentialization of the cultures under study. As Sherry Ortner (1984) has noted, anthropologists during the past decades have found actor-oriented practice theories helpful in accounting for variation within a culture and for contesting monolithic models that do not reflect reality (see also Vayda 1994). The influence of Giddens's and Bourdieu's (1984, 1991; 1977) approaches—not to mention Leach's path-breaking work (1954)—aided anthropologists in deconstructing, casting into doubt, and delimiting the usefulness of the culture concept (Yengoyan 1986). They learned from scientific study, personal encounters, and textual reflections that the "Bongo-Bongo"—the

Mundugumor, the Cherokee, and the Nuer—do not exist except as abstractions. Even as anthropologists used such categorizations, they understood that there are different worlds, events, and realities for different individuals, statuses, and positions. Yet in the beginning of anthropological inquiry, historical nominalism and structural-function-alism gave but one model of synthetic, synchronic description. It took decades to establish that approach as "scientific"; to ensconce anthropology in universities; and to produce texts that responded to, reflected, and advanced that model. Only after its establishment could it be contested. Anthropology can now turn in upon itself not as a form of navel-gazing but to evaluate its past and prospects without fear of being labeled as either nonscientific or insensitive. In other words, the emergence of books such as this volume indicates that the discipline is mature enough for sober (or even lighthearted) self-examination and solid enough to withstand the blows of fashion and political correctness.

Conflict theories, symbolic analysis, theories of practice, and the most recent emphasis on Foucauldian-influenced resistance have challenged and denounced essentialism as the sole paradigm for anthropological inquiry; it is now only one model from among a wider, more varied and fertile field of heuristic devices in the study of culture. These theoretical shifts have been accompanied, perhaps even caused, by anthropologists' confrontations with global-local and state-community intersections, whether in the most remote jungles of Amazonia, the most isolated, icy tundras of eastern Siberia, the most inaccessible chateaux of the French aristocracy, or the most ominous gangs of America's inner cities. The culture concept, and not just anthropology's writing culture, has come under attack as discipline-wide, self-reflection reveals its failure to account for fissures in the cultural fabric and the dynamic relations of power in these holes.

3. Just as their ethnographic inquiries led anthropologists to transform Culture to cultures, so must they recognize that there is no one generic, de-culturated "Anthropologist." Many, as the essays in this volume reflect, have been misled in that regard. Most ethnographers have thus far not changed their self-image to jibe with how they experience and describe natives of the cultures they study—as self-conscious actors. They may experiment with ethnographic genres but usually are reticent to admit to experimenting with the ethnographic experience. The current reflexive turn in anthropology, with its postmodern, new-wave attractiveness, relies more on textual constructions than on prac-

tices in the field (Poewe 1996). With rare exceptions that reflexivity and attached deconstruction of "the anthropologist," beginning with Lévi-Strauss's literary opus *Tristes Tropiques* (1975), derives more from the anthropologist's abstract pondering of the ethnographic venture than from relationships with people in the field. Culture, power, politics, economy, history, philosophy, and humanity are the stuff of such reflexivity.

That stance originates at least in part from how people have been represented in ethnographic fieldwork—as "informants," channels of access to culture. Because they are decidedly not individuals imbued with likable and detestable characteristics, no informant can be the object of an anthropologist's personal desire, distaste, or apathy. Thus, when anthropologists such as Malinowski find themselves filled with longing for informants' slim bodies, attractive good looks, or winning smiles, they shamefully hide those feelings in a personal diary or attempt to repress them altogether (Wengle 1988). Anthropologists strive to overcome carnal thoughts in order to view the natives not as they view themselves. Anthropological reflexivity perpetuates this stance by directing attention to the causes and effects of the cross-cultural enterprise—to French culture while sitting in the middle of the Amazon, to colonialism, to the imbalance of power between the researched and the researcher, and to the nature of knowledge, epistemes, paradigms, and the Panopticon rather than to personal relationships (and most certainly not to erotic relationships) with people in the field.

A recent development mitigating against such reflexivity is that anthropologists as well as their field partners have realized that they are imbued with specific characteristics, or positioned. Abu-Lughod (1991), after Narayan, points to the bias (for good and for bad) in being a "halfie" anthropologist, and certainly natives (such as Chao in this volume) and near-natives (such as Huseby-Darvas in this volume, who lived away from her native Hungary for some thirty years before returning to conduct fieldwork) enter the field with different skills and expectations from their (mainly) American and British counterparts. The agenda of many native, and perhaps near-native and halfie, anthropologists is to decolonialize the discipline and claim it for the people, nation, and political agenda that their position within the culture demands. In their decision to reclaim traditions via anthropology, these native ethnographers announce decidedly positioned stances.

Although pioneers such as Sol Tax (1975) practiced and wrote of "action anthropology," not until the clear agenda of Marcus and Fischer's *Anthropology as Cultural Critique* (1986) articulated a mandate for taking, developing, and defending a stand did "committed anthropology" (Shokeid 1992), "engaged anthropology" (Rappaport 1994), and "militant anthropology" (Scheper-Hughes 1995)—along with feminist anthropology, which had fought for several years for acceptance—emerge as legitimate alternatives to the relativistic-objectivist positioning dominant in the field. These political agendas linked happily with the ascendance of hermeneutics and its attached calls for "thick description," multivocality, and intersubjectivity. Anthropologists and anthropology were developing a sound theoretical base from which to move from stances of passivity and immaturity to adult self-awareness and critical perception.

By the middle of the 1990s anthropologists possessed a history and justification for acting and representing themselves as self-conscious, political, and politicized actors, even in the field (Feldman 1991:13). They are finally beginning to catch up in their presentations of self to the representation of those under study. Social forces, both in and outside of the discipline, mitigated for decades against the personhood, especially the sexed personhood, of anthropologists. But now the felicitous convergence of the discovery of new models and approaches with the establishment of a place in the academy for the study of sex, "which no longer marginalizes discussions of sexuality in science but increasingly views it as being significant in understanding problems of culture, history, and the world system" (Herdt 1994:xii), invites placing themselves within the purview of participant-observation, anthropology's distinguishing method and epistemology. It may still be a risky proposition (see Poewe in this volume), but the time has come to consider if—and if so, how—an anthropologist's personhood, in particular sexed personhood, impedes or promotes ethnographic endeavors—or does both.

Why is the discussion of the sexuality of field ethnographers still risky? By writing about sex, anthropologists expose themselves, their informants, and their partners to the "little dangers" wrapped up in the rubric of personal and professional reputations. In revealing our sexual encounters (not just their "sexual customs")—how we were unwilling dupes in someone else's game of conquest, how we actively pursued sexual relationships, and how we used the field for personal growth and sexual experimentation—anthropologists may jeopardize the integrity of previously published work. Although more than thirty years separates the publication of this volume from that of Malinowski's diary, it would be imprudent to forget that many luminaries in the field challenged his entire corpus of ethnography because of its revelations. Beyond prudishness, another cause for anxiety is writing in an experimental genre that treads the line between "ethnography" and "autobiography" (Hastrup 1992), thereby inviting criticisms of self-indulgence and irresponsibility for combining species that may better be left alone. Finally, discussions of their sexuality may endanger anthropologists' carefully cultivated relationships with informants—"What?! You were carrying on with X all this time and never told me after all the things I've told you!"—as well as cause pain to spouses or lovers who did not share all aspects of the field experience.

We believe that these risks are worth taking. By adding sex and sexuality to discussions of participant-observation, we hope to demystify the field and show it as a process of intersubjective communications that sometimes work and sometimes do not. Sexuality, according to the dictionary, is "the expression of sexual receptivity or interest"; it becomes a key element of this communicative process because our bodies, voices, facial expressions, clothing and accouterments send and receive messages about which we are not always aware. Pheromone research and the biological basis of sexual reproduction notwithstanding, sexuality is culture-, incident-, and person-specific. Moreover, as Karla Poewe tells us in this volume, it "has frequently to do with things other than sexuality, for example with ethnicity, religion, love, alternative consciousness, and new insight." Ignoring its role in the interactions of field ethnographers is dangerous as well as naive. Many of the essays that follow give specific examples of why that is so.

The essays in this book ponder various intersections of sex, sexuality, and the enterprise of fieldwork. The authors were charged with analyzing their experiences from a theoretical perspective to include discussions of desire and passion, the power components of gendered interactions, the temporal nature of the field, and participant-observation as a life-style. Like many of our contemporaries, our hope is that the issues we raise will result in the writing of grounded ethnographies, those that derive from particular encounters and impart a positioned knowledge. We have taken risks in the hope of encouraging the move toward historically deep, politically informed, "full-bodied ethnographies" situated in time, space, and emotion between self-aware, sexed ethnographers and their equally self-conscious, gendered field partners.

## A Call for Grounded Theory

To put this book into a broader context, it is worth asking two fundamental questions: Is sex important enough to be dealt with as a theoretical and empirical issue in anthropology, and what has anthropology, as a social sciences discipline, had to say about sex? Most readers,
we suspect, would answer yes to the first but would need to take a deep
breath and some time to consider the second.

In practice, anthropology as a discipline has rarely dealt with sex
and sexual desire. Anthropologists have, unquestionably, cornered the
market in such ancillary issues as kinship, descent, and marriage, but
most writings on these issues have avoided dealing with sex—human
mating—as a hot and lusty phenomenon. Instead, sanitized sex is
termed "courtship" behavior, "marriage" practices, or "alliance." Human beings can identify all these categories of behavior and engage
in their related practices, yet they are also driven by and engage in
"love," "lust," and "pleasure," emotions or psychobiological states that
anthropologists are apparently ill-equipped to study. Robert J. Smith
once mused (1978) that anthropologists have no grasp on a fundamental human concept, which every normal human being experiences,
called "fun." Similarly, anthropologists find it hard to come to grips
with other sensual and emotional issues such as ecstasy and pleasure,
which, although experienced and even documented (e.g., Macaloon
and Csikszentmihalyi 1983), they do not deal with seriously if at all.
The same is undoubtedly true regarding sex and sexuality, which perhaps in the interest of "scientific objectivity" have been translated from
bodily experience into the theoretical realms of "kinship," "marriage,"
and "alliance." The few classical anthropologists who have tried to
portray sexual attractiveness and the practices of sex did so in "throw-
away papers" hidden in obscure journals and never, ever cited.

But "sexuality" is not "kinship" nor "marriage" nor "alliance"; it is
more and less than all of these concepts. Nor, for that matter, is sex a
purely biological process by which the human species reproduces itself. It is partly a form of entertainment (see, for example, Gregor
1985), partly a means to create and sustain the self, and partly a way
to reproduce and create, display, distribute, and reinforce power. In
these attributes it shares with many realms of human activity and
thought. By burying sexuality in an unseen category because it is also
a facet of other categories and institutions, anthropologists have hidden an area of study from themselves. That is not terribly surprising,

because in most societies sexual behavior—both the mechanics and the associated emotions—is hidden and covert (Friedl 1994). And anthropology has a dismal record of dealing with such hidden phenomena. Organized crime, incest, the very, very rich, and international business, to cite but a few, have been virtually unknown and forbidden territories to anthropologists, no matter how much they affect to deal with the institutions that direct human lives. Why should sex and sexuality be any different?

Like teasing out the meanings of symbols—which anthropologists learned to do with non-Western societies and only later applied to their own—they can and should apply insights learned from searching out other hidden data to the issue of sexuality. By doing so, anthropologists will refuse to accept no-go areas, starting with themselves and their ethnographies.

All the contributors to this book stubbornly demonstrate their dedication to ethnography. As they make their way through field encounters, deal with people and situations they never anticipated, and then return to reflect, they reassess and ultimately celebrate "the attempt to understand another life world using the self as the instrument of knowing" (Ortner 1995:173).

Ethnography demands the grounding of theory in practical action; sensual experience, including but not limited to I/eye-witnessing, does for anthropologists what surveys and statistical analyses accomplish for political scientists, sociologists, and social psychologists. An ethnographer's physical move from the personal to the political to the general and back again gives anthropology its excitement and "really real" essence. But that present-tense involvement also leaves ethnography vulnerable to charges of distortion, manipulation, and violence. Psychology has already taught that it is hard if not impossible to know the self. How much more difficult must be the task of knowing the other?

One way that anthropologists do come to know the other is through unexpected events. The serendipity of fieldwork often provides revelations and directions that could not have been imagined in its planning stages. Certainly, Paul Stoller had no premonition that he would become a sorcerer's apprentice as he set out to study ethnicity in Niger (Stoller and Olkes 1989), nor did Susan Harding (1987) expect to hear the Holy Spirit call her as she prepared for her study of born-again Christianity. Once in the field, these pivotal moments not only charged the researchers, causing them to reassess their role as ethnographers, but also provided firsthand, experiential illumination into alien phenomena that others had told them about but they had barely believed possible. Poignantly faced with the internalization of a bit of the culture that they came to study but not import, Stoller and Harding mounted a decided struggle against "going native." In the process, they turned their doubts into understanding and their bad faith into good. These embodied experiences led them to decouple what were once merely heuristic concepts from theoretical proclamations and replant them on more solid theoretical ground.

In like fashion, Don Kulick (1995:20) points out that sexual experiences in the field hold a promise for epistemological productivity. Being displayed as a sex object and buffeted about in a power play (Huseby-Darvas); propositioned or rebuffed (Salamone, Climo, and Winkelman); exoticized due to one's naked body (Ashkenazi and Rotenberg); inserted into the native gender system (Jones); encountering misconceptions about shared sexual identities (Fitzgerald and Chao); challenged on the grounds of asexuality (Markowitz); or embraced because of sexual activity (Lunsing) provided illuminating moments that pushed each of this volume's contributors to transcend daily data collection tasks and think further about the nature of cross-cultural knowledge.

The sexual encounters we have each experienced and managed lead us to a different notion of culture than that proposed by our forebears. For some, culture remains Kroeber's "superorganic" that supersedes the individual and predetermines both behavior and the meaning of behavior. That concept is most evident in Winkelman's contribution; he shows clearly how his sexuality was misread because his culturally shaped cues were out of place.

But many more essays describe how culture is up for negotiation. After they arrive in the field, anthropologists often select what they deem to be a suitable native role and then learn to manage that artificial or authentic identity (Lewin and Leap, eds. 1996). Meanwhile, natives at various rungs of the social scale, of different genders, and at different times may contest or accommodate this role selection. Culture, in such an experience, is slippery, inconsistent, not necessarily predictable, and internally varied. It is certainly portrayed more saliently by Roger Keesing's (1994) cultural model than by the culture concept.

This book, therefore, is just as much about anthropology as it is about sex, and two general theoretical points emerge from these intersections. First, conventional anthropological wisdom that dictates a genderless stance in ethnographic research is not only untenable but also impossible to sustain. We argue, therefore, that the issue of gendered research must always be addressed; as Foucault (1980) has taught, gender and sex in both the ethnographers' and the natives' life worlds are ideologically immersed social constructs constituted so "that we can never know in advance what will 'count' as sexual in another culture" (Kulick 1995:7). That suggests the importance of ethnographies as well as theories; sexuality must always be a part of the contextualizing process by which ethnographers place themselves in a defined and visible position concerning the two "significant others" in anthropology: natives and readers. For natives, an anthropologist is, willy-nilly, a sexual person, and both anthropologists and natives ought to recognize that fact overtly and negotiate their positions consciously from the start. For readers, the process of recognition and negotiation must be visible so the empirical and theoretical outcomes will be clear and integrated into the published results of the process. By doing so, anthropologists continue the trend started by Geertz (1973) of "thickening" ethnographies and making them valid representations of real activities of real people in which the anthropologist, whether an outsider, a marginal native, a halfie, or a member of the community, is embedded. Second, despite the outpouring of self-castigating critiques of anthropology as a colonialist enterprise, most anthropologists in the late twentieth century are not representatives of overwhelming power, wealth, or other means of coercion. That makes the sexual stance they adopt more a matter of negotiation than intimidation, a common ground rather than one of absolute dominance or the power relations of subordination. With luck and care, both ethnographer and field partner may emerge from fieldwork with enhanced mutual understanding.

That leads to our methodological conclusion: The chapters of this book provide evidence to suggest that ethnographers ought to address the sexual issue proactively, both as an ethnographic tool and as a way of making the "participant" part of participant-observation operational. An anthropologist might not be sexually alert at all times, but sexuality cannot be brushed aside as ethnographers construct their in-the-field persona and draw conclusions from their mounds of data.

Whatever theories have been explored by or derive from the research represented in this volume, they are grounded in the intimacy of experience. And it is the intimacy of experience, ours as individuals and members of what, for lack of a better term, we call a culture, that drives anthropology, particularly as synthetic experiences through television and other media become the staple diet of many. Synthetic experience—whether the censored reports of orthodox anthropology (e.g., compare *Sex and Repression in Savage Society* with *Diary* [Malinowski 1955, 1967]), edited "ethnographic" films, or computer-generated multi-media—does not allow for real intimacy, only the appearance thereof. It is precisely the most intimate issues, such as sexuality, that are edited out, vanished, and made as-if-not. The making of as-if-not bedevils anthropology at all stages. Moreover, synthetic experience is a malleable item. As students, certain issues are not discussed; as fieldworkers, certain things are not to be mentioned; and as exponents of our experience, certain things are not to be published. By synthesizing without consciously acknowledging the manipulation, anthropologists warp the procedure from start to finish.

The usually unsolicited sexual experiences of anthropologists provide insights because they hit where they most hurt. When anthropologists are gazed at and teased or fondled in a sauna, on a village dance floor, in an office, or in a bar, they are vulnerable to both the public and private eye. Their self-confidence falters. They are forced to consider issues that they might have preferred to overlook. In all probability, Mexican gay men would have been invisible to Winkelman had he not been propositioned, Salamone may not have considered the impact of missionaries in the arcane realm of witchcraft had he not felt chastised by them for his sexual adventures, and certainly Ashkenazi and Rotenberg would never have known that social acceptance cancels bodily strangeness had they not ventured into public baths at various stages in their fieldwork. From firsthand sexual contacts with people in the field, anthropologists learn that they are not agents of domination; indeed, they are not in charge. These incidents alert anthropology to the need for amending and revising models of culture and the cultural. Until recently, anthropologists have ignored these challenges, or at least their sexual sources. What this book urges is grounding theory in them.

## Organization of Chapters

Our understanding of the issues drives the organization of this volume. The authors are largely self-selected, but their work represents a cross-section of the anthropological community in areas of theoretical and geographical interest, in years of research, and in background. For more experienced anthropologists, field events are part of a continuum, and they are able to see their experiences as part of the continuing evolution of their lives and careers. Thus, some essays are by experienced fieldworkers and theorists who see themselves, their careers, and their ethnographic ventures through the perspective of time. Others are by beginning anthropologists, for whom heretofore hidden issues of sexuality emerge onto their perception of a critical stage of professional life—entry into the field. The diversity extends also to the personal positioning of the writers. Some are outsiders exploring cultures in which they are strangers, yet others are positioned between two worlds and exploring each—that of natives and that of anthropologists—with reference to the other.

Part 1 examines the experiences of beginning and veteran anthropologists who, following the dictates of orthodoxy, find it lacking as they deal with the conflicting demands of sexuality (in its varied aspects) and field experience. The opening essay exemplifies our earlier conclusions. Rose Jones entered the field to study aspects of social behavior for orthodox reasons (AIDS research). In an orthodox fashion, too, she created for herself a sexless field persona, as was proper by the anthropological canons, only to discover that "they" (the natives, the informants, the field) had different ideas about her sexuality. They were also better placed to insist on their ideas than she was on hers. Jones found that her declared sexual position was unacceptable and that it must be negotiated. She had to cater to and adjust to her hosts' ideas. In the final analysis, she found herself, her relationships with her hosts, and the quality of her fieldwork enhanced precisely because she was sensitized to the nuances and costs of particular sexual stances open to her. It is useful to contrast Jones's evolving position with that of the writer of the final essay in this volume, Wim Lunsing, who started from an opposite point of departure and yet came to many of the same conclusions and results.

Jacob Climo, his career steeped in the orthodox approach to sexual issues in the field, which dictated formal denial of both sexual activity and personal feelings, recalls the difficulties of a conflict between his sexual and his field relations. The discord caused distress and stress to Climo as he tried to come to terms with his repressed sexuality in Mexico. This reflection has caused him to think hard about the general applicability of the denial of sex (seen broadly as sexual activity, sexual relations, and presentation of gender) in the field.

Frank Salamone closes Part 1 by portraying his evolution as an anthropologist—from the footloose adventure of graduate student days to the responsible existence as spouse, father, and master of his craft—which parallels his continuing evolution as a sexual being. His essay demonstrates that trying to maintain an orthodox adherence to the forms of asexual ethnographic presence is not possible.

Read together, Climo and Salamone illustrate how much anthropologists are bound by their natal cultures, no less in the realm of sex than in any other. Neither of these researchers was in any way a liberated anthropologist. Rather, they were strangers attempting to cope, within the strictures of time, gender, and culture, with the sexual aspect of their professional lives. "Anthropologist" does not necessarily equate with "liberated."

In Part 2, Michael Winkleman discusses how the kinds of sexual partners he selected or who selected him emphasized his marginality as an anthropologist. He found soon after beginning research in Mexico that either he had to adapt to others' definitions of himself or be threatened physically and emotionally. His sexual adaptation was only one element in the general difficulties of becoming a fieldworker, but it shows the discomfort engendered by the lack of theoretical tutelage from his discipline.

Michael Ashkenazi and Robert Rotenberg, on either sides of the Eurasian continent, had to work through feelings of discomfort in order to accept new definitions of themselves and their social roles. Their chapter, like Climo's, is less about overt sexual activity than about internal, sexually tinged emotions and feelings aroused by the clash of the behavioral expectations of their natal cultures (in which nudity equalled sexual activity) and those of their hosts, for whom nudity, under the circumstances of public bathing, was hardly a sexual event at all. Their experience struck deeply at personal issues relating to sexuality, concepts of maleness, and identification of nudity with sex and shame.

As anthropologists developed and later shed some of Malinowski's pioneering ideas about fieldwork, they sought and found a role that would justify their embryonic, emerging, partnership with the subjects of their study. This—what Marx would perhaps have excoriated as a form of false consciousness—has been upstaged by halfie anthropologists—the "natives" returning to study their own (Abu-Lughod 1991). Tom Fitzgerald, Antonia Chao, and Éva Huseby-Darvas did so, each in different ways and from different perspectives, and examine their experiences in Part 3.

Significantly, they each found that the basis on which they had constituted their sameness was one the studied population would not accept, and it was the natives who decided which half of the halfie was valid. Fitzgerald, who had been heavily involved in gay issues in the United States, assumed a similarity and therefore community of interest with Scandinavian gays. He was nonplused at being rejected by informants who shared both his sexual orientation and commitment to social action because, upon examination, both commitment and orientation had specific local values and expressions. Common sexual orientation does not, in and of itself, ensure good field rapport. In contrast, Chao found herself uncomfortable in the role assigned her as *P'o* (feminine gay) in Taiwan and only through much groping managed to find, or accept being assigned, two roles that made sense to her informants: "American" and "elder sister." That placed formal limits on her erotic relations with informants while strengthening her rapport with them. In describing the lesbian scene in Taiwan, she demonstrates strongly how same-sex orientations are interpreted in different ways and how formal definitions of those roles impose freedoms and limitations that an anthropologist must comprehend and adapt to.

The degree to which informants (broadly speaking) control the definition of an anthropologist's self increases as the anthropologist is immersed into the community studied. Huseby-Darvas, unlike Chao and Fitzgerald, did not have the luxury of stepping back from the field into a cosmopolitan background where she could assume or not assume an assigned gender or sexual identity. A native of Hungary yet a stranger to the village culture in which she lived and worked, Huseby-Darvas was "on stage" and had to manage her self-display at all times. Doing so strongly limited her ability to resist or accept, without "stepping out of character" (and thus being pushed out of the field), the sexual definitions and their consequences that informants imposed upon her. Huseby-Darvas's experience highlights the impossibility of always managing and controlling a sexual neutrality or even a locally appropriate social role when specific native individuals' interests intervene.

In Part 3, Fran Markowitz's and Wim Lunsing's essays illustrate that not only must ethnographers come to terms with their sexuality in the field but also that consciously coming to terms with it (in Markowitz's case) or actively participating in the sexual life of informants can be productive and beneficial. That is not to say that this approach (one hesitates to use the word *strategy*) is not without hazards. Colleagues and superiors carp, and sources of information may be compromised or refuse cooperation. On the whole, however, these two essays illustrate the potential (and, in their cases, actual) benefits that can accrue both in the external and internal realms from being a sexual person in the field. Externally, both Lunsing and Markowitz had access to, or came across, data that otherwise would not been available to them. Internally, their stress and feelings of loneliness and social and personal frustration were ameliorated and released by forming stable, loving sexual relations. In practicing as social and sexual individuals, they preceded Winkelman's exhortation earlier in this volume—to explore by participation in the sexual realm.

The differences between these two chapters are instructive. Although Markowitz gradually realized that she had to assume a sexual point of view because her Russian-immigrant informants refused to accept any other, Lunsing began by encouraging and exploiting sexual relationships as an element of data collection. Markowitz's experience characterizes a mainstream step in the evolution of ethnographic fieldwork. It demonstrates that even in the folds of orthodox fieldwork approaches, where the researcher is relatively passive and adapts to the requirements of informants' society, there is need to recognize and act upon the sexual element rather than hide it.

Lunsing's implied proposal is far more radical, controversial, and pro-active. His management of his sexuality, refusal to compromise it even in the face of professional objections, and use of it as a research method provide a different model of approaching sex in the field. Although he emphatically states that in many situations flagrantly displaying sexuality can be harmful and must be avoided, he widens potential sexual attitudes to include not only abstinence (which he does not accept) but also wide-reaching, even public, sexuality, which in certain situations may well propel fieldwork forward to greater quality of data, breadth of informants, and speed of access.

Karla Poewe, much more than Malinowski, has been a far-reaching influence in making the hidden, sexualized aspect of anthropology an overt recognized element of the ethnographic experience. As Manda Cesara (1982), she embodies the critique of the ethnographer-as-asexual-being that hallmarked anthropology during the twentieth century. Her comments epitomized a threshold work, for on the one hand she wrote fully and honestly of her inner life, while on the other, because of the strictures of the discipline at the time—as represented by her publisher, something Jones encountered two decades later—she published under a pseudonym. In this volume she constructs a meta-comment on her earlier meta-comment on the process of fieldwork. One of her conclusions—that anthropology needs full-bodied accounts of the field—has served as a guideline for what we argue throughout.

Overall, the following essays suggest a number of main points that must be considered against the background of the theoretical position we discussed in the first part of this introduction.

First, it is clear from all the contributions that the standard or orthodox or patriarchal model of fieldwork, in its sexual aspect, is dead (if it ever had any more than a simulacrum of life). People—informants and interviewees—will not accept the anthropological protestation or presumption that an anthropologist in the field is mentally and culturally devoid of sexuality. In retrospect, that idea is laughable, and it caused sexual reality to go underground.

Second, there is good reason to suggest that this particular stance, because it went largely unexamined and was the product of Christian, white, middle-aged, middle-class males, may well have done the discipline an extreme disservice. It dissociated women, blacks, gays—anyone not of the power-controlling mainstream—from themselves, forced them into an inauthentic mold, and thereby reduced points of view. This had a direct effect on the reliability claims of anthropology, which avows to be a holistic discipline and whose theoretical and empirical value derives from that holism. Holism is not possible when multiple points of view are denied. Moreover, the orthodox stance violated another fundamental methodological tenet central to ethnographic research. It caused fieldworkers to prevaricate about the real process of data collection, affecting the validity of the research to an unknown degree.

Third, the essays that follow suggest strongly that multiple points of view must be considered within the framework of multiple experiences. Salamone discusses research spread over time and several cultures, and Ashkenazi and Rotenberg achronically compare two bathing cultures, both contributions demonstrating how ethnographers must be flexible in approaching the sexual issue. What answers at one point—in time or space—will not answer at another. Salamone's sexuality was perfectly acceptable to his native informants, yet Ashkenazi and Rotenberg's was dismissed completely. As a rule, anthropologists have accepted relativism as a given but not when applied to sex. Relativism, with all its surrounding controversy, must be extended to sex as well, because sex—as orientation, practice, and motive—is such a fundamental human issue.

Fourth, the following discussions illuminate a fact that anthropologists have known, discussed, and yet tended to ignore in many ways: The natives are not dumb—a word used in both its senses. The natives, the people whom anthropologists study and who become grist for their ethnographic descriptions and theoretical vaporings, have voices. Those voices, if one listens, are opinionated, personal ones and have their own agendas. In fact, it is often those agendas that predominate, whether in the form of determining legitimate sexual partners for Climo in Mexico or denying sexuality altogether for Ashkenazi and Rotenberg in Japan and Austria. It, and the natives, make objects of anthropologists for their own manipulation and use. The time when Malinowski could sit comfortably in his tent and order informants to appear before him is long past. Anyone doing so without considering that the natives have their own agendas, and without catering to that agenda, is likely to be faced with a quick "fuck off, Jack." That is a positive development not only because it makes a balanced dialogue of the anthropological exercise but also because that dialogue means, methodologically, that anthropologists are perturbing data to a much lesser degree. Researchers are as much the subjects of their informants as the informants are of them and become part of a fabric that yields, if they observe as carefully as the writers here have done, magnificent rewards.

The breadth of the essays that follow is, ultimately, no more than a skeletal indication of what needs to, and can, be accomplished. The contributions cross-cut a number of anthropological "things." Different geographical areas are represented, as are varying fields of interest, some directly related to sex and gender, others not at all. The theoretical positions are also diverse, as are the researchers' sexual orientations, personal circumstances, and sexual situations they faced during research. We have brought them together because they share a feeling of unease about the way in which anthropology has developed methodologically. The skeleton we have provided, which ranges from a retrospective consideration of "how I could have done things better" to the strong advocacy of a pro-sexual approach to fieldwork, rests on good methodological reasoning and should be expanded by future publications and research.

NOTE

This essay is a combined effort, and the authors' names are listed alphabetically.

## PART 1

# REFLECTIONS: LIFE STAGES AND FIELDS OF DREAMS

1

# Husbands and Lovers: Gender Construction and the Ethnography of Sex Research

*Rose Jones*

Anthropologists have inherited a discourse that not only relegates sex and sexuality to the confessional but also demands that a strict distance be maintained between their sex and sexuality and the sex and sexuality of those they study. Through my experiences in St. Lucia, West Indies, I have become convinced that an anthropologist's sex and sexuality cannot be successfully integrated into the research process unless this discourse is abandoned. I have therefore resisted the temptation to confess and have permitted the boundary between my sex and sexuality and the sex and sexuality of the people with whom I lived to become blurred and distorted. What follows is a chronology of sexual events and experiences that occurred within the context of the ethnographic process. It is also a record of how I used these experiences to generate and assess anthropological data successfully.

## Awakenings: Learning to Unlearn

I went to St. Lucia for the explicit purpose of conducting research on sexually transmitted diseases (STDs), with a focus on HIV/AIDS. Although I left the island with an ample set of STD data, I also departed convinced that the basic tenets of the ethnographic inquiry had to be redirected, particularly that which requires an anthropologist to maintain a boundary between her sex and sexuality and the sex and the sexuality of the people among whom she lives and studies.

When I arrived in St. Lucia, issues of sex and sexuality manifested themselves almost immediately. Before even attempting to compile data for my study, I noticed that topics that seemed to be only marginally connected (or completely disconnected) to sex invariably resulted in sexual comments and insights. If, for example, I made inquiries about gender and economic relations, sexual themes were typically discussed. They were also likely to emerge from conversations regarding ethnicity and class. In general, who one had sex with, who one did not have sex with, who one might have sex with, who one should not have sex with, and the conditions under which one should have sex appeared to assume a central role in how Lucian women and men ordered, conducted, and discussed their lives.

Although I did not expect that issues of sex and sexuality would occupy a central role in my research because I intended to focus on the biomedical and ethnomedical dimensions of STDs, I was, at least initially, delighted by the prospect of integrating sexual data into my research. The data appeared easy to elicit and collect, and in the post-AIDS era of the late 1980s the topics of sex and sexuality were, after a long academic hiatus, once again beginning to captivate the attention of anthropologists. I took comfort in the knowledge that my research would have popular and academic appeal. In all honesty, exotic images of West Indian sexual tales and antics titillated me, infusing me with hope for a successful dissertation and career. What could be more alluring, I pondered, than a dissertation-turned-book filled with data on sexual customs and practices from the West Indies?

What I did not know then was that my aspirations, as well as my avariciousness, were to be both tempered and challenged by the reality of understanding sex and sexuality in Lucian society. The comfort and delight I initially experienced over the prospect of being able to integrate sexual data into my research was, I would come to learn, contingent on the fact that I was collecting data on "them." My sex and sexuality were, I erroneously and naively thought, safely removed from the data-collecting process. Like most anthropologists, I unwittingly embraced the notion that my sex and sexuality were separate from their sex and sexuality. I was to find, however, that the dichotomy between their sexuality and mine was difficult to erect and maintain and in attempting to do so I undermined my ability to collect the data I was charged to collect.

## The First Step: Acquiring a Husband

The first clue concerning the fact that it was going to be problematic to maintain a distance between my sex and sexuality and theirs occurred shortly after I arrived in "Springfield," a rural village on the island's western shore, where I conducted the bulk of my ethnographic research.[1] After settling into the rhythms of village life, I was encouraged by several women in my communal yard to initiate and establish a quasi-economic relationship with an elderly man whose yard abutted ours. He carried water for me, and I began to prepare and serve breakfast and dinner for him in exchange. He eventually began to clean and sweep my portion of the communal yard, while I, in return, shared luxury food items with him. We eventually established a comfortable routine whereby morning and early-evening hours were spent informally discussing household matters and gossiping about village events.

After a few months, the women in my yard began to refer to this old man as my husband (*mawi ou*). Surprised and somewhat confused by their perceptions, I protested. I informed the women that he could not be my husband because I already had one and explained that my husband and I were still very much married, although he remained in the United States. Amused yet clearly confounded by my perception of the husband-wife relationship, the women pointed out that they knew I had a husband. They did, however, pose some leading questions: "Does your husband carry water for you? Does he bring you things to cook? Will he be here to defend you when other men talk bad on you?" I was, of course, forced to concede that my far-away husband did none of these things.

In addition to labor, my adopted husband and I also, as these women's comments foreshadowed, came to exchange important social resources within the community. In particular, he, as do Lucian husbands in general, protected my sexual reputation while I, as do Lucian wives, extended social respect and prestige to him. In St. Lucia as in other West Indian societies, female and male roles and relations are governed and regulated by a gender-based value system largely predicated on the dyad between male reputation and female respect (Wilson 1973). Accordingly, husbands safeguard wives' sexual reputation while wives confer social status on husbands.

On the one occasion when my sexual reputation was, like that of most women, called into question, my adopted husband gallantly and nobly defended it. In a somewhat comical albeit sincere manner, he used a machete to threaten a young man who had been telling people that "he take me on," a euphemism for a sexual liaison. Although the machete challenge produced a humorous response from me and the women in my yard (being near blind he was incapable of actually engaging in a dueling match), his threat did stop the young man from continuing to gossip about our alleged sexual encounter.

Similarly, as a woman who not only regularly attended church services but was also known not to run around "with all kinds of men," I conferred respect upon my adopted husband. The fact that I, a woman who was perceived to have "good morals," accorded respect toward him, as evidenced by the food I prepared for him as well as the time we spent together, necessarily meant that respect was accorded to him by other members of the community.[2] It was always with great delight that I watched him derive community respect through our ascribed relationship. On more than one occasion I heard him tell his buddies at the rum shop that I had brought home store-bought chicken for us, a treat that elicited envy and respect from his cronies.

In acquiring a local husband I came to have a greater understanding of the dynamics of husband-wife roles and relations in Lucian society. In contrast to other types of heterosexual unions, husband and wife unions usually require that social and economic resources be exchanged on a reciprocal and regular basis. Such unions, therefore, tend to provide optimal security. Thus, by assigning me a husband, my female neighbors had effectively solved two imminent problems—the acquisition of male labor and sexual protection—that my U.S. husband, due to his distance, was unable to provide. Similarly, my adopted husband, who had no wife, benefited from the labor I provided as well as the respect I bestowed upon him.

As time passed, I would, however, also come to learn that in addition to establishing and sustaining a primary heterosexual relationship such as the husband-wife alliance, Lucian women and men also tend to generate and secure social and economic resources by establishing sexual and reproductive alliances with multiple partners. In contrast to husband-wife types of unions, multiple sexual and reproductive alliances constitute economic strategies that permit women and men to achieve greater degrees of economic autonomy. Accordingly, sexual unions in Lucian society are often not mutually exclusive, but rather dynamic and flexible. Women and men in Springfield might therefore engage in several sexual unions simultaneously. Thus, unbeknown to me at the time, although I had acquired a husband I was also in search of a male lover.

## The Second Step: Searching for a Male Lover

I realized that the women in my yard were vested in securing a male lover for me several weeks after my U.S. husband departed the island. Subsequent to his one-week visit I made my usual trip to the health center in town to collect data on STDs. There, I was approached by a male health-care worker, a British volunteer with whom I had occasionally socialized.[3] He informed me that several women from Springfield had recently visited him and asked him to make a baby with me. "She is a good woman for you," they apparently told my British friend. "She has a husband who lives in the United States and she doesn't run around with all kinds of men." "She does not," they appear to have emphasized, "have any children yet and neither do you so it would be good for you to make a baby with her."

Somewhat daunted but intrigued by this conversation, I returned to the village that night and related my encounter to the women I suspected of having made the trip to town. "Yes," they sheepishly nodded, they had visited my friend at the clinic. "It is not good," they told me, "you have no baby . . . and we see that your husband has come and gone and still you are without child . . . the man you work with in town," they explained "is good . . . he has a car and money and if you make a baby for him, he will give you money now, and when you reach old age your child will give you money."

As I had done earlier, I protested their attempts to insert me into their gender and sex system. I told the women that bringing a baby back to the United States would create many problems for my husband and me. My husband, I emphasized, would not be pleased if I had a baby by another man. Again, they were amused by my apparent naivete. "You have been gone so long from your home," the women explained, "that surely by now your husband has made many babies with many women . . . you cannot trust men not to do so. You will have trouble and problems only if you do not bring a baby home since your husband will be giving all of his money to the women and children he has got since you left."

The concern these women expressed over the fact that I had failed to establish a sexual and reproductive alliance with a male lover reflects, as did their concern over my not having established a viable husband-wife relationship, their sense of how gender roles and relations transpire. Such roles and relations are predicated on the notion that women and men are mutually dependent, yet they cannot always trust each other. There is, as has been reported for other areas in the West Indies (Sobo 1993), suspicion and mistrust between Lucian women and men, and it is manifested and attenuated through the acquisition of multiple sexual and reproductive alliances.

In Lucian society, women and men often generate and secure social and economic resources through a tripartite scheme in which sex, reproduction, and economics converge. Integral to that scheme are issues concerning parentage. Reproductive alliances provide individuals with the means to secure short-term and long-term economic resources, and there are disparate gender-based strategies for how they secure the resources generated through such reproductive alliances. Such strategies not only explain the suspicion that characterizes male and female sexual relations but also why some women and men are motivated to form multiple sexual and reproductive alliances.

For most men, reproductive alliances generate long-term economic resources. As are gender relations, parent-child relations are based on precepts of interdependency and reciprocity. Thus, when a man provides resources to a woman for the care of a child he has sired with her, that child, according to the basic tenets of parent-child economic relationships, becomes obligated to lend support to him in old age. Conversely, when a man does not (or cannot) provide a woman with the economic resources necessary to ensure his child's welfare, he is not entitled to receive economic support from that child in old age.

Notably, women have a distinct advantage when it comes to defining and regulating father-child economic relations. As is true for the West Indies in general, children in Springfield tend to live in matrifocal households in which men assume transitory domestic roles. Households, particularly early in the life-cycle, are usually composed of a mother and her children. Accordingly, women are, as men in Springfield are quick to point out, in an optimal position for defining and regulating children's burgeoning perceptions of their fathers' economic roles.

When men do not (or cannot) provide women with economic resources for the support of their mutual children, or when women deem that the resources men provide are insufficient, they apprise the children of their fathers' economic failure. Such knowledge means that a child is not obligated to provide economic support to a father in old age. The strategic advantage women have in defining father-child economic relations is, of course, problematic for men, who are consequently inclined to form multiple sexual-reproductive alliances (Jones 1994). Siring children with multiple women in separate households is, in other words, a strategy they can use to safeguard their economic interests in old age. From a male perspective, siring children in multiple households makes it less likely that any one woman will be able to undermine a man's ability to reap economic resources in old age. As one old man explained, "Many children with many different women means you kin to all and at least one of your children bound to help you when you old."

As is true for men, forming multiple sexual and reproductive alliances is also an economic strategy women can employ. In contrast to men, who primarily derive long-term economic resources (e.g., securing economic support from children in old age) from the sexual and reproductive alliances they form, women also derive short-term economic resources from sexual/reproductive alliances. Because fathers are expected to provide mothers with economic resources for child care, women can expect to derive economic benefits from sexual and reproduction alliances early in the life-cycle. As a form of subsistence, childbearing can, however, be a precarious occupation (Handwerker 1989). From a woman's perspective, the more men she has children with, the more likely it is she will receive economic support. If one man cannot provide resources one week another may be able to do so, and if one man can only provide food, another may be able to provide cash. As one woman succinctly explained this scheme, "When one man not feeding his child, you have to get pregnant for a next man in order to feed the first one [child]."

Sexual and reproductive alliances constitute one of the primary means by which women and men in Springfield generate and secure economic resources, and forming multiple sexual and reproductive alliances is fundamental to the way Springfield residents understand and order gender roles and relations. It was, I would eventually come to understand, that dimension of the gender and sex system that had motivated the women in my yard to secure a male lover for me. From their perspective, my U.S. husband was, as Springfield men generally do, promoting his own economic self-interest and siring children with women in multiple households in my absence. Accordingly, the women assumed that I would return to the United States to find that his money was being diverted to several households to which he had established a series of sexual and reproductive ties. In an earnest attempt to compensate for what they perceived to be an imminently bleak economic situation for me, they tried to insert me into their gender system. From their perspective, forming a sexual and reproductive alliance with a male lover was not, as I initially assumed, a matter of sex itself, but rather a matter of economic survival. In forming such an alliance, I could, they reasoned, generate economic resources independent of the ones my husband provided.

## The Third Step: Acquiring a Female Lover

The women in my yard eventually stopped sending potential male lovers my way, and I thought I had sufficiently laid the matter of my sex and sexuality to rest. I was mistaken. Once again I was to discover that the boundary between my sex and sexuality and theirs was not so easily dismissed. And once again I was to learn that this conventional sexual division impeded my ability to understand gender roles and relations in Lucian society, a perspective that was critical for the study of STDs and HIV/AIDS.[4]

For the residents of Springfield, I had, in the six months I lived with them, become *un 'ti madame* (little woman), a title and status that affectionately articulates role ambiguity. From their perspective, I was neither an adult nor a child but somewhere between—a little woman or a little wife. On the one hand, I was adultlike in terms of my marital status, age, and occupation. As a legally wed female approaching thirty and also economically self-reliant, I was, as were other females in the community, an adult. On the other hand, I was also childlike, as evidenced by my fertility status, asexuality, and level of domestic incompetence. As a thirty-year-old female who had borne no children, had yet to establish a viable sexual and reproductive alliance, and was miserably inept at performing simple household chores, I was, like other prepubescent females in the community, childlike.

Although the role and status of little woman was at times frustrating, it was at other times advantageous. Although I lamented the many hours I spent learning to wash my underwear properly, loathed the incessant scoldings I received for improperly preparing and serving meals, and was sometimes embarrassed to be introduced to adult women in other villages as "little woman," I relished the detailed explanations my childlike questions and inquiries generated. In having acquired the dubious status of little woman, I had also unwittingly become a student of Lucian culture. I was mentored, taught, and counseled.

Although I thought that my refusal to cultivate and establish a sexual and reproductive alliance with a male lover ended all discussion and concern with my sex and sexuality, that line of thinking was erroneous. Although the women in my yard accepted, albeit reluctantly and with grave reservations, my refusal to establish an alliance with a male lover, they sought other alternatives for me, their little woman. Thus, near the end of my field stay I found that I was in search of a female lover.

One balmy Saturday evening I attended a community fete where there was much drinking and dancing and found myself arm in arm with a woman who taught me a dance. As the lesson progressed, she became amorous, caressing my hips and thighs. Feeling pangs of discomfort and dubious about how to respond to this novel situation, I fled from the arms of this woman, who I would later learn was *zameze* (a woman who takes female lovers).

The next night in my yard, as had become my habit I related, albeit timidly and awkwardly, my encounter. To my astonishment the women had witnessed it—indeed, they had initiated it. "We saw you run from her," they told me, "but why we do not know . . . if you will not have a baby for a man who is not your husband, why not take a zameze?" "Zameze is," the women gleefully explained, "women's secret . . . some women do take on female lovers, but it's not for men's ears."

Subsequent to this conversation, I had encounters with other zameze. One sent, for example, a friend to speak for her: "Mauvis is liking you a lot . . . she saying I should come by and tell you she sweet on you and thinking you looking nice." Dora, the zameze I met at the dance, did not send anyone to speak for her. In contrast to Mauvis, she was, as she had been at the dance, less subtle and continued to express sexual interest through body language. She winked at me openly and touched me when we met at other community dances.

All in all, I was approached by three zameze. Although I had come to know each as co-workers, neighbors, and social acquaintances, I had not, before the conversation with the women in my yard, known them to be zameze. I had, as my encounters with zameze would prove, formed an erroneous and misleading understanding of the role they assume in Lucian society.

My response to zameze invitations and encounters was withdrawal. Relying upon the ascribed status and role of little woman, I feigned sexual ignorance when advances were made and pretended not to understand nuances in sexual language when talk of me cultivating a zameze liaison was broached. I retreated, as would a child, to the safety and sanctity of the women in my yard when approached and did not attempt, as I had earlier, to explain why I would not or could not take a female lover. For their part, the women in my yard failed to understand my refusal to do so but continued to accept my sexual decisions, regardless of how dubious and irrational they appeared to be.

The encounters I had with the zameze and also the discussions they generated proved invaluable to my research. Through this ethnographic experience and the others that preceded it I came to understand more fully the structure and dynamics of gender roles and relations in Lucian society. As are husbands and male lovers, zameze are defined by precepts contained within the system of gender and sex. In contrast to other women, they are generally older, often approaching menopause, and have already fulfilled expected gender roles; they have generated and secured social and economic resources through stable heterosexual partners, fertility, and the acquisition of male lovers. Because zameze have, in contrast to other women, usually established some degree of economic security, they are permitted more sexual options. Because the notion of women taking women as lovers undermines the system of gender and sex whereby women and men access and secure resources through each other, zameze is "women's secret."

As was the case with securing a husband and searching for a male lover, the zameze option was extended to me because precepts of my sex and sexuality had been inserted into their scheme. In retrospect, I believe the option was extended for several overlapping reasons. First, my failure to establish a reproductive alliance with a male lover and my apparent ability to generate social and economic resources independently made the zameze option, to their way of thinking, a suitable alternative for me. It is a sexual option Lucian women can draw upon given similar social and economic circumstances.

Second, because I had explained that my U.S. husband would not be happy to learn that I had a male lover, as would be evident by the progeny we produced, the zameze option would compensate for my perceived dilemma. As a "woman's secret," he need never know about my sexual habits on the island. Because no progeny would result from such an encounter, my secret would be safe. Inherent to this rationale is the concomitant conviction that humans are sexual creatures. In Lucian society, adults are expected to engage in sexual activities, and those who do not are generally viewed suspiciously and classified as social deviants. Moreover, because the women in my yard knew that I had been sexually active before arriving on the island, as evident by my marital status, they understood that I, like most human beings, was sexual. Thus, extending the zameze option, they apparently reasoned, would allow me to engage in sexual relations and know that my U.S. husband would never learn of my secret.

Third, I suspect that the women considered that I might prefer female lovers. For Lucians, sex and sexuality are not defined dichotomously. Heterosexuality and homosexuality do not constitute, as they typically do in American society, separate sexual identities and entities; rather, there is much overlap between them. In Lucian society, sexuality is more aptly viewed on a continuum that is often determined by stages in the life-cycle, as the case of the zameze suggests (Jones 1994). Thus, it was quite plausible from their perspective that I might engage in sexual relations with both men and women. Even though it would not have been optimal for me to establish a zameze relationship without having first established a reproductive and sexual alliance with a male lover, my role and status as little woman accounted for that breach in tradition.

### Sex and the Anthropologist: The Ethnographic Lesson

My ethnographic experiences with husbands, male lovers, and female lovers lead me to believe that had I not permitted, albeit often unwittingly, precepts of my sex and sexuality to be inserted into the Lucian system of gender and sex I would have come away with a less complete and less accurate understanding of female and male roles and relations in Lucian society, a situation that would have adversely affected my ability to understand STDs there.

Had I not engaged in a quasi-economic relationship with the old man in my yard, a process that resulted in acquiring a local husband, I would not have come to understand the dyad between gender and interdependency. Had I failed to discuss openly the sexual relationship I have with my U.S. husband (e.g., potential problems with bringing home a baby he and I did not make together), I would not have fully understood the sexual strategies women and men in Springfield employ within the reproductive domain. And if I had failed to permit the zameze issue to become personalized I would have failed to understand how Lucians perceive sexuality and how gender and sexuality are defined and influenced by stages in the life-cycle.

Like most anthropologists, I relied on a series of formal and informal interview schedules to gather data. Although the information I collected in that manner produced a wealth of data, it did not provide the same types of insights and knowledge I gained through ethnographic experiences with husbands and lovers. The survey data only provided a script or blueprint. Although the structure of the Lucian system of gender and sex manifested itself in the survey data, the dynamics of the system were not revealed through such inquiries (Bolton 1995; Parker, Herdt, and Carballo 1991).

Although I had, for example, documented the term *zameze* in survey data before the dance at which I encountered Dora, it was only through interactions with zameze and the dialogue these experiences set in motion that I came to understand the concept fully and accurately. In the survey data, for example, I asked a representative sample of Springfield residents, stratified by age and gender, to define zameze. Without exception they all responded "a woman who loves other women" or "a lesbian." Although those definitions are technically correct, they can also promote a misleading perspective, as I was guilty of doing. In particular, zameze is not, as I initially concluded from the survey data, synonymous with the concept of "lesbian" as it is commonly understood in the United States. When all respondents reported that the zameze was lesbian, I erroneously concluded that sexual classification was mutually exclusive.

It is important to realize that the insight I gained into the vital role of husbands and lovers in Lucian society was manifested in the field. I was initially delighted to collect data on "their" sex and sexuality and often unsettled by their attempts to sexualize me. I came to realize, however, that my understanding of "them" was largely contingent on their understanding of me. My knowledge of the system of gender and sex in their society derived more from the fact that precepts of my sex and sexuality were being inserted into that system than from the multiple surveys I was simultaneously collecting.

In particular, I was apprehensive about relying on data obtained in a manner that deviated from anthropology's sexual discourse. Although I had successfully collected the data I sought, I had, albeit often unwittingly, permitted the boundary between my sex and sexuality and theirs to become distorted. Even at that point in my fledgling career I implicitly understood the academic risks of permitting an anthropologist's sex and sexuality to assume a visible role in the data-collecting process. Because my field concerns have become a reality, I have concluded that the discipline's sexual discourse must be redirected. Had I constructed and maintained a boundary between their sex and sexuality and mine—the critical issue challenging the discipline—I would have come away with a less accurate, perhaps erroneous, understanding of female and male sexual roles and relations in Lucian society.

## Sex and the Anthropologist: Rethinking the Discourse

In the years since I completed my doctoral research I have come to realize that the anxiety I experienced in the field over permitting my sex and sexuality to be integrated into the data-collecting process was, unfortunately, warranted. In response to a solicitation for articles on ethnography and sex research I submitted the ethnographic research recounted here to a prestigious journal. In declining to publish my submission, one reviewer articulated the sentiments of two others and questioned my data and research methods because my sex and sexuality had assumed an active role in the ethnographic process. In recommending that my article not be published, the reviewer wrote: "Although I appreciate the author's candidness about her [ethnographic] experiences [including] . . . her discovery that female lovers would approach her . . . [this] do[es] not need to be recounted in the *active voice*. Some researchers may be concerned about the ethics of that [and] since the author may have a long and interesting career, she may wish to preserve some *anonymity*" (emphasis added).

As I initially suspected, it appears that my credibility and career would be enhanced if, as the reviewer suggested, I would adopt a passive voice and assume an anonymous persona. In essence, the reviewer was demanding that I embrace anthropology's conventional sexual discourse—that which separates our sex and sexuality from theirs. Although it would have been relatively easy for me to do so, erasure of my sex and sexuality from the research would have been unethical, misleading, and counterproductive. Rather than removing the ethnographer from the ethnography, I believe it is time that the ethnographer be integrated into the ethnography. I also believe that anthropology's sexual discourse should be reevaluated, a task that has not been seriously or earnestly undertaken since the discourse on sex was developed during the late nineteenth and early twentieth centuries. It was during that period when anthropology was beginning to emerge as a viable academic discipline, that the notion that "our" sex and sexuality being separate and distant from "their" sex and sexuality was defined and legitimated. That dual concept emanated largely from the work of social evolutionists (Bachofen 1861; Morgan 1978[1878]). Arguing that societies evolve through a series of progressive stages of development, social evolutionists posited that social progress be measured through sexuality and that social progress was contingent on sexual lasciviousness being transformed into sexual control.

Lewis Henry Morgan's work effectively illustrates how the sexual dyad between "us" and "them" came to be defined. In *Ancient Society*, he proposed a fifteen-stage evolutionary scheme. Ranking societies from "Promiscuous Intercourse," the "lowest conceivable stage of savagery" to the "Monogamian Family," the apex of the social scale, Morgan advanced a sexual scheme that separated various cultures into sexual categories and advanced the notion that "our" sex and sexuality is separate from "theirs."

Although anthropological research on sex and sexuality was greatly transformed through the ethnographies of Malinowski (1929) and Mead (1961[1929]), their work, like that of the social evolutionists, embraced and promoted a dual view of sex and sexuality. Malinowski perpetuated, for example, the natural versus civilized sexual dichotomy. By contrasting the carefree, nonauthoritarian father-son relationships among the Trobriand Islanders to those of the authoritarian, neurotic, father-son relationships in Europe, Malinowski embraced a sexual dichotomy in which "western culture is [considered] complex and veiled, [while] Trobriand culture [is considered] simple and direct" (Fisher 1980:170). Accordingly, the distance between "our" sex and sexuality and "theirs" was largely affirmed (Caplan, ed. 1987; Fisher 1980; Weeks 1986:22). Mead's work also promoted the notion of a distance in sex and sexuality. In *Coming of Age in Samoa*, she, like Malinowski, implicitly advanced the natural versus civilized ("them" versus "us") dichotomy. As Jeffrey Weeks (1986:39) notes, "One of the attractions of her [Mead's] portrayal of Samoan life was precisely the idea that Samoans were in some indefinable sense . . . closer to nature than contemporary Americans."

Subsequent to Malinowski and Mead's work, anthropological sex research took a long hiatus, one that would not seriously be awakened until the onset of the HIV/AIDS epidemic in the late 1980s. Although anthropologists continued to collect data on sex and sexuality (Davis and Whitten 1987), sex did not constitute a primary area of focus or interest (Caplan, ed. 1987:13; Whitehead 1986:109). Consequently, the dual view was neither questioned nor challenged.

It was during the 1960s, a time of sexual awakenings in the United States, that interest in anthropological sex research was rekindled. Recognizing that sex had been relegated to a status "second only to basket weaving" (Associated Press 1975:23), the first plenary session on human sexual behavior was organized by the American Anthropological Association in 1961 (Davis and Whitten 1987:70). One of the most significant, albeit unrealized, effects of this rekindled interest was a dialogue that examined the role anthropologists assume in sex research. In particular, attention was accorded to issues concerning personal and disciplinary biases and prejudices. For the first time, anthropologists began to discuss openly the degree to which personal sexual biases had adversely affected research. Miriam Slater, for example, conceded that she had not collected data on sex while conducting research in the West Indies because "[if] I had asked them about their sexual practices, they would have asked me and my husband about ours" (Associated Press 1975:23). Indeed, the boundary that separated "our" sex and sexuality from "their" sex and sexuality appeared to have become a basic tenet of ethnographic research.

Through such revelations it became clear that sex and sex research were uniquely problematic in spite of the discipline's commitment to cultural relativism and rejection of ethnocentrism. As Frayser (1985:13–14) comments, "Americans are ambivalent in their attitudes about sex. This general ambivalence about sex has hampered the scientific study of sexuality. Researchers are scientists, but they are also members of American culture and are subject to many of the beliefs of the general public."

Anthropologists soon began to link personal sexual bias to the discipline (Broude and Greene 1976:411; Hovedt 1983:14; Marshall and Suggs 1971:xii). Noting that research on sex and sexuality could jeopardize or compromise a professional career (Broude and Greene 1976:636; Davis and Whitten 1987:72; Frayser 1985:13), anthropologists who had studied those topics openly discussed being ridiculed by colleagues (Suggs and Marshall 1971:220).

Although such insights offered a rich context for evaluating the sexual discourse anthropology had created as well as anthropologists' role in sex research, these issues and the fledging dialogues they generated were eventually muted and abandoned (Jones 1994). Consequently, the dichotomy and distance between "our" sex and sexuality and "theirs" continued. The few anthropologists who challenged and deviated from that discourse (Cesara 1982; Donner 1982) typically did so anonymously.

Although the HIV/AIDS epidemic once again placed issues of sex and sexuality at the forefront, sex research remains at an embryonic stage of development. The discourse created by the social evolutionists in the nineteenth century and legitimated by Malinowski and Mead in the twentieth remains largely intact. Anthropologists are still expected to maintain a boundary between their sex and sexuality and those they study, and the discipline continues to be biased against sex research and sex researchers (Abramson 1990:149; Zick and Temoshok 1986:77).

## Reflections and Conclusions

My research experiences in St. Lucia convinced me that the conventional boundary that isolates and separates "our" sex and sexuality from "their" sex and sexuality must be rethought and redirected. That anthropology and anthropologists have permitted a discourse—one notably problematic and long recognized as being infused with personal, disciplinary, and cultural biases—to continue without reproach or redress is unacceptable.

Although the prospect of critically evaluating anthropological sex research is disturbing to some because it requires personalizing sex and calls the basic tenets of the discipline into question, it is critical that such a process be set in motion. Continuing to demand that anthropologists remove their sex and sexuality from the ethnographic process and erecting boundaries between "our" sex and sexuality and "theirs" make a mockery of the discipline. In addition to obfuscating theoretical development, such an approach promotes prejudices and biases, which in turn conflict with anthropology's philosophy and pedagogy.

Although I went to St. Lucia to learn about "them," I found that was impossible without also permitting them to learn about me. The women in Springfield did not allow me to erect or maintain a boundary between their sex and sexuality and mine, and it was equally clear that my initial attempts to do so adversely affected my ability to collect the data I sought. By allowing myself, albeit often unwittingly and reluctantly, to be inserted into their gender and sex system I eventually came to understand the structure and dynamics of gender roles and relations in Lucian society, a perspective that proved inextricable to collecting data on STDs and HIV.

Despite the attractiveness of postmodernism and reflexivity for anthropologists struggling with dilemmas of colonialism, exploitation, and the subaltern, the intersubjectivity of self with other continues to be tacitly forbidden in anthropological studies of sex and sexuality.[5] That the discipline would still require anthropologists to recreate and rewrite their ethnographic experiences so the boundary between "our" sex and sexuality and "theirs" continue to be maintained is unethical as well as unconscionable. Anthropology, long renowned for objectivity and sensitivity and committed to empowering others and creating a cacophony of diversity, is, it would appear, the same discipline that would seek to suppress and oppress its own.

NOTES

Research was conducted in conjunction with a project concerning fertility and demographic transition in the West Indies. It was supported by NSF Grant BNS 8804719 (W. Penn Handwerker, PI). The opinions, findings, and conclusions expressed in this essay do not necessarily reflect those of the National Science Foundation.

I extend my deepest and most sincere appreciation to the people of St. Lucia, particularly the women and men of Springfield. They taught me much more than is contained in these pages. I am grateful to W. Penn Handwerker, Marsha Prior, and Karen Kleinfelder for reading early drafts of this essay. Their individual and collective comments and insights were helpful and instructive. I am also grateful to Fran Markowitz and Mike Ashkenazi for helpful editorial comments and assistance.

1. Springfield is, as are all names and locales in this essay, a pseudonym. Notably, Springfield is the name several women suggested I use to refer to their village because "it is a long-ago name."

2. For Lucian women, respect is primarily measured according to sexual history/activity. The madame, or wife is typically accorded the highest respect, whereas the *jamete*, a woman who openly has sex and babies with many different men, is generally accorded the lowest social respect (Jones 1994).

3. The national identity of this volunteer has been altered to protect his anonymity.

4. In St. Lucia as in the vast majority of other West Indian societies HIV/AIDS is primarily spread through heterosexual contact; other patterns of trans-

mission, particularly that which occurs through needle-sharing and blood transfusions, were negligible at the time of research.

5. This sentence was written by Fran Markowitz. An exception concerns the work of gay and lesbian anthropologists who are using the reflexive narrative to reexamine the discipline's traditional discourse on sex and sexuality (Lewin and Leap, eds. 1996).

2

# A Memory of Intimacy in Liminal Space
*Jacob Climo*

In an important sense anthropology's long fascination and capacity to understand the sexual other ultimately depends on anthropologists' willingness to engage in self-examination: How can ethnographers expect to inquire about the sexuality of the self and the other, increasingly a central task, if they do not have the courage to confront their own? Richard Shweder, for example, argues that good ethnography is a kind of causistry, an intellectual exorcism in which ethnographers are wrenched out of themselves:

> Since there is always some point of view from which things seem alike, and some other point of view from which things seem different, the causistry is in how the ethnographer chooses to portray the apparent differences between self and other. The choices are limited. Either the other is the same as us and the differences are merely apparent, superficial or trivial, or the other is other than us and the differences are real, deep, and important . . . when it comes to the best ethnographies of the 1970s and 80s . . . in each case there is a deliberate challenge to our sense of self, as the difference between self and other is either celebrated, elevated, or denied. (1986:39)

In fact, although the self/other dichotomy may play an important role in ethnographic theory (Crapanzano 1980, 1994) it rarely accounts for the variety of "others" present in the field. The decision to conduct concerted field research with one group of others does not account for the complexity of those who occupy many local situations. An ethnographer who reduces the disparate voices of the field to a single dialogue with the other has certainly oversimplified the field-worker's role, and that becomes a special problem when considering the ethnographer as a sexual subject.

Octavio Paz, a Mexican philosopher, has observed that romantic love, a key motive for sexual relationships, requires by definition the social improbability and incompatibility of the partners—in ethnographic terms, their cultural otherness:

> To realize itself, love must violate the laws of our world. It is scandalous and disorderly, a transgression committed by two stars that break out of their predestined orbit and rush together in the midst of space. The romantic expression of love, which implies a breaking away and a catastrophe, is the only one we know today because everything in our society prevents love from being a free choice. We have to adjust our profoundest affections to the image of what our social group approves in a woman. It is difficult to love persons of other races, cultures, or classes, even though it is perfectly possible. (1961:198)

In complex field situations love and sexual relationships often parallel or correspond to the ethnographer's work and interest in the other, hence the convergence of intellectual and romantic interests may lead to sexual relationships with others in the culture under investigation. For a variety of reasons, the emotional and sexual desires that govern an anthropologist's conduct in the field may also lead to sexual and love relationships with others not in the group under investigation, among people who would be improbable, inappropriate, or even forbidden in both their home culture and the culture they study.

Anthropologists tend to remember their fieldwork either implicitly or explicitly as a rite of passage (Abbott 1982) that includes, first, a stage of detachment from previous statuses; second, a transition or liminal phase, a nebulous period corresponding to fieldwork itself (Wengle 1988:5) and characterized by symbolic status-death and an absence of the traits from the past and future; and, third, a reintegration phase that marks the end of the status passage and the inclusion of the individual in a new position that carries new rights and duties.

Time and distance from this field experience have enabled me to construct a bridge between the past and the present, yet for several reasons following Turner's (1974) and Wengle's (1988) elaborations I prefer to identify the events as transpiring in liminal social space. First, memories are nebulous, and reconstructing them suspends a normal sense of chronological time and space. Liminality is also characterized by a lack of past and future status; it is a condition of paradox, ambiguity, contradiction, individual isolation, and symbolic social death. Liminal social space suggests a breakdown of cognitive schematic frameworks; an absence of status, anonymity, sexual continence, or excess; loss of a sense of self and identity; emotional pressure and collapse; the stripping of ego defenses and a heightened sense of vulnerability and suggestibility; and, as Wengle notes, a willingness to accept pain and suffering and be unselfish, humble, and obedient. An individual's sense of identity in liminal social space depends significantly on reactions from other people. The individual desires autonomy, independence, and growth through status mobility. Yet there is also dependence on a "sacra," the ritual and esoteric knowledge of the larger group (in anthropology, the discipline of fieldwork itself) that provides a larger framework of meaning. Without a sense of relatedness to another human who is relatively similar, the sense of identity collapses (Wengle).

As I reconstruct it, my field experience provided a social haven, a liminal space, where my family and community were absent and unknown. Although such intimate relationships transpire in liminal social space, they nevertheless reveal personal values, and their impact in shaping a new identity can be profound. The enduring emotions these memories still evoke attest to the power of the past in the present. Although it is a difficult process, reconstructing the past permits me to identify some cultural and psychological attitudes I brought to the field about sexuality, and thus my understanding of intimacy in liminal space might be instructive to the present ethnographic enterprise.

## The Background

Over many years my sexual life involved an effort to express freedom from a confining childhood filled with frustration and ambivalence about my development as an American Jewish male. The traditional American Jewish ideal requires religious endogamy. Dating and marrying Jewish women is required, whereas marrying Christian women is a cultural taboo. A major difficulty in my development centered on that conflict. On the one hand, my family approved of secular education as a means of upward mobility; on the other hand, Christian women were forbidden.

Perhaps the best analogy for my experience is Philip Roth's novel *Portnoy's Complaint,* in which sexuality and ethnicity first come together explicitly in "The Jewboy" as opposed to "The Nice Jewish Boy" (Gottfried 1988:38–39), terms that designate Roth's understanding of the dilemma in American Jewish masculinity. "The Jewboy (with all that word signifies to Jew and Gentile alike about aggression, appetite, and marginality) and 'the Nice Jewish Boy' (and what that epithet implies about repression, respectability, and social acceptance) . . . were the Abel and Cain of my own respectable middle-class background" (Roth 1985:161–62).

According to Gottfried (1988:39), Roth's protagonist Alexander Portnoy is required to be both The Nice Jewish Boy, a gentleman, respectful and naively helpful to women, and The Jewboy, who looks for sexual intercourse with non-Jewish girls. But he cannot be both. "What makes men of boys, Portnoy believes is the capacity to 'be bad—and enjoy it . . . to be able to stop being a Jewish mother's well-behaved son and let the Jewboy in himself go.' In the context of the novel this primarily means eating what is forbidden, whether it is unkosher meat. . . . or an unkosher woman, a *shikse,* without guilt."

As Maurice Charney (1981:124) explains the desire to achieve manhood by breaking the sexual taboo, "A guiltless, spontaneous sexuality becomes the ideal of the guilty, who seem to forget that it is their guilt that endows forbidden sexuality with such exciting resonance. It is only through guilt that sex can be felt so intensely, since guilt makes sex a cultural, ideational, cognitive artifact and not simply a physical transaction."

By the end of college I met and fell in love with my opposite, an attractive Christian whose father, a not totally successful businessman, was my father's counterpart: an anti-Semitic urban Christian. Although Kym's last name sounded Jewish it was German. She brought me home, and at dinner, because in public I am so much The Nice Jewish Boy, her father forgave my being Jewish. "I suppose we have to accept the unethical Jewish businessmen since they donate so much money to the university," he observed. I stared at Kym, and my jaw dropped. "Just smile, we'll be out of here soon," her look communicated. And so we were.

After college I felt I had three choices: I could die in Vietnam, take drugs and make sandals in California, or become an anthropology graduate student. On learning that I had chosen the latter, a close friend of my family's said, "You are looking for your Jewish roots indirectly, seeking your Jewish identity in anthropology by studying Indians, a circuitous route; but that is not your problem. Your problem is that you lack faith; you don't really believe you will find your identity at all. And maybe you fear that if and when you do find it you will not love it."

When I was an undistinguished graduate student reaching the end of coursework my professors did what any self-respecting department must do—sent me to the field. In my new status as an objective participant-observer I went off to a country where the other knew themselves fairly well—at least so I thought. They had some notion of how to deal with their sexuality, but they certainly were not prepared for mine.

## The Field

Finding my Jewish background impossible to eliminate, my anthropology professor decided that it would be a smart strategy to involve me in something urban and Jewish. My advisor remembered that two years earlier in a Mexican city he had noticed that a few Jewish merchants and some other people were wearing Stars of David. Accordingly, I was sent to investigate something resembling a Jewish sect, poor urban people whose personal and family conflicts had motivated them to leave the Catholic Church. The group of fifty or sixty individuals ranged in age from an old man in his eighties and a few women in their seventies to teenagers and some young adults who were especially friendly with me, a self-supporting American student.

The Jewish merchants were no longer there, but they had left a legacy of symbols and customs still followed by this sect of Pentecostal Protestants in an otherwise Catholic city. They used kosher wine from Central city, wore Stars of David, and celebrated the Sabbath on Saturday. They also had a strong feeling for Israel and for Jews. They called themselves spiritual Jews (*Judios espirituales*) rather than Jews of the flesh (*Judios carnales*). Aside from that, they were like other Protestant fundamentalists, believing in Jesus Christ but with a twist: They took communion with matzoh imported from Israel. They welcomed me into their church and homes, and I quickly learned to sing their melodies and the Psalms in Spanish as I participated in their celebrations.

It was one of the happiest times in my life. I rented a room for $2 a day in a small hotel located on a main street that ended up the coast. The hotel had three floors and no elevators, and my room was on the second floor at the top of a wide marble staircase. It had a bed and a bathroom with a shower. A sliding glass door opened onto a balcony that faced the ocean across the street.

People didn't swim in the water, which was rumored to be full of sharks. But fishermen went out in boats every morning, and the view from my window was the most glorious I'd ever seen. I loved my accommodations but could not stay there between one and four in the afternoon because the sun came over the water then, and the room became unbearably hot.

It began to feel like "my city," with its smell of salt air and clear water. I lay in bed in the evening, listening to the sound of the waves splashing against the shore, lapping, then flowing backward. In such quiet moments I felt an inner peace I had never known. The motion soothed me, and even my desire for rebellion turned calm. It was also a time of freedom. I was away from my family and the university. Both had oppressed me.

I made friends with local tourist shop owners and some of the fishermen and took buses to visit people from the religious group in their houses inland. I also spent hours meeting people in restaurants, bars, and cafes. My favorite restaurant was a few blocks from the hotel, and I learned to eat local food in nearby family restaurants. They served eggs sunny-side up, along with refried beans and rice, jalapeños, tortillas, and cola or strong coffee. I ate hamburgers or beefsteak and onions and devoured fresh juices from every delicious tropical fruit. Cantaloupe and grapefruit were my favorites, but I also drank juice from mangos, papayas, tamarinds, pineapples, watermelons, and oranges. I liked a popular cold drink called Horchata made with raw rice and vanilla and always ate flan—custard covered with burnt sugar—for dessert.

During weekday mornings and in the afternoons I would interview my "brothers and sisters" from the religious community in their homes. But on Friday and Saturday nights I met them at religious services held in the small, single-room Pentecostal church. When we arrived on Friday nights to open the church's door it was so hot inside that we had to wait at least twenty minutes before entering.

On week nights I loved walking along the pier near my hotel because it had a red light district. I made the acquaintance of a group of prostitutes and had almost decided to study them but could not persuade the woman who managed the house to allow them to talk to me or take a walk with me. They were too frightened. I was nervous also, filled with anxiety and frustration because the girls always invited me to have sex. And I was willing. Great desire drew me to one woman in particular; she was exotic, different, mysterious, and Christian.

Although I felt guilty for feeling such desire, I didn't allow myself to have sex with her. I was frightened and ashamed. The girls were fourteen or fifteen, and most couldn't or wouldn't talk much about themselves. Three of them told me variations on the same story, portraying themselves as victims in a ruthless, callous world. They said they had run from village homes where they suffered hunger, poverty, and physical and sexual abuse, and in the city the house of prostitution was the only home they knew. The house men protected them from abuse by clients. I was amazed that a prostitute could be so attached to her "home" and that the "house mother" could be so concerned and strict about her welfare and behavior. In one of my fantasies I would seduce the girl and convince her to leave the house. We would fall in love. I would enroll her in a school in the States. My family would accept her.

Several weeks into my research with the Pentecostals I received a call from Kym. Her voice sounded strained. She was coming to visit. I told the hotel owner that my wife would be visiting so he would not object when she stayed in my room. The day after she arrived we attended a spiritualist healing meeting that a hotel acquaintance had told me about. I had not yet visited such a ceremony, but, more important, I did not want to introduce Kym to the Pentecostals. First, I had told them I was not married. Living with Kym in the hotel would be totally inappropriate, an affront to their system of beliefs, and I feared that my ability to continue working with them would be threatened. At the very least they would question my moral status. Second, the fact that Kym was Christian was a major problem for me, as I feared it would be for them. I had told them that I was a Jew of the flesh, a role with which I felt satisfied as an anthropologist because they called themselves Jews of the spirit. I was in the ballpark of their ideological universe, similar yet not identical. The older members remembered when Jews like me had lived in the city. They accepted me as a Jew, took me to their services without trying to convert me, told me of their political intrigues, and welcomed me into their homes. Because I was afraid that Kym's Christianity would jeopardize my status in the group I avoided any potential problems by keeping her away from them.

Most of the participants at the healing group were poor and pregnant. Their extended bellies and swollen ankles spoke of their need for attention. The women spiritualists nurtured them by rubbing their bodies and legs with oils and scents, and then they chanted and brushed and hit them gently with palm branches. As they massaged those who sought healing, they spoke in tones of kindness and friendship.

I became skeptical as I sat watching the two men who controlled the healing ceremony. The first seemed quiet and did not involve himself in the general cleansing ritual, but only with each woman as she walked up for advice. He sat in the middle of a small group on a wooden chair and encouraged each to come forward, one at a time. Then he would put his hands on her shoulders and speak softly. In a kind of a personal consultation he was providing help and encouragement.

But the second healer, who assumed to know in advance what people needed and why they were there, seemed to be running a much more questionable ceremony. He would extend his hands as if laying them on a piano and focus them on a specific person in the semicircle that faced him. He would then push his hands forward and shake them, pointing at that individual. He made a loud sound—"whoosh-shsh"—and the person would assume a kind of trance, often staring off in a daze and seeming dizzy or bewildered. Then, within everyone's hearing, he would ask questions about their problems. The subject would respond from the trance.

After I observed what he was doing I developed a stomachache similar to that I had experienced as a teenager in synagogue with my father, anticipating being called up for the honor of reading the Torah. I always had a moment of anxiety before they asked me. Now I felt the same gnawing stomach cramp. What, I thought, if he were to do that to me? I became nervous and leaned over to ask Kym if she wanted to stay much longer. Maybe she was ready to leave. But I was too late.

Before I realized what the healer was doing, I heard the whooshing sound and, looking up, saw he had turned his hands on me and was looking directly at me and making the sound. I could see drops of white spittle cling to his chin as he licked his lips to do it again. I was stuck. I broke into a cold sweat and thought, What am I going to do? Without understanding how or why, I became afraid that he would take advantage of me. In desperation, I pretended to go into a trance. Imitating the others, I moved my head around a little as if I felt dizzy, and the healer asked in a loud, clear voice, "What is your mission?"

I began with my anthropology answer: "I am visiting to try to understand how you heal and help people." What a fraud, I thought as I said it, that man is turning his attention to me because he wants money. Of all the people there he seemed the least helpful. When I had ceased talking the healer said, "I bet you're thinking that I'm just try-ing to take money from you." His ability to know what I was thinking disturbed me greatly.

"Well I want you to know you're wrong," the healer continued. "We are here to help in any way we possibly can. We are not doing this in order to get rich. Look behind you at the door." I turned and he said, "You see those baskets on the ledge of the door, those baskets are for donations. People who come here can donate whatever they want, whatever they feel they can share with us. There is no price. And if a person can't pay they don't have to pay."

As he spoke, I felt ashamed because I realized that he was telling me the truth. I nodded. I must have put my head down because a strange fatigue came over me, and I heard a soft, low hum.

He looked at Kym and asked, "Is she your wife?"

"She is my girlfriend," I replied.

"Do you have trouble copulating with her?"

"No," I mumbled, realizing the reason men came to him and feel-ing pleased to have discovered an ethnographic reality.

"Well, if you have any problems," he continued, "I want you to feel comfortable to come here and tell us because we will do everything in our power to help you with those problems." I promised I would come.

I thought the healer had turned his attention to someone else even though his distant-sounding voice kept questioning me. Quietly, I be-gan to retreat into myself. I sank into a trance and heard my voice, talking from a distance. I heard myself speaking Spanish fluently. I was talking freely about my relationship with Kym. I was saying:

We took a class together. She finished her quiz early. There was some-thing about the way she moved her body. She walked to the door but then turned back and looked at me for an instant. She was beautiful, slender with a pale, white skin, light brown hair with red highlights, and thick, long hair falling over her shoulders. Her dark-green eyes sparkled with life; when she looked at me they said something that ignited me. After the next class I walked up to her and said I thought the way she had looked at me indicated that maybe she wanted to meet me, that I wanted to meet her. I spoke quietly and intensely, convey-ing the image of a man who knew what he wanted. My palms were cold and sweating. She laughed nervously at my seriousness but began talk-ing to me, and then we were walking together. Our conversation quick-ly turned to argument. I had never before met anyone who felt so antagonistic about Jews and was able to talk about it to a Jew. It was also my first affair that lasted more than a short time. Kym had been married but had divorced her husband a few months earlier. She was twenty-seven, and I was twenty-two.

I told the healer that when my parents came to visit they were cordial even though doing so was difficult for them. We had gone out for ice cream, an un-adult activity for my family, so they could see the relationship as an immature one. A smart uncle had told them that a relationship such as mine with Kym was necessary for many young Jewish men. But the man who had told me I was seeking my roots in anthropology wrote to express shock and disbelief that I could have a relationship with a Christian woman given my background and the love of my family. My parents and their friends agonized over the problems of young Jewish men and women meeting and marrying Christians. His letter hurt me because I felt my relationship with Kym was a natural culmination of the values I had learned at home. Passion prevailed.

When I awoke from my trance I was surprised to have told the healer so much. It was late in the afternoon when we returned to the hotel and climbed the cold, marble staircase to my room. "Do you have trouble copulating with your girlfriend?" Kym teased me on the second-floor landing.

Our relationship continued for a while, but we grew apart shortly after I revealed to the healer, the last person I expected to be my confidant or confessor, something I had never consciously expressed—my relationship with Kym was a rebellion against my family. It took the discomforting presence of an anonymous other for me to articulate and ultimately understand that fact. Soon after, our loving changed. Now there was no hint of tenderness and communion, only raw defiance—our bold assertion that love could prevail over culture and our defiant losing battle to prove that passion could dominate the forces that controlled us.

## The Unconscious Sexual Self and Others in Liminal Space

Current ethnographic discussion of fieldwork primarily takes place on the level of what Anthony Giddens (following existential phenomenology and Wittgensteinian philosophy) calls "practical consciousness": "We begin from the premise that to be human is to know, virtually all of the time, in terms of some description or other, both what one is doing and why one is doing it. . . . In other words, agents are normally able, if asked, to provide discursive interpretations . . . for the behavior in which they engage" (1991:35).

Colin Turnbull (1986) provides a good example of this practical-consciousness approach in his focus on field researchers' mobility through ascribed gender roles. Because researchers' gender beliefs and practices are deeply embedded yet seldom coincide with those of the host culture, Turnbull observes, their dedication to detachment and objectivity may be a hindrance. Ultimate objectivity may arise from an immediate subjectivity, which, for him, is always conscious and controlled. Through participant observation fieldworkers can arrive at an understanding of an appropriate sexual role and present it truthfully and accurately by making a total sacrifice of self (and cultural expectations) by becoming something like an actor on a stage. For Turnbull, the different expectations of sexuality that anthropologists face create a real form of culture shock. But a successful fieldworker, always conscious and in control, "can train himself/herself, as the actor often does, to voluntarily and totally relinquish the former self and discover a new self. . . . the self that is right for that particular context. Such mobility . . . offers the fieldworker the greatest opportunity for participating while observing, the one self observing the other while still being the self of the moment" (1986:26).

On one level, fieldworkers must approach their sexual roles consciously and through such practical consciousness attempt to comprehend the sexuality of the other. In my narrative, for example, I began to comprehend the sexual role of the other when the healer attributed impotence to me and I realized that it was a common sexual problem in that area. Yet by itself the practical-consciousness approach to sexuality is incomplete. It neither reveals nor attempts to comprehend the equally important, although largely neglected, unconscious level of sexuality that is also present in fieldwork. Sexual roles and sexuality involve unconscious subjective behaviors and thoughts that have no formal expression in ethnographic discourse or everyday speech because of cultural taboos.

Such unconscious modes of cognition and emotional governance, as a matter of definition, specifically resist being brought into consciousness and appear there only in a distorted or transposed way. As sexual subjects, anthropologists bring unconscious sexual baggage and desires to the field. Moreover, it is not surprising that some people seek and find the other in liminal space as a way of dealing with sexual taboos and unconscious desires from their backgrounds. At the time I lived the events in my narrative I was unaware that my sexuality involved strong overtones of rebellion from my family's demands for religious endogamy. I now understand the field site as a liminal social space, a safe haven, an unexpected place in which I played out issues of my sexuality and the sexual taboos from my culture. Understanding unconscious as well as conscious motives are vital in fieldwork.

In this narrative and much of my work (Climo 1992, 1995), I prefer to represent the other as a conversation with multiple voices, several others, rather than as a single-stranded dialogue. Such a conversation would first include the formal other, the Pentecostal religious sect I went to study but whose actions are almost totally absent from this narrative and whose members, to my knowledge, were completely unaware of my sexual involvement. On an unconscious level, the sect represented my family's formal Jewish religious commitments and beliefs. Thus, even though I was light-years away from home in a geographical sense I was unable to introduce Kym to the Pentecostal group for fear they would respond negatively to our relationship, just as my parents had rejected her as a Christian.

The prostitutes I met represented a second other whose voice in the field was nevertheless important. As I projected fantasies of rescuing one of them and "legitimizing" her by taking her to the States and enrolling her in school, I also came in touch with my desires, ambivalence, fear, and guilt about having sexual relations with the other. What caused my inhibitions included anxiety about sexual involvements, religious prohibitions that included the demeaning of women and sexual relationships through money exchange, fears of disease, and ethical considerations when I realized most of the prostitutes were only fourteen or fifteen.

The third other was my girlfriend, Kym, whose voice and image are clearly other than mine on one level and the same on another. My family and home culture condemned our relationship, and our sexual connection was further complicated by social, ethnic, and religious differences. Yet we also shared a common culture that distinguished us from the other I was studying and mirrored our differences back to me in liminal social space. I hid my true relationship with Kym from the Pentecostals in the same way that I hid it from my family. I did not feel capable of juggling the social and emotional turmoil it would cause.

Yet a fourth other appears in the voice of the healer who came from the urban culture I studied but from a different sect. His impact on the narrative is of a different sort entirely but significant in that the healing event marked a change in my relationship with Kym. Perhaps more than any other, the healer's voice and my trance established the environment of my field experience in liminal social space that was unknown. I entered a trance in a vulnerable state, without preparation and without past or future social roles or understanding of the cultural meanings behind the trance. It culminated in symbolic death, that of my relationship with Kym, as well as the death of my rebellion against my family. It also initiated me in the sacra of anthropology as I learned painfully to accept the dominion of culture over nature and discipline over passion and so developed a new sense of myself as an ethnographer.

Time and distance have permitted me to acknowledge my continuing ambivalence about the meaning of these events. I agree with Crapanzano (1994) that closure or the possibility of ultimately coming to a full and adequate explanation is antithetical to anthropological engagements as well as to all social engagements. Among other problems, closure ignores the open-ended nature of anthropology and the continuity of a creative dialogue over time. It is ironic that so many written presentations in anthropology terminate in well-organized, elegant explanations, whereas so many emotional relationships in the field lack closure and are inelegant. They confound fieldworkers and evoke frustration, awkwardness, guilt, ambivalence, and even chaos.

A major challenge of contemporary ethnography is that ethnographers in many intellectual and academic circles are held to standards of political correctness that forbid or discourage them from perceiving themselves as sexual beings in the process of developing. Consequently, individual ethnographers may censor the discussion of themselves as sexual subjects out of fear of cultural taboos or retribution. Yet by refusing or denying the need to examine their sexuality in the field they threaten the very freedom of inquiry that the discipline requires. No department of anthropology or granting agency would accept my narrative as an appropriate professional use of a field site, but it happened nevertheless. Moreover, because public discussion of anthropologists as sexual subjects was taboo at the time—indeed, it still remains so in many circles—I did not ponder or try to understand the meaning of these events in any legitimate anthropological context. They never appeared in my scholarly writings (Climo 1968, 1971) or took concrete shape in my thoughts.

I do not agree completely with the position that ethnographers should be psychoanalyzed before conducting field research (Wengle

1988). Yet if at all possible it is best that they know and understand the unconscious sexual baggage they bring to the field and then analyze it once there and from afar as they write ethnographies. Of course, therapy is the most obvious way to uncover one's past, although autobiographical knowledge about one's sexuality can be gained in several alternative ways. One could maintain a private journal, speak about intimate experiences with trusted friends willing to be sympathetic listeners, or, particularly, recall and write about memories of sexual incidents that taught how a culture approaches the intimacies of human life.

I have always admired the common practice of anthropologists who maintain communications and contacts with people from a village or city and follow them when they migrate and over time. Here, I used the less common practice of reinterpreting the meaning of a particular field experience over time, especially over the course of my life. Barbara Myerhoff has referred to the creative product of collaboration between the ethnographer and informant as the "third voice" (Kaminsky 1992:5–11). A similar product emerges as the past self and the present self collaborate to construct the remembered self. Doing so requires liminality in space and time, but the product is worth the effort. Psychologists often regard autobiography as a necessary process in the growth of an individual. For field ethnographers concerned with issues of sexuality, the same process may help reveal more intimate levels of their own culture, that of the other, and the sexual baggage they bring to the field.

NOTE

I wish to thank Fran Markowitz and Michael Ashkenazi for their written comments and suggestions on earlier drafts of this essay.

3

# "Oh, *There* You Are!" Sex and the Heterosexual Anthropologist

*Frank A. Salamone*

"**O**h, *there* you are!" The voice was that of Philip, my dissertation director's "houseboy." He had been looking for me and had, much to my embarrassment, found me in bed with my companion, a married adult student who had accompanied me to Nigeria. Although my dark-olive skin does not blush, it came close at that moment. I saw my academic life pass before me, ending in a flaming crash.

I was already edgy enough, knowing that this, my second field trip to Nigeria, was a do-or-die predicament. I had to finish my fieldwork and dissertation within a year or be denied tenure at SUNY-Brockport, where I was teaching. I felt good about the fact that my mentor would be in Nigeria to launch me back into the field and look over my notes. Now, I worried that I had lost my chance to make a good impression and, hence, my legitimacy as an anthropologist.

I needn't have worried so much. Philip certainly had no intention of reporting my behavior to my *oga* (chief). In fact, his opinion of me soared because my sexual conduct with a beautiful blonde showed me to be normal in his eyes. I had a lot of learning to do about the African view of Euro-Americans, who were expected to lust after beautiful blondes. Chuck Frantz, my dissertation advisor, certainly was not naive about my relationship, indeed, he and his wife were having their own problems. He shocked my somewhat puritanical ears with stories of his own desires and attempted escapades in the field after his family left for Europe and the United States.

I offer this vignette more than twenty years after its occurrence as an introduction to the intricacies of understanding sexuality in fieldwork. In the incident, there are three anthropologists at various stages of their careers. Chuck was about fourteen years older than I, established in the profession, and had already chaired a major department of anthropology. I was in my early thirties, teaching at a state college, published, and on the line for a tenure decision. "Andrea" was in her early twenties, unhappily married, and majoring in anthropology.[1] Each of us was at a different part of our lives and careers, both professionally and developmentally.

Because intense reflections over the course of several years about this incident have provided me with insight into the role of sexuality in my field trips, I have also been encouraged to apply that insight to heterosexual males in similar developmental and professional circumstances. It is important, for example, to understand why I feared recriminations. In spite of the fact that sexual encounters with locals, students, and colleagues had been a matter of course, the received wisdom in the 1970s was that an anthropologist should refrain from sexual activity in the field unless with a spouse. An anthropologist, in other words, was supposed to be asexual, at least for official consumption.

That contradiction between real and ideal, between what really happened to me in fieldwork and what is supposed to happen, has profound methodological and theoretical consequences. A good deal of the poststructural, postmodernist movement was anticipated in the writings of those who noted an inherent contradiction between the objective pose of the ideal and idealized fieldworker and the ambiguity and subjectivity inherent in the fieldwork process itself.[2] It was never quite what fieldworkers expected, and eventually some learned that to know that fact was truly the beginning of wisdom.

I learned, for example, that what people say and what they actually do are quite different. Because I was studying ethnic identity I learned that all identities are only masks donned and shed as the occasion demands. Perhaps my lesson made me cynical, yet it also made me more humanistic and forgiving. Now, symbolic-interactionist approaches, combined with action theory with Marxist praxis overtones, are routine. In the 1970s they were almost heretical, as was the idea that nothing is permanent and process is everything.

Anthropologists presented such a "correct" view of their conduct to counter the image of being adventurers jotting down impressions. Even the most qualitatively inclined argued for the validity of an ethnographic record that reality often belied. Although structural functionalists were attacked for oversimplifying and creating straw people, their descriptions had a certain solidity and wholeness that distorted reality in the field. Deeper knowledge brought more questions and, on a significant level, less understanding and certainty than mere surface knowledge. Consequently, the ethnographic products of that period, admirable and well written as many were, tended to hide their authors' uncertainties and shortcomings. Many who entered the field in the late 1960s and early 1970s felt inadequate and deemed themselves failures for having normal imperfections and urges, including sexual desires.

## The First Trip

Certainly, those who became anthropologists in the early 1970s share similar tales of being unprepared for their first field trip. Methods courses, alas, did not really teach the pragmatics of fieldwork, but rather related anecdotal tales that made the field appear an exotic adventure (Salamone, ed. 1974, 1979, 1982, 1983–84, ed. 1985, 1986, 1995). We had heard of Evans-Pritchard's presumed sexual adventures, and Malinowski's diary (1967) had also created a stir among the troops. These legends, however, were so vague that when I met Barbara Pym, with whom Evans-Pritchard indeed did have an affair (described in her novel *Less Than Angels*), I did not recognize her name. Many anthropologists were titillated by tales of how the "natives" would find them irresistible, and, consequently, they "would never have to sleep alone."

Despite my lack of any real preparation for fieldwork, I was excited about my first trip in 1970. It was, however, but one more element in an impossibly overcrowded period. During the previous six months I had become a father for the fifth time, secured a new teaching position, finally passed statistics, also passed my doctoral comps, moved to a brand-new house that cost far more than I could afford, and continued to have marital problems. Going to the field was, and continues to be, an escape from the drudgery of daily existence.

At a Hausa-language class at Duquesne University in Pittsburgh in 1967 I had met three priests of the Dominican Order. One of them, Fr. James Dempsey, invited me to visit him in Nigeria. Before the summer was over, he had been named Bishop of Sokoto. Three years later I managed to reach the bishop's residence, where I was reunited with "Father Hex," who had also been at Duquesne.[3] After a few days he advised me to hitch a ride with a friend of his to the mission station at Yelwa. I did so, and after a bumpy ride over the red laterite roads we arrived there covered in red dust.

There I began my long association with Fr. Peter Otillio. Although I enjoyed the Dominicans' company, traveled with Pete extensively, and conducted this first fieldwork from the mission station, I did not see myself as a monk-in-training. Therefore, during a trip to Ibadan I slipped away from the Dominicans to visit a brothel because I felt a need to distinguish myself, somehow, from the priests and brothers. The fact that I had five children was not tattooed on my head, and many indigenous people regarded me as simply one more missionary.

Soon I was approached by a young man who wanted to sell me pencils, pens, or whatever else I wanted. Half-jokingly, I told him that I wanted a woman. He did a double take and then led me to a bar. In those days, 1970, every bar was a brothel. I soon had some young women around me, chose one, bought her a beer, and negotiated a price, about $10. We left our beers unfinished and retired to her room, which she shared with another professional.

I still think I remember every detail of the room. We climbed a small ladder to an upper berth. There was a small curtain around our bed. The young woman's name was Agnes, which she pronounced with an extra syllable, "Ag-en-es." Agnes's roommate entered the room. To her surprise I was involved in a conversation that was a Nigerian version of "how did a nice girl like you get to work in a place like this." I was and was not present in that room. My participant-observation had extended into Nigerian sexuality but at a cost to my emotional involvement, for I could no longer be a detached observer, coldly recording data.

I managed to meet the good fathers on time and returned with them to the seminary. After dinner Father Peter asked someone to drive me to a bar because he knew of my interest in music and felt I should have a chance to hear it in the big city. I was driven to a bar and arranged for a pick-up time. Because the seminarian felt his reputation would be compromised if he were seen in such a place, he left me seated comfortably at a table near the band. I ordered a beer and had barely sipped my first drink when another young man inched over and again asked whether I wanted a woman. She, his girlfriend, was not eager for the transaction, fearing the "white man's sexual potency." After a half-hearted attempt at conversation in the big room I walked away feeling a strange sense of failure and repugnance. I was not sure of what I was attempting to prove—my independence, need for sexual adventure, or desire for further adventures.

That first trip was a comedy of sexual errors and miscommunications. Each error, however, taught me something about the people with whom I was dealing as well as about myself. I did, for example, separate my sexual needs from fieldwork. I was able to assume appropriate asexuality when required. I was not, however, able to live in a totally celibate fashion, and because I had internalized the myth of the sexless anthropologist I berated myself for my dreams and even failed schemes. On another occasion, for example, I went to a *bikin aure* (wedding feast) with my Dominican friends. Geni, an attractive Dukawa woman whose picture my wife has since destroyed, was in the group attending the party. Her brother Jude was close to the Dominicans, and he and I have remained friends. The young woman walked close to me in the dark, an action I took to be an advance. Unfortunately, I was not aware of Dukawa courtship practices, and my attempts to flirt back by holding her hand or putting my arm around her were repelled with giggles but not discouraged. Our flirtations were out of synch. Something was expected of me, but I was not sure what. Both of us tried to understand the other's courtship practices, but I was not sure what to do. Given the circumstances, there probably was little that I could have done. In addition, I had to be careful not to scandalize the Dominicans. Fortunately, Jude approached me politely and asked me to come into the light. By staying in the shadows, he said, I was frightening the youngsters. He apologized for restricting my freedom but assured me that I had free reign of the interior of the village. I complied with his wishes, and my feelings were partially assuaged by noting that Geni had followed me back into the village.

I returned to the United States and secured a tenure-track position at the State University at Brockport. While there, I became good friends with a number of adult students and recruited many into anthropology. Andrea was one. She and another student, Scotty, had asked whether they could come along on my next field trip. I had joked about it and said that if they could get funding they could. Scotty did receive a grant but failed to get a Nigerian visa. Andrea, who had a full-time job, financed herself.

## Andrea

I had not expected my student to travel with me to Nigeria and was ambivalent about her doing so. I was flattered to have her attention but worried about my tenure, dissertation, and the wreck of my first marriage. After some preparation in London, however, we continued on to Nigeria. Eventually, we arrived in Zaria. Soon my dissertation director had me reading tomes on the area I was to revisit. He pretended not to know what was going on between Andrea and me, but that was just a pretext.

I have already referred to the cheerful reaction of one Nigerian to our relationship, that of Philip, Chuck's servant. A more ominous response came from a photographer in Zaria. Andrea had entered his photo booth to have pictures taken for the multiple residence forms we needed to scatter across Nigeria's military bureaucratic landscape before undertaking field research. I heard sounds of a scuffle, some noises, and then saw Andrea exiting hurriedly from the booth. I confess that my first thoughts focused on whether she had bungled getting her pictures, thus further delaying our entrance to the field. She appeared shaken and pale and asked to leave as soon as our photos were ready. We did so, and then she told me what I should have known. The seemingly friendly Hausa photographer had attacked her. She was torn between yelling, thereby directly involving me in a brawl, letting him fondle her a bit and easing her way out without further incident, or killing the smallish man. Andrea was a tall, full-figured woman in her early twenties in 1972. She opted for a relatively silent struggle, keeping her dignity intact and enabling us to get the pictures. It was a bravura performance that displayed grace under pressure.

Sadly, I acted appallingly out of a misplaced concern for a successful field trip. I berated her for not dressing as I had instructed her, in modified Hausa clothing. In her diary, she recorded her version of my inexcusable behavior:

> What I like about Frank is that he always comes through when you need him. Had a bad experience today. Had pictures taken for registration as alien and with U.S. Embassy, and picture taker made overt passes. Cannot understand my reactions, although it was typical of other similar experience I've had. I'm not used to people making passes and at first I refuse to believe that that was what it was. Then when I understand, my brain seems to suddenly go numb and I'm paralyzed. I re-

act like a robot answering questions that I'm asked. Instead of scream-
ing, running or smashing the guy, I sit paralyzed like a fool. The ter-
ror starts as a numb, paralyzing thing and then changes into the shakes
after I'm out of it and realize what could have happened. Explaining
that to a man is, I suppose, impossible, for they are seldom on the
receiving end of a solicitation, and their "status" enables them to reject it if it is unwanted without resorting to physical violence. I don't
know if I insulted Frank's masculinity by not calling him or what, but
he was furious with me, not the guy. That was just what I needed, since
I already had the shakes. I don't think they showed. In a way, it's amusing since he claims he doesn't want any responsibility for me. Why
should he expect me to call him to my aid? (June 9, 1972)

From that day until we returned from Yauri, Andrea dressed in
Hausa clothing. A female anthropologist teaching at Ahmadu Bello
University aided her in the selection and use of appropriate cloth. She
also gave Andrea good advice regarding our relationship. Although
Andrea was known on the campus as my friend, she insisted that off
campus she be introduced as my wife, a situation that with poetic justice caused me serious problems in subsequent years. The idea must
have been germinating in her mind for some time, as a later study of
her diary suggests, but my first conscious awareness of her plan came
in Yauri after a trip that reached epic proportions in my mind.

Our journey to Yauri began with a ride to a junction at a town
named Tegina. I suspect that my dissertation advisor thought it droll
to imagine us making our way across Northern Nigeria with no set travel plans while he took the departmental van in the exact opposite direction. Moreover, Andrea and I were just young enough to regard the
trip as a glorious adventure and one more challenge to overcome. I
know I viewed it as part of the mandatory rite of passage into anthropology. After all, we had journeyed back and forth to Sokoto twice in
order to please bureaucratic procedure. We were finally on our way
to the field.

We arrived later than we expected—hot, tired, and frightened from
being abandoned in a lorry park. A hotel manager sent his boys to take
us to his rustic establishment, where we spent a memorable few hours.
Accordingly, when later that morning we checked in with the divisional
police officer, Ali, we accepted his invitation to help us find accommodations. He had already saved us from yet another trip to Sokoto to
straighten out our residence requirements through taking our passports and forms and sending them there under his authority. He

winked at our relationship and, for a number of reasons, wanted to become our friend. He had come to Yauri, at that time a place without public electrical power, from big cities and had spent time in Rome and London in training for the police force. In 1972 he was part of Nigeria's deputation to INTERPOL. To put it bluntly, there were few people in Yauri with whom he could carry on the type of conversations he wished: the missionaries, a Welsh schoolteacher, occasional visitors, and very few others.

The house Ali found was roomy and in generally good repair. It was on top of an enormous hill at the end of a gravel road. There was a kitchen with a wood stove, a bedroom with a large bed under mosquito netting, and a bathroom with no piped water. There was no electric or gas lighting. Neither of us knew how to use the stove, but the outdoor barbecue held promise for hot meals. After one night in the hot bedroom we decided we would sleep outdoors in a net hut. There were a few holes in the netting, but we felt that a liberal use of spray and mosquito repellent would lessen our chances for being bitten. In fact, neither of us did contract malaria.

Our use of the outdoor hut made us appear more human to the Gungawa who lived near us in resettlement villages. We were not sure how to dress in such an open area. During our first night in the hut we were also unaware of just how close we were to other people, nor did we realize that our hut was on the main road for water. We discovered on our first morning there that village's inhabitants woke a lot earlier than we did. I opened my eyes to see women and young children staring and giggling at us. Andrea had on a revealing negligee, and I, under a white sheet, was wearing but a sheepish smile. Somehow, I carried off the obligatory *"ina kwanas"* with some aplomb. Eventually, the last giggling youngster left, looking back over his shoulder. Dressing rapidly, I left the hut, washed, and started the day—or continued it.

There were other embarrassing incidents in the hut. Each, however, aided the fieldwork and my understanding of what processes were taking place in the area. Because the indigenous people thought we were married they shared stories with us that they would not have otherwise. Andrea was told how birth control and abortion were carried out, facts only a married woman could easily obtain. Her presence made me "normal," something important to successful work. Moreover, because the chief of police regarded me as a married man with easy access to sex he could question me about the missionaries. Because I was studying missionary influence in the area it helped to have access to Muslims who would speak to me freely, a condition my being so obviously not a missionary aided.

Eventually, the summer ended. My dissertation on religious and ethnic change in Yauri was completed. Andrea came to my dissertation defense and to the celebratory dinner with Chuck Frantz that followed. We have kept in sporadic contact over the years, following one another's progress. She is happily married and has a son.

## The Dead *Bori*

In 1976 I returned to Yauri. I had learned that one of the people with whom I had been close was reputed to be one of the more powerful priests in Nigeria. Eagerly, I wrote a grant to the American Philosophical Society based on a Lévi-Straussian approach applying liminal categories to the realm of the sacred for the study of this *bori* (traditional doctor). The grant was funded, and I was granted an NEH endowment as well.

At the mission center I immediately felt a change in atmosphere. Father Peter, my old friend Pete, had become cool to me. He asked me why I had not told him the truth about Andrea, for, he asserted, he could have accepted our sleeping together but not our lying to him about this relationship. He had disregarded the chief of police's statements regarding our relationship. Old Ali Kunde, the chief, had told him our passports bore different names. Other hints were also overlooked. Yet despite his anger he helped me get settled with an Irish schoolteacher across the road from him. I had more privacy than in the 1972 trip but had to be more careful to be on good behavior or else risk losing his help permanently.

There were some embarrassments. One of the professional women had met me on the streets of Yauri and followed me home, but I had to refuse her in spite of my worldly desires. The Nigerian cook, a world-wise Igbo, gave me knowing looks. Even more embarrassing than having a professional prostitute come looking for me and sending her friends—somehow I was never home when they came—was having the sister of a young man who had worked for me in 1972 came looking for me too. I did not recognize the younger sister, nor did I immediately understand that her brother was ill and needed money. Slowly, I began to realize that she had become a "courtesan" and was available. I was tempted but did not understand how to court the Hausa professional. Again, I was told that she had come looking for me, an expression I began to detest.

My sexual needs were not met in any manner during that summer—in fact, my primary professional needs were also not met. Jugun Hella, the *bori* priest whom I had come to study, had died, poisoned by his Muslim enemies. Unlike the panic I had felt in 1972 when things had not proceeded according to schedule, I simply switched to study other things, primarily Dukawa marriage relationships. Certainly, my removal from sexual intrigue forced me to concentrate harder on my fieldwork.

My time in Zaria educated me in other ways, too. I watched the ethnic rivalries in the academic sector, and Hausa male-female relationships unfolded openly in front of me. My classmate, for example, had sought unsuccessfully to find me female companionship, a claim my newspaper friend scoffed at. He publicly upbraided my academic colleague for leaving me to spend my last night in Nigeria alone in the governor's retreat. I had learned, however, that I worked better without official ties, including those to women. In a Freudian manner I found that lack of sex meant that creativity was channeled in other ways. Some of my better fieldwork emerged from that trip. I had finally discovered that there was good reason for field ethnographers to become temporarily asexual.

## A Honeymoon in Jos

In 1977 I remarried and went to teach in Nigeria with my wife, Virginia, who was excited about leaving the United States and getting some international experience. I, however, was ambivalent. Warning signals had been ringing, but I chose to underplay them. In our defense, we had other things on our minds. There had been a difficult divorce, angry children, financial problems, and professional problems, as well as a church annulment to secure and marriage plans and housing arrangements to make.

We were to live in temporary quarters for an undetermined time, which proved to be for the remainder of our stay. At first we felt things were not too bad. We lived in the VIP guest house and had excellent food. After a few weeks, however, we guests evidently began to grow tiresome, and we were moved to what had been a one-family home that had been converted to hold more than twenty people. Later, we discovered that the staff had concocted a sad scheme. They had begun to serve us food that had been condemned for the students as spoiled.

Virginia became ill with what was diagnosed, treated, and cured in the United States as a kidney infection. In Nigeria, every doctor treated her for malaria or pregnancy. She was not pregnant, and, fortunately, neither of us had malaria that trip. Her illness and low spirits in our crowded environment brought us closer yet inhibited my movements. Virginia proved an excellent fieldworker and carried out her own research while offering suggestions on mine. Once again, however, I found myself being concerned about two people and not sure what to do. I was deeply concerned for Virginia's welfare and angry with myself for worrying about my fieldwork. I believed that her presence kept me from doing my work properly and at the same time hated myself for being concerned with that worry. I longed to do one thing or the other, to resolve the ambiguity of the situation.

Virginia, meanwhile, had secured a position supervising student teachers. Although she is a magnificent teacher and an excellent supervisor, she found that students took to checking her statements with "The Prof." Furthermore, the head of her department had me teach her class when it was being videotaped. The greatest embarrassments, however, were yet to come.

We decided to go to Yauri for Christmas to do a bit of research and to visit "my" field site. The ride was, in fact, enjoyable. It was the season for camel caravans, and we began to feel romantic again. Exotic birds were being hawked in gas stations, and Fulani tending their cows crowded the highways. When we got to Yauri, however, Virginia noticed Andrea's name in the mission register she had signed in 1972. I had to show Father Peter our wedding license and bear his hurt look once again. The bishop had already refused to see us in Sokoto. A police woman who had been friends with Andrea asked for her, caught herself, and made matters worse by saying, "Oh, you have a new wife!" I was indeed a true Hausa in her eyes, for I had exchanged a younger wife for an older one.

Often the fact that a wife was with me made me appear more human than working alone would have. We established a relationship with an Afusare family after we saved a young child from being killed on the ring road. The child had crawled out of the village, and we stopped our blue Volkswagen and carried him back. Later we returned and were thanked by Joseph and his wife, both of whom worked in the Murtallah Muhammad Hospital in Jos.

## The Last Trips

I had gone to Nigeria in May 1989 to decide whether to accept a Fulbright Fellowship. My major concern was whether my family would be able to accompany me. I had discovered over the years that trips generally worked out better if I were alone and able to focus totally on my work, floating easily with time and tide. Worrying about others placed me in a position I do not like—having to conduct research while being concerned with the welfare of loved ones.

I did not require another Nigerian experience. Personal and professional reasons, in fact, contested against it. Professionally, my fieldwork among American jazz musicians was progressing well, and there was no reason to imagine that it would not continue to prosper. But even if I didn't need another Nigerian experience, I wanted one. The prestige of being a Fulbrighter and returning to Nigeria appealed to me, as did the possibility of working among the Yoruba, whose art and music I had long admired. Previous experiences in Nigeria, however, made me cautious. I had not had much personal luck when women were with me in Nigeria, and my once great physical stamina was not so great any longer. True, in the past I had managed to conduct reputable fieldwork under difficult personal conditions. Nevertheless, I was aware that on this occasion I would be responsible for a ten-year-old boy and a six-year-old girl as well as my wife. Therefore, I decided to take a brief, solitary exploratory trip.

I arrived in Ife to stay with one of my former students. Unfortunately, my presence seemed to sharpen the problems between him and his wife. I had paid more attention to his two elder children than he did, a fact his wife sadly brought to his attention. I helped clean up dishes, made my own bed, and talked to his wife about intellectual matters and her job as a radiologist. She was concerned that he left me alone for long periods without either company or transportation. After he had disappeared for an entire Sunday and failed to introduce me to the traditional ruler of Ife, her relative, she began to berate him in Yoruba. She pointed out to him that she had entertained me all day, driving me to where she worked. She did not mind entertaining me because I had been a gentleman and an "uncle" to her children. I was, she stated, his former teacher, after all. I had always supported his work, helped him to get into an American doctoral program, helped him get published, and in so many other ways aided his career. In fact, that was the core of his concern. People were already chiding him for wanting to bring his "Godfather" to Ife. On and on she prodded him, hitting his sore spots as only a spouse can do who has been long-neglected and unloved.

I did not have to be a Freudian scholar to recognize her sexual frustration. I retreated quickly to my room and read some mystery novel or other to escape. Suddenly, screams and blows drove away all hope of escape. Foolishly, in retrospect, I placed myself between the antagonists, trusting that enough Yoruba sense of hospitality remained for me to risk my safety. Fortunately, it did. A fist stopped inches from my face. Yoruba neighbors and relatives swarmed into the apartment to stop this round of a never-ending fight. I had witnessed "experientially" the horrible relationship between Yoruba men and women.

My last field trip to Nigeria was supposed to be a family affair, but Virginia returned to the United States with the children, despite my earlier visit to prepare the way and after several failed attempts to locate housing. I returned to Ibadan and stayed on until early April. Ironically, Pete came up with a two-bedroom apartment behind the Dominican House of Studies. I still had no transportation, however, until I let out that I was willing to pay someone to provide me with a set number of rides for a weekly rate. Virginia has teasingly accused me of not arriving at these solutions while she might have stayed in Nigeria, and there may be some truth in her allegations.

I do know that I was miserable but busy for the next three months. My field notes show a driven man who concentrated on a number of matters dealing with male-female relationships, artistic issues, and healing. Nigerian colleagues teased me about buying potency medicine, and one healer gave me a packet of such medicine. I made a point of not trying out the medicine, this time happily, and sublimated my energy into intense work.

## Conclusion

The assumption on the part of many feminist and gay authors that being a male heterosexual in the field is nonproblematic is wrong if not wrong-headed. Angrosino (1986), McKeganey and Bloom (1991), and Moffat (1989) indicate otherwise, and my experiences in different settings tend to support their findings. Certainly, the meaning of being a heterosexual male varies situationally. Most Africans regard it as essential for a man to be accompanied by a woman. When a male anthropologist, unaccompanied by a woman, works in a polygynous society, he is often viewed as abnormal. Such societies encourage polygyny as a civic duty for the wealthy and even encourage male sexual escapades as proof that a man is a sexually functioning being. Because a male anthropologist from a developed country is considered as wealthy, his failure to have a female with him leaves him open to charges of being antisocial and homosexual—in sum, "abnormal." Therefore, subtle pressures regarding his interest in local women may be raised, especially when he is away from his wife. Refusal must be couched in careful terms lest one be labeled racist or "not male." In addition, passes directed to his spouse or female friend must be deflected with skill.

As other research (McKeganey and Bloom 1991) indicates, the age and status of a male heterosexual anthropologist is even more critical than his sexual orientation, at least in certain settings. Sexuality cannot and should not be considered separately from the overall situation. Therefore, a young, anxious, and unproven anthropologist is a different person from a middle-aged, established scholar on the seventh trip to the same area. In Nigerian societies, for example, less intrusion will be made into one's private life, including one's sexual life. The presence of a wife and family, however, will tend to weaken a male anthropologist's freedom of movement and may be used against him in the strange world of Nigerian academics (Salamone 1992, 1993).

Yet some anthropologists argue that an ideal anthropologist must be reflective at all times and, if possible, be a woman, gay, and a minority. Somehow a white male anthropologist is "unproblematically" perceived as being insensitive, unreflective, and domineering. My experiences, and I am sure those of others, argue strongly against such a facile and biased position. Indeed, my reflections upon my fieldwork tend to argue in a somewhat different vein. All fieldwork is problematic and subjective. In contrast to much postmodernist deconstruction, however, my generation and the one immediately preceding it sought to understand the subjectivity of fieldwork in order to control for it.[4] We sought to alert readers and ourselves to our biases and perspectives, a position championed by Robert Redfield in his classic *The Little Community* (1960). In contrast with current positions that often lapse into solipsism, we affirmed that our enterprise, in spite of its relativistic nature, was worth pursuing in the field, conducting our own fieldwork and not merely using that of others as a literary text.

We never held that absolute truth could be found this side of the grave. In fact, we stated explicitly that it could not. Nevertheless, we maintained that seeking truth was a worthy enterprise and that whatever partial truth could be viewed was found in praxis in fieldwork. Unlike many postmodernists, therefore, we did not avoid the adventure of fieldwork. We did not decide in an absolute fashion that belies the essence of postmodernism's dogma that no truth is ever possible and thus no effort is worth the energy. We tried to save the field, knowing that it is ever so much easier to destroy than to create. In doing so, we know that we risked being criticized, in fact, we were often our own worst critics. But along the way we learned some things about ourselves and the field.

I have learned that I have the need to lose myself in my work without distraction. I have also learned that real life, however, is a matter of compromise. Until I learned that—and I came to understand that fact in the field—my fieldwork lacked a vital part of its humanity. Until I realized that my need to be alone in the field conflicted with my longing for my wife and family, my education was incomplete. Observing the manner in which others responded to my situation taught me a great deal about their own culture.

I learned that real life is both this and that. Therefore, meaning cannot be separated from its contexts. If I have contradicted myself here and there, then (following Walt Whitman) I respond, very well, I contradict myself. Each oscillation holds some truth. Each period of my fieldwork holds some truth about my sexuality. Each occurred at a different stage of my personal and professional development and in interaction with others who were also at different stages of their developments.

Thus, my first field experience was my rite of passage in which I had to learn what it was to be an anthropologist and in which I felt the need to distinguish myself from my missionary friends. Later, with Andrea, three anthropologists were involved, each at a different stage of development and each seeking to carve out a particular identity. Finally, my last trip to Nigeria saw a more mature anthropologist seeking to keep his family with him and helpless to do so. While using frustrated energy to propel his fieldwork he at last began to understand the ambivalent nature of fieldwork and of his life.

## NOTES

1. "Andrea" was not her real name.

2. An interview with Clifford Geertz (Beereby 1995) provides an exact example of what I mean. Geertz clearly draws the theoretical consequences of his field ambiguity. His generation was the one immediately preceding mine. With Geertz, I am not sure that the other extreme, the deconstructionist one, is correct, but—also with Geertz—I am also not sure that it is wrong (see also Geertz 1995).

3. I have changed this priest's name, and some other names, to protect them from undue embarrassment.

4. See the bibliography of Salamone (1979) for sources investigating the epistemological meaning of subjectivity in the field.

# PART 2

# PRACTICING CROSS-CULTURAL SEXUAL ADAPTATIONS

4

# Cross-Cultural Social-Sexual Adaptations in Fieldwork: Perspectives from Mexican Field Settings

*Michael Winkelman*

Sexuality is a biologically based aspect of human experience and behavior, but one subject to extreme modification by culture. The concept of social-sexual relations emphasizes normative cultural issues of appropriate sexual role behavior and social expectations regarding sexual (coital) behavior, both within the culture and with respect to outsiders (perhaps including anthropologists). Social-sexual relations are also part of the overall intrapsychic and behavioral dynamics that precede coitus and may exist in its absence. The intrapsychic dynamics of intimacy and sexual (coital) behavior are also important for anthropologists' personal field adaptation. Sexual impulses and needs, their own and those of the other, should be addressed in field settings. That is facilitated by knowledge of culturally specific patterns and mores regarding social-sexual behavior, the patterns typical of anthropologists' social-sexual relations in a field setting, and the psychodynamic implications of various social-sexual relations for an anthropologist's personal adaptations.

My assessment of the advantages and disadvantages of different adaptations to sexual relations in field settings is based on analysis of my experiences in Mexico as student fieldworker and as manager of a field school. It is also based on accounts of other anthropologists. My emphasis is on the psychological and social aspects of sexual relationships, including the broader context of individual psychodynamics and interpersonal aspects of social relations within which sexual interaction may take place.

Making an appropriate field adaptation requires understanding the nature of sexual mores in a foreign culture and adapting personally and culturally influenced sexuality to the demands and limitations of new cultural and interpersonal contexts. Anthropologists have to balance different personal, cultural, and professional frames of reference as well as a range of conscious and unconscious cultural factors that guide sexual behavior and intimacy. Managing sexual relations in the field may involve a variety of adaptations that can contribute to or detract from an anthropological enterprise, depending upon individual and cultural circumstances.

## The Context of Social-Sexual Relationships in Fieldwork

Although anthropologists have led the way in many aspects of research into cross-cultural variations in sexuality (Tuzin 1991; Vance 1991), they have been much more reluctant to direct attention toward their own sexual behavior, especially in terms of sexual relations in the field and with the people in the communities they study. As Okami and Pendleton (1994:85) point out, "The topic of human sexuality . . . [i]n anthropology . . . is typically ascribed the status of illegitimate child." While anthropological ideals have often suggested avoiding sexual relations with the people being studied, sexual behavior (or its repression) is nonetheless a part of anthropologists' field experiences. The anthropological tradition of prolonged residence in the field, away from familiar cultural contexts, makes sexual adaptation inevitable. Anthropologists' avoidance of public and professional discussion of issues of sex in the field has left the management of powerful human drives and emotions largely outside conscious deliberation. That lack of attention reflects not only societal avoidance of public discussion of issues surrounding sexual relations but also theoretical anthropology's history of general avoidance of the issues of sex (Lindenbaum 1991; Tuzin 1991).

A more direct consideration of sexual relationships in field settings is occurring, however (Abramson and Pinkerton, eds. 1995; Kulick and Willson, eds. 1995; Lewin and Leap, eds. 1996; Sorenson 1993; Whitehead and Conaway 1996, eds.; Whitehead and Price 1986). Anthropological approaches to the study of sex have typically emphasized an "interactionist" perspective, recognizing the synergistic interaction of psychobiological and cultural factors in the displays of sexual behavior (Tuzin [1991], but see Vance [1991] for a review of the constructivist view). Sex is a powerful human drive and emotion. It is tied to biologically based aspects of social behavior, attachment, reproductive success, and species survival and constitutes a pervasive factor in the motivation of human behavior (Okami and Pendleton 1994). Yet human sexual behavior is subjected to considerable plasticity, and needs are created and met through the shaping and controlling influences of cultural, social, and individual factors (Dubisch 1995; Erchak 1992; Okami and Pendleton 1994).

An anthropologist must manage personal intrapsychic sexual needs as does any person. The management of human drives and needs for intimacy and sexuality are central to the maintenance of a sense of personal integrity, security, identity, and social stability, especially in fieldwork settings (Wengle 1988). Consequently, sexual adaptation plays a role in field adaptations. There, managing one's sexual nature requires a particular adaptation and structuring of sexual and gender identity to create a relationship with the other (Wade 1993).

Sex is central to some of the most intimate of human relations and bonds, but its expression is also often subjected to some of the strictest of cultural controls, among other reasons because sex is also a source of conflict. The necessary social control of sex was the topic of *Civilization and Its Discontents,* in which Freud (1930) suggested that societal control of sexual behavior was necessary in order to avoid conflicts that would otherwise undermine social relations with others. It is apparent that anthropologists have also considered these repressions as an ideal professional necessity, because avoiding sexual relations in a fieldwork location is the professional norm (Dubisch 1995; Wengle 1988). So much is sexual repression considered an ideal norm for anthropologists in field settings that disclosure of Malinowski's dairy (1967) and its accounts of his "sexual needs, longings and desires . . . shocked the pure and chaste anthropological community" (Wengle 1988:123).

Avoidance of the issues of sexuality comes at a cost, because these universal, biologically based drives have powerful influences on social behavior and are often intertwined with cultural values of central importance. Anthropologists confront issues of intimacy and sexual relations in the field, even if through abstinence and celibacy. Although a local culture may have permissive mores about sex and view sexual relationships with anthropologists in open and accepting terms, that does not eliminate sexual adaptation as a source of concern or problems. An anthropologist must still decide what is appropriate and the consequences of that action.

Sexual intimacy can play a number of roles affecting interpersonal adaptation and cultural identity in foreign cultural contexts. Abstinence is a way of maintaining cultural identity and intercultural barriers, whereas intimate relationships with locals can be a mechanism for enhancing cross-cultural development. Sexual relations in the field can potentially contribute to cultural learning and cross-cultural development in terms of how sexual intimacy provides a bonding and fusing of identities. That can facilitate internalization of the other and enhance transference of positive affective relations to the new culture. The dynamics created in field sexual relations can enhance an anthropological enterprise, directly contributing to learning about the other and their culture. But sexual mores constitute an important aspect of cultural behavior, and adoption of appropriate sexual behavior can be crucial to anthropologists' acceptance and success. Their very lives may depend upon their choices, because some groups kill men who have unlicensed sex with their females and consequently violate a family's honor.

## Sexual Adaptations during Fieldwork in Mexico

My first field experiences in rural Mexico were preceded by a brief preparation, orientation, and adjustment period in Mexico City. The initial contact period involved an enthusiastic immersion into the national culture through museums, studying public monuments, and social activities. My efforts at language and cultural learning made me receptive to invitations to meals, drinks, and other social engagements. My perspective on my position in this society—as a young, tall, white, blond male—was largely unreflexive and naive. I was even largely unaware that my relaxed appearance caused many Mexicans to classify me, from their cultural perspective, as a hippy.

During my first days in Mexico City I found to my surprise that on several occasions I was the object of explicit homosexual propositions. Given my exclusively heterosexual orientation, these repeated solicitations by Mexican gays and bisexuals became a source of personal concern. I could not understand why so many men were propositioning me, because I was exclusively heterosexual in my home culture, where I had rarely been propositioned by gays. One evening I confronted my propositioner. I wanted him to tell me what I was doing that (falsely) signaled my interest in a homosexual relationship.

While the initial explanations I received had focused upon their perception of my attractiveness as a blond, one propositioner revealed that my nonverbal behavior signaled, from his point of view, my interest in homosexual relations. Apparently the miscommunications resulted from my (perhaps excessive or extreme) American style of establishing and maintaining direct eye contact. That, augmented by the intense focus of attention caused by my struggle to understand a new language, was communicating sexual interest within the context of the social interaction rules of Mexican gay culture. Although I had recognized that similar interaction patterns involving eye contact occurred in North American heterosexual relations, I had not anticipated how they might operate in the context of homosexual signaling among Mexican males.

Because these social-sexual communication issues were not directly related to the research in which I was engaged (Winkelman 1982, 1986, 1989) I did not pursue them further. I also successfully managed to prevent further encounters and misunderstandings by deliberately avoiding the more direct, prolonged eye contact typical in North American interaction. Furthermore, when Mexican gays signaled interest through eye contact and facial expressions (e.g., "lecherous" smiles), I was now able to communicate disinterest through behavioral and nonverbal avoidances. Male propositions ended and faded from my concern, remaining only as a source of examples of cross-cultural miscommunication and cultural differences.

## Norms Regarding Appearances: Social-Sexual Propriety

Mexican sexual norms are often characterized as more traditional and restrictive than U.S. sexual norms, particularly in regard to women. In contrast to a liberal American view influenced by feminism, woman's rights, and somewhat more open expression, traditional Mexican culture maintains a more restrictive view of women's sexuality. A good woman is a reflection of the ideal of Mary in the Holy Family—chaste, devout, self-sacrificing, and devoted to her family.

Males are generally socialized to take responsibility for the maintenance of the honor and virtue of their families through defending the sexual honor of female kin at the risk of disintegration of a respectable social self (Winkelman 1993:ch. 27). Traditionally, a man was considered responsible for the chastity of wife, mother, daughter, and sisters and their social-sexual behavior, which was seen as reflecting upon the family's honor as a whole. The importance of female social-sexual behavior with respect to family honor is closely tied to a male value complex and identity referred to as machismo ("maleness"). Violation of the honor of one's family normally requires men to act violently in revenge. Diaz-Guerrero (1961), a Mexican psychologist, considered preoccupation and anxiety regarding the maintenance of family honor to be a central theme of the male Mexican personality. He noted their consequences in hypersensitivity regarding sexual issues, particularly personal sexual potency and the female kin's sexual behavior.

I had prepared somewhat more adequately for adapting to the social interaction dynamics, values, and norms regarding heterosexual relations in Mexican culture. Recognizing the life-and-death cultural importance of these sexual mores and the possibly violent responses to violation of honor, I had planned to abstain from sexual relations with local women while in the field. Yet I was unprepared for the social behaviors I experienced. I had anticipated the formality of social relations and a preference for group gatherings over one-on-one meetings with professional colleagues. Nonetheless, the emphasis on being chaperoned, even in the most public of contexts, was still more than I had expected. Years later, Condon (1985:34–35) drove home the principles that had guided these social relations: "There is the suspicion of an almost inevitable sexual attraction between a man and a woman when they are together alone. . . . we must not only avoid scandal, we must avoid the appearance of scandal."

Although the people with whom I had contact did not explicitly state such concerns, they were clearly manifested in their behavior. I learned in time that women would never meet me alone to discuss topics of professional interest. On occasions when I had made plans to meet with women at their places of residence, the meetings were abruptly postponed or altered because "nobody else was at home." When I attended professional conferences, my invitations to women colleagues to share taxis when returning from the meetings to hotels were declined with the explanation, "It doesn't look right." Other women would arrive for meetings in public places accompanied by relatives or friends acting as chaperones.

Cultural emphases on norms regarding relations between unmarried people of the opposite sex were brought directly to my attention when I received permission from local political authorities to reside and study in a remote mountain village, Ozolco, in the state of Puebla, southeast of Mexico City. Several adult males of the village made it a point to tell me, "Don't do anything with the young ladies" (¡No hagas nada con las muchachas!). Published accounts of the villagers' murder of outside meddlers—religious proselytizers and government officials—coupled with local accounts of assault and murder over romantic liaisons made it clear that the consequences of sexual relations in this particular field setting could be fatal. My initial disinclination for sexual relations in a field context was as much motivated by personal and moral concerns as by potential threats to my well-being. I was concerned about the possibility of pregnancy and its implications—a spouse socially and culturally quite different from myself or a child abandoned in a foreign culture.

Although my conviction held, my initial impressions about female honor and sexual behavior were eventually challenged. During my second summer of field research I lived in a small town, Marquelia in Guerrero, that was a rapidly growing transit point on the main coastal highway about 125 miles south of Acapulco. Habitations in the area were largely family residences, but a few hotels and boardinghouses also provided residences for a more mobile population. These included some bar and restaurant employees, particularly a female population not related to people in the town. The behavior of several of these women with publicly recognized "loose" morality contradicted ideal norms. They told me, in what appeared to be uncharacteristic cultural behavior, that they wanted me to give them a child with blond hair and blue eyes like my own. That behavior reflects long-standing positive evaluations of outsiders in Mexican culture, particularly blonds (*guerro/a* or *rubia/o*), a reflection of "sexual colonization" or exploitation. It emphasizes the need of differentiating cultural norms for sexual behavior with respect to in-group and out-group members.

The behavior of these women also suggested something of which I was unaware at the time. My notions about the monolithic restrictive norms regarding females' sexual behavior were not as uniform as the stereotyped ideals might have suggested. Subsequent experiences led to a growing realization that these ideal norms were not uniformly upheld, even among women who might otherwise have been considered respectable and reputable.

My commitment to avoid sexual relations in a field setting, as well as my expectations about monolithic Mexican norms for female behavior, were eventually undermined. During two periods (2½ and 5 months) of fieldwork focused in rural settings (Ozolco and Marquelia), various factors led me to make occasional trips to urban areas (Cholula, Puebla, and Mexico City, respectively). Social contacts with women in urban contexts involved what I correctly perceived as nonverbal and contextual invitations to intimate relationships. Direct eye contact, lingering gazes, smiles, and facial expressions communicated a mutual attraction that transcended cultural differences. During each of these two periods of fieldwork, the urban visits led to developing an intimate relationship with a Mexican woman.

I developed relationships with women who were distinctly different from the traditional Mexican profile in several important ways. Most important, they were outside my immediate field settings and had life-style characteristics that placed them between Mexico and the United States. Both had visited or lived in the United States and did not reside with their fathers (who were deceased or divorced from their mothers), nor did they have older male relatives living in the household.

My first social-sexual relation in the field was with a woman in her mid-twenties, the daughter of a woman from the United States and a Mexican man. I met with her on several occasions during trips away from my field site to obtain supplies in Cholula, Puebla. She had spent some years of her early life in the United States but had primarily lived in Mexico. She was pursuing an advanced degree at the University of the Americas and lived on her own. Although she was in many respects Mexican, her life history and personal dynamics deviated from the Mexican norm. Her mother's decision to divorce her father and return to the United States had led to her own brief return to the United States during late adolescence. But stigmatized as a Mexican in her mother's elite community, she decide to return to Mexico, where she lived apart from family with her mother's financial support. Her preference for living in Mexico did not, however, reflect a compatible personal psychosocial dynamic.

The woman exemplified the characteristics of marginalization in her inability to establish stable intimate relationships with either Mexican or North Americans. She had discovered that Mexican men generally found her intimidating, and she confided that prospective partners were often incapable of establishing or maintaining an erection or else had difficulty penetrating her. Those not intimidated tended to view her as immoral, an "American whore" (a conclusion she did not accept), generally because she had independent residence and lived alone. She had attempted to develop stable intimate relationships with several American (U.S.) students from the university, but those had also been short-lived.

A year later, during a second period of field research focused in Marquelia, Guerrero, I developed a relationship with a woman whom I met during a trip to Mexico City. Attractive and sociable, she was introduced to me by her male cousin, an acquaintance who was a government employee assigned to the same rural field setting where I had been conducting research. I was immediately attracted to her, as she was to me. Our intense mutual attraction was expressed in nonverbal communication dynamics paralleling American norms and led to frank disclosure of attraction. Yet I initially avoided intimacy out of a personal concern for her emotional well-being; I knew I would be leaving Mexico within months. She, however, discounted my concerns and emphasized enjoying the present rather than preoccupying myself about the future.

My woman friend was an executive secretary in a government bureaucracy and worked evenings on her own as a licensed dentist. She was the primary provider for her family, which had lost their father and husband when she was a child. Her mother had planned my friend's career as a means of providing for the family. In her late twenties, she remained unmarried not so much out of her or her family's interest in her remaining single, but out of an inability to establish a marital relation. Although on several occasions she entered into intimate relationships with Mexican men, these were short-lived and characterized by mutual incompatibility. She recognized that her difficulties stemmed from the typical expectations placed upon wives in Mexico and her lack of availability, disposition, and even training to accept the roles. Apart from the life-style demands imposed by her two-career work schedule, her stubborn independence and lack of domestic skills made her an unsuitable spouse for typical Mexican males, who likewise failed to meet her needs.

## Discussion

Power is an important issue in the relations between people of countries that have unequal economic and political potential. An examination of the events I have described also shows the relative similarity of class status between the anthropologist and the field partners. Although I do not believe that my involvements were motivated by power factors, power issues could have played some role in my partner's involvements with me because of my status as a representative of a powerful foreign country. I could have represented a "ticket to a better life," even though both women had traveled extensively outside of Mexico, were capable of leaving again if they wished, and were economically much better off than the poor graduate student with whom they became involved. Their involvements, however, were more than an issue of potential upward mobility. I believe that both women were also availing themselves of the opportunity to associate with the outsider norms I represented. That involvement may have validated some sense of self in providing a personal relationship they could not achieve with compatriots. The social-sexual relationships that students in my field school program in Mexico established with locals also conform in general ways to that characterization of marginalization. Many relationships have been with locals who spoke some English or had been to the United States, skills and experiences that provided a basis for establishing relationships with students in the program.

Characteristics of marginality appear typical of what other anthropologists have reported about their sexual relationships in the field although not characterized in such terms. Field sexual relations with natives of similar class and education to the anthropologist have been noted (Dubisch 1995; Wade 1993). The characteristics of the Mexican women with whom I was involved reflect in important ways the characteristics of the partners Wade (1993:203) reported: "relatively well educated by local standards . . . not from the poorest families and . . . not particularly attached to [the] culture and identity . . . [and] not regarded as too far 'beneath me' by local people." Ideologies of male dominance, machismo, and sexual conquest have often been seen as a primary motivation for males' sexual relations, particularly in the field (cf. Wade). Wade's assessment indicates that his encounters were mediated by class factors that made the relationships more similar rather than more distant.

Although Dubisch (a female anthropologist) may reject the notion that her field sexual partners in Greece were marginalized people, they nonetheless appear to have similar parallels. In particular, they were people accustomed to encounters with foreigners. One, a multilingual businessman, worked regularly with tourists and had a reputation for initiating sexual relationships with foreign women visiting the country. The other had been married to a foreigner, worked in the tourist business, and had considerable contact with other foreigners as well.

Their multicultural characteristics are typical of those of my field lovers and also reflect Wade's assessments of his field partners being more similar to him than the other in general. These characteristics suggest that foreign anthropologists are likely to develop social-sexual relationships with host nationals who are somewhat alienated from aspects of their native cultures. Both parties seek partners with whom they have greater compatibility.

The stereotype of an anthropologist as a "professional stranger" may have its counterpart in field sexual partners being "marginalized natives." The characteristics of the women in my field relationships, as well as their similarity to the accounts provided by other anthropologists discussed previously and those of my students, lead me to hypothesize that the partners with whom anthropologists (male or female) most readily establish social-sexual relationships in a field setting may be characterized as marginalized natives. That marginality is reflected in personal characteristics that make them poorly adapted for stable conjugal relations in their own cultures and yet more similar socially, economically, and educationally to a foreign anthropologist—and therefore more interpersonally compatible.

I use the term *marginal* not in a pejorative sense but to refer to the relationship of the individual psychodynamics to the normative expectations of the others' cultural reference group. Marginality has been used to refer to a condition in which an individual is caught between different identities, norms, and beliefs; it occurs as a consequence of incomplete adaptation to different and conflicting value systems. Everett Stonequist (1937) characterized such a marginalized person as a cultural hybrid. But Stonequist contended that a marginalized person cannot accommodate to contradictory systems and generally suffered psychic consequences and alienation. Marginalization creates a tendency to personal maladjustment and deviant behavior, particularly when an individual does not have a personal reference group to relate to and identify with. Marginality may be managed through an effort to assume and live with an identity referenced to another culture. That referencing may also involve the seeking of partners from that other culture.

## Consequences of Field Social-Sexual Relationships

Like most aspects of life, social-sexual relations in fieldwork settings can have advantages as well as disadvantages. Determining what adaptation is most appropriate and advantageous and what is advisable in adapting requires deliberate assessment. Adaptation is influenced by a number of factors, including marital status, long-term goals, and what is expected in the host culture. Independent of how one views the morality of sexual relations with people under study, sexuality and intimacy are central issues for psychoemotional adaptation. The needs for intimacy and personal support are a central part of long-term cross-cultural adjustment (Winkelman 1994) and therefore important to adjustment issues in the field. Two related psychoemotional issues should be considered: that of the fieldworker and that of the local partner and his or her expectations.

Trips away from the field, and my first social-sexual relationship, provided important social, personal, and emotional support and the chance to escape the challenges of coping with Spanish, Nauhatl and the dramatic cultural differences of my rural living situation. Showers, a bed with a mattress, and foods unavailable in my research site made these interludes particularly important. They also provided welcome opportunities to leave the immediate site of my field research without leaving the field. That may reflect a typical pattern of anthropologists' sexual relations in the field in locations outside of the direct field re-search settings (cf. Dubisch 1995). The escapes provided what Bernard (1988:168) discusses as the "break" stage of participant observation, a time when an anthropologist leaves a field site to find physical and emotional distance from the demands of research, put things into perspective, and "just take a vacation without thinking about research at all" (Bernard 1988:168).

Enhancement of emotional well-being and reduction of role am-biguity can also be achieved by a relationship with a significant other in the host culture, which may facilitate fieldwork in a number of ways (Wade 1993). Sexual relations were an important aspect of social iden-tity in the culture Wade studied, and his relationship with a local wom-an communicated his commitment to that culture. It also provided a socially safe identity and defused the potential threat sex differences posed in interaction with female informants. Moreover, the relation-ship provided a basis for establishing kin relations that facilitated in-terviewing others and led to participation in aspects of the culture that would have otherwise been unavailable. Likewise, the social-sexual relations I established in the field were beneficial to me not just from a hedonistic perspective but because they were a channel for inclusion in cultural dynamics and social life. My partners opened new areas of cultural understanding while providing desired intimacy, a social network, the opportunity to learn about other aspects of cultural life, and rapidly accelerated language learning and comprehension. The positive self-regard that loving relationships tend to induce also helped me maintain a positive attitude about cross-cultural adaptation, cultural shock, and challenging learning experiences.

Anthropologists have pointed out that the intense involvement of sexual relations can also open an individual to other dimensions of cultural knowing and identity. As Cesara (1982) explains, emotional involvement and love relationships with persons in another culture can serve as means of learning about that culture. Wade suggests that his relationships with women in the field were linked to an "impulse of transcendence and union" (1993:205) and reflected a "desire to transcend the separateness that I perceived as distancing me from the constructed otherness of black culture, by participating in a relationship classed as most intimate in my own culture, one not just of sex, but of 'love'" (203). Sorenson (1993) discusses how sensual and sexual experiences can serve as a means of grasping central aspects of a culture and its members' ways of life. He contends that without these experiences, core features of the pre-modern way of life would have remained unknown to him and that the hypersensuality that pervaded the society he studied would have remained invisible to him as an outsider.

Field sexual relationships may create important changes in the sense of self and identity that have far-reaching implications for cross-cultural development and adaptation. They enhance the importance of a significant other from the culture under study, facilitating the internalization of norms, behaviors, and ideas of that culture through deeper identification with the new cultural reference group enhanced by the bonding with lover/other. Rapport, cultural empathy, and affective interactions in intense interpersonal relationships smooth internalization of new social roles through identification with the other.

In achieving this internalization of identification, an anthropologist will necessarily undergo personal changes that may have important implications for self-concept, result in intrapersonal changes, and contribute to changes in self that affect identity and cross-cultural adaptation. Intercultural effectiveness (Abe and Wiseman 1983; Cui and Van den Berg 1991; Hammer 1987; Hammer, Gudykunst, and Wiseman 1978) involves a range of personal changes likely to be augmented by the internalization of the cultural other. That can be enhanced by stable social-sexual relations and support with someone from that culture (Winkelman 1994). The phenomena of the "anthropologist gone native" reflects the extent to which internalization of the cultural other may transform one's sense of self and life objectives.

The rewards to an anthropologist in the field must be balanced by a recognition that the benefits to the parties in social-sexual relationships may be asymmetrical. That was not so evident in my first field relationship as in the second. The reasons for what I considered to be somewhat uncharacteristic Mexican behavior with my second relationship later became apparent because her relationship with me paralleled her previous relations and offered, in her view, what could have been her only avenue to an acceptable marriage. Although she knew that in all likelihood her relationships with foreigners living in Mexico for protracted periods would not lead to marriage, she felt that such a union was the only way she would find a spouse.

The second relationship also provided an opportunity for observing and participating in Mexican culture and family relations and to a rapid improvement in my Spanish conversational skills. After finishing research in rural Guerrero, I returned to Mexico City to pursue interests in spiritualist healing. I initially established residence in a boardinghouse, but my partner invited me to reside with her and her mother and younger siblings. Other members of the nonresidential extended family (especially visiting brothers-in-law) were not always reserved in expressing opinions about the inappropriateness of my presence and living situation. On one occasion a brother-in-law emphasized disapproval by bringing a loaded pistol to a family meal. His arrival during my absence enabled female kin to hide the ammunition clip before my return, averting what could have been a violent incident.

Students in my field school in Mexico, especially American female students, quickly learned that local males had different cultural expectations and tended to make exclusive social claims that went far beyond the expectation of exclusive intimacy. Conflicts erupted as a consequence of the continuing platonic friendships that female students had previously established with other Mexican or American males. Female students have also discovered that intimate relationships that involve (or imply) sex can be counterproductive in terms of maintaining their reputation and the community relations necessary for carrying out research. When one student anthropologist's intimate relationships with a local male became obvious, members of the community gossiped about that student, who felt the need to withdraw as a consequence of embarrassment. Another, the subject of inaccurate rumors of being pregnant, was unable to comfortably pursue her research project in the community. Those females with publicly recognized intimate relationships with locals have received hostile rejections and reprimands, especially from male adults of their host families. Dubisch (1995) also points out that cultural concepts of honor and shame made her anxious about causing a scandal that might have undermined her reputation and ability to carry out fieldwork in the community. Sexual advances by male anthropologists in societies where there are strong controls and restrictions on female sexuality could as well lead to the need to terminate fieldwork.

Field intimacy may create expectations about more serious and lasting relationships than a foreigner intends. Male students of my program who established intimate relationships with host nationals faced broaching the topic of marriage and return to the United States, a negotiation that might occur in initial days of contact, before intimate relations, or even in the absence of coitus. This pattern of behavior reflects issues of power and the notion that an American may be a "passport" or "ticket" to a better life, as was possibly the case with my second relationship. Locals may not accept a limited relationship but rather may instead continue to pursue a long-term commitment. In one case, a male student abruptly left the field program early for reasons directly related to the difficulties encountered in disengaging from an intimate relationship with a local person.

## Conclusions

Anthropologists must address the social and cultural shaping of biologically based needs for intimacy and sexuality and the inevitable social-sexual dynamics that underlie cross-sex interpersonal behavior in fieldwork. Although the idea that anthropologists might deliberately engage in sexual relationships as a tool of field research runs counter to the normative ethical positions of the profession, such relationships should be evaluated on the basis of cultural compatibility, merits, and practical advantages and disadvantages rather than strictly on moralistic bases. The multiple audiences and reference groups that affect anthropologists indicate that the regulation of sexual behavior in the field should be the product of a deliberate strategy rather than as a consequence of unconscious intercultural dynamics operating outside conscious awareness or biological impulses. Clear rationales for one's field sexual adaptations are important because personal conflicts about the management of sexual relations can be disastrous, as illustrated in Wengle's discussion of the psychosomatic consequences of the internal conflicts between maintaining celibacy and establishing liaisons. Anthropologists should consciously assess the nature of their intrapsychic sexual dynamics and local social-sexual mores in planning field adaptations. The decisions that result must be based upon cultural conditions, professional criteria, and contextually relevant ethical evaluations rather than personal or circumstantial factors alone. Political dimension must be considered as well. I find the degree of my political power with respect to my two partners arguable, but my experience as well as that of my students requires a sensitivity to the politics inherent in sociosexual relations between partners of two unequal economic and political expectations and potentials.

The issue of sexual relations while in the field cannot be appropriately decided without awareness of local personal and cultural circumstances and appropriate behavior and an understanding of the personal consequences of different means of managing sexuality. Information about the host society can yield culturally and situationally appropriate responses. Consequently, the students' relationships with locals have appear to have declined as I have advised new generations of field school students about the unexpected and disadvantageous consequences of field social-sexual relations that previous students have experienced.

In contrast to the traditional ideal of remaining abstinent in the field, there are grounds to suggest that sexual relationships can play an important role in helping anthropologists adapt to and learn about another culture. Therefore, they ought to be managed deliberately rather than left to happenstance or unconscious personal or intercultural dynamics. As in all cross-cultural adaptation, it is necessary to have knowledge of personal values and characteristics, cross-cultural interaction patterns, and others' values and characteristics. Sexual behavior is widely subjected to moral evaluation, but anthropologists should not base their field adaptation on unexamined moral bases. Rather, the appropriate role of sexuality and intimacy has to be assessed on the basis of the individual circumstances, cultural mores, and intercultural dynamics.

Intimate relationships can open many avenues for cultural adaptation and learning through additional social contexts and the personal relationships that serve as a source of insider perspectives and positive emotional transference. Although the power relationships inherent in an anthropological enterprise may foster caution about the ethicality of field sexual relationships, such concerns should not preclude establishing those relationships as a part of bicultural development. Anthropologists should, however, be aware of the powerful effects of such liasons upon self-concepts and subsequent development, as well as well-being and local relationships.

## NOTES

I want to acknowledge and thank those who have offered assistance in the construction of this account and its analysis. The first are the individuals whose intimate relationships with me provided the basis for the experiences and learning related here. I also thank Margaret Willson for the initial encouragement to write this essay; John Chance, Jim Eder, and Cindy Winkelman for discussing some of these issues with me and sharing their insights; and Betsy Brandt, Jill Dubisch, Michael Ashkenazi, and Fran Markowitz for insightful comments and constructive criticism. I especially thank Cindy Winkelman for allowing me to share personal insights and assisting in facilitating my field adaptations while administering a field school program for almost a decade (the Arizona State University Ethnographic Field School in Ensenada, Baja California, Mexico).

5

# Cleansing Cultures: Public Bathing and the Naked Anthropologist in Japan and Austria

*Michael Ashkenazi and Robert Rotenberg*

Human societies differ in their tolerance of nudity. The range of reactions varies from complete prohibition in public (as in Jewish and Christian fundamentalist groups) to complete public nudity (such as rain forest communities in Africa and South America). The social rules that determine how one reacts, or is expected to react, to the nude human body become apparent when someone violates those rules, especially when the violator is foreign or different.

Societies with strong nudity taboos may have specific licensed zones or activities where nudity is acceptable and even encouraged. Public bathing is one such activity. This discussion will explore our problems in engaging informants during public bathing activities in two cultures. Observing, participating with, and interviewing nude people of both genders while nude oneself has unexpected consequences. We hope to provide the opportunity to reflect on those consequences, as well as on the understandings of local culture that only became possible through such research. Specifically, we are interested in exploring whether crossing action boundaries in sexually charged domains enables fieldworkers to make more critical observations and what the ethical implications of doing so are for the profession of anthropology. In the following text, the authorial "I" and "my" in the Japanese context refers to Ashkenazi; in the Viennese context it refers to Rotenberg.

## The Japanese *Sento*

Public bathing has been common in Japan since the eighteenth century. It is still practiced, although its heyday—when private baths were few—has passed. There are two common bath locations: the *ofuro* (also called *sento*) and the hot springs (*onsen*). Ofuro are ostensibly for hygienic purposes, although, as Clark (1994) notes, they also have an important emotional context.[1] Onsen are for relaxation and pleasure. They are associated, appropriately, with play and what the Japanese call "water trade"—leisure activities such as public drinking, eating, and merrymaking.

Bathing etiquette is superficially similar for all baths, although social circumstances differ. The Japanese see this etiquette, and the bathing experience itself, as one of the prominent activities that define "Japanese-ness." It is thus difficult for a foreigner to participate fully because of external constraints and subjective emotions and feelings. These two issues can be distilled into two questions. One is asked, sometimes overtly, sometimes using circumlocutions, by the Japanese. The other is asked by non-Japanese participants (or at least by this participant). The Japanese are concerned with the ability of non-Japanese to participate in, understand, and accept public baths fully. Non-Japanese are concerned with how to endure, and perhaps enjoy, an experience that is unfamiliar and sometimes difficult for them. Both questions have an ambiguous sexual dimension: Is the situation of public nudity a sexual one? If so, how does one define those rules in addition to other rules having to do with nonsexual comportment? To illustrate some of those dilemmas it is necessary to understand something of the circumstances, both generalized and personal, as well as my experiences and their consequences.

Until fairly recently, most urban neighborhoods in Japan included a public bathhouse. Most private homes were without baths until well into the twentieth century, and sento served a multiple role as a place for bathing, relaxation, and gossip. Mixed bathing was common (although there were also sexually segregated baths or bathing times in some places) until new municipal ordinances promulgated during the American Occupation forbade the practice, at least in most urban areas.

Parents teach the etiquette of hygiene in the bath to children early (Hendry 1986) and impress them with the need for hygiene. Even a public bath begins in the home. There people change into bathwear, such as a traditional light robe (*yukata*) or a track suit. Bathers carry a small basin containing towel, soaps, and other toiletries.

A sento structure is recognizable by its tall chimney. A bath attendant sits on a raised dais inside, receives a fee equivalent to $2, and supervises cleanliness and order. People put their shoes in numbered, locked bins and undress in areas that in sento, although not always in onsen, are separated by sex. Often the separation is a matter of appearances (*tatemae*), because the barrier between the two sections may be minimal. Nude and carrying basins, towels, and toiletries, men and women enter separate bathrooms.

Conceptually and socially a bathroom is divided into two sections. One is the washing area and the other is the ofuro proper, which may include more than one tub. The washing area is equipped with knee-high taps, mirrors, small plastic stools, and sometimes showers. Bathers sit on the stools, fill their basins with water, slosh it over their bodies, and then soap up entirely and rinse again. Clark notes (1994:68) that bathers prefer tub water over tap water for the initial soaking. I admit that I never noted that phenomenon, which points out how externalized my observations were. To me, although not to the Japanese, one sort of water was the same as the other. The bath is filled with water that is usually hotter than is comfortable for most non-Japanese. Bathers immerse themselves and sit with knees drawn up if the bath is crowded and legs extended if there is room, although spreading out completely is a social solecism.

There are interactional differences between the washing and tub areas. The wash area is functional. People are engaged with themselves, often fairly intimately. There is little interaction. Those who are well acquainted or members of the same family might talk quietly. On the whole, complete display of the body is accompanied by a closure of social interaction. In the tub, the pattern reverses. Strangers whose gazes cross might initiate conversations. There is laughter and general discussion. The atmosphere is convivial. In most neighborhoods people know each other. For them, the bath is a forum for discussion and debate carried over from the outside.

The daily bath ritual, whether in private or public, is an important personal and emotional experience for most Japanese. The closeness of shared bathing, the physical effects of soaking, and a sense of cleanliness are highly valued. The desire goes beyond hygiene. For many, participation in this very Japanese activity defines comfort and belonging to a group of those who bathe together (family, neighbors, or a formal group) and to the larger classification of "Japanese."

## At the Onsen

All classes of Japanese have patronized hot springs as a form of entertainment from prehistoric times. There are many of them, particularly along the mountainous spine of Japan. Different spring waters have different qualities, and onsen operators make different claims for their properties. Some onsen have great fame as places for therapy of specific sorts. Others have reputations as places of relaxation and entertainment, running the gamut from the familial to the raunchy. A number of onsen, particularly but not exclusively those in more remote, rural areas, have mixed-bathing facilities.

The layout and etiquette of most onsen differ little in their basics from sento. Yet there are some differences. Onsen are usually attached to a hotel or inn. That changes the atmosphere of the familial and community processes in the sento to what the Japanese call *asobi* (roughly, "play" but with a hint of relaxed rules and behavioral license). The bath and fittings of onsen tend to be more elaborate than those of sento and may include aquariums, plants, waterfalls, oddly shaped tubs, and mud baths. Behavior in the washing area is similar to that in sento, but tub behavior is radically different. Bathers may be drunk. They arrive in large groups intent on merrymaking and splash noisily, make jokes, and sing. In many onsen bathing goes on around the clock. Parties or individual merrymakers may spend twenty-four hours or more in an unending series of eating, bathing, mah-jongg, catnapping, and more bathing. Some hotels run floor shows that add to the merriment and excitement. Washing is not the object. Enjoying the conviviality of participating in a social and personal sybaritic exercise is.

A few onsen have mixed-sex baths. Dressing rooms may or may not be separate. If they are, men and women tend to undress on opposite sides of the room. Groups, usually single-sex groups but sometimes families, bathe during the day. Even mixed-sex groups who arrive together tend to split into single-sex groups for washing purposes. Groups also maintain distance while in the water. Such mixed-sex bathing also tends to be far less rambunctious than onsen bathing usually is.

Toward evening, and particularly toward the early hours of the morning, the situation changes. There are far more single bathers of either sex. Quite often the exchanges are subtly (or not so subtly) erotic, and members of either sex might, provided they are not crowded by others, solicit or be solicited sexually. Because of their locations, most mixed-sex onsen are patronized, particularly in winter, by farmers, road workers, and outdoor laborers seeking a cheap and enjoyable form of relaxation. From casual conversations with other bathers it appeared that most were blue-collar workers, an observation reinforced by their appearance and language.

## The Towel

The description of public bathing behavior hints at the complexity of rules that must be known before becoming a bather. To illustrate only one set, consider the small towel (*shibori*) that people carry into the tub and that does double duty as a washcloth and a towel. Hendry (1990) has discussed the uses of shibori as gifts and wrappings in Japanese society; they are used in many ways and possess large domains of implicit meanings. In bathing a shibori is a masking device. Most individuals use the thirty-by-forty-five centimeter cloth to shield their privates when walking into the ofuro. The covering is minimal, but proper etiquette requires that the towel be held casually over the pubis to obscure, if not cover, that area. When washing, the towel is used as a cloth. When not in use it is always placed in the lap. In the tub, the towel has multiple uses, and its manipulation indicates a bather's knowledge of social rules. Rinsed, squeezed, and folded, it may be placed on the head as a means of cooling. Individuals who are weary, hard-working, or not interested in being interrupted are likely to place a folded towel over their foreheads and rest their heads on the back of the bathing pool. One acquaintance rather acidly remarked that those with towels on their foreheads were usually those who had done nothing the whole day but wanted to prove the reverse. Some men spread the towel handkerchief-wise over their faces, obscuring them completely. The rolled-up towels may also be used to emphasize a point or to make shapes to entertain a child.

All of these various uses have parallels in Japanese society outside the bath. There, the gestures involved in folding, pointing, and otherwise using a fan as a communication device are practically hieratic. That is, a manipulated fan or towel signals ideas and themes that occur often in Japanese conversations. Their use in the bath is a marker of participation in Japanese culture as a whole and in its subgenres.

## Baths and Foreigners

The preceding description has been a distancing description. It reduces an activity weighted with emotional and personal issues to a formal set of descriptive statements. Within that context, any Japanese can recognize some variation of his or her daily activities. But the bridge between the normative and the personal is no less important. It maintains distance between an anthropologist and the subject of his or her discourse. At the personal level, anthropologists tend to avoid exposure to informants. The bathing situation creates an exposure of two sorts. First, physical and visual exposure made me more obvious than I would have been clothed; second, there is anxiety about violating unknown rules of propriety when there is little room to hide. Violations of rules are a horror from which anthropologists are professionally enjoined to recoil. That anxiety must also factor into the creation of the anthropological product: an interpretation of what constitutes an other. The introduction of a foreigner into a bath thus creates obvious problems for both native and stranger.

I knew to expect public, even mixed, bathing when I went to Japan as a student and wondered how I would react. My introduction came soon after I arrived. Before then, nude bathing with others had been an unavoidable but not particularly sought-after experience (I had served in the military, for example), and since reaching adulthood I had associated mixed nude bathing with sex play.

I knew from my reading, even before arrival, what "the rules" were. The washing area provided the sort of privacy that allowed me to concentrate on my own affairs. As a single foreigner traveling alone, I attracted attention in any case and had become accustomed to that. The washing area, paradoxically, allowed me to isolate myself from the usual stares. Because I was also concerned to show that I knew the proper etiquette, I washed myself thoroughly in as ostentatious a manner as possible. Entering the bath was difficult physically. The water was too hot, but I put up with it.

It was the towel that caused problems. It took a fairly long time, and hints from an acquaintance, to realize that nudity was controlled. One did not simply walk around naked, but rather protected privacy, more so than privates, with the towel. Spreading it over my face was uncomfortable. Moreover, I wanted to see what was happening. Putting it on top of my head felt ridiculous, although Japanese bathers could carry off the maneuver with aplomb. I compromised by using the towel to wipe my face from time to time, otherwise leaving it in my hand or perching it nonchalantly (I hoped) on my shoulder. Nevertheless, I never grew adept at its use. No matter how proficient I grew at performing the expected behaviors I was always a foreigner.

There were other indications of my strangeness as object and subject. Other men would stare quite openly at my circumcised penis, an oddity in Japan. Their gaze could have a number of subjective implications, none of which were resolved. Did an open stare constitute the start of a sexual proposition? As a heterosexual, that made me uncomfortable. Did they stare for purposes of comparison? Japanese have commented to me and to other foreigners that Japanese were "smaller." Was it envy that motivated the glances? On the other hand, perhaps they were looking at my circumcision. One close friend could not resist asking, when seeing my young son, whether he had been in an accident. He was horrified to learn that babies were subjected to cruel mutilation when I tried go explain the Jewish ritual of circumcision after birth (*mila*). I felt strange and at the same time I was an object of inquiries about strangeness.

Etiquette in the tub was even more confusing, albeit in subtler ways. Could I look directly into people's eyes? Invite conversation? This was, after all, a bath, a private place. Should I sit with my legs (longer and less limber than most Japanese) folded all the time? Other bathers were stretching out.

None of the feelings of discomfort stopped me from using public baths, however. Greater ease in public bathing occurred under two circumstances. The first was going to an onsen as a member of a group. The group was highly structured and had a recognized position in Japanese society. The fact that I was a foreigner was not significant for members of my group and, it appeared, for other bathers. In the somewhat noisy atmosphere of the onsen, when most bathers were slightly (or very) drunk and sang their school songs, horseplay made my strangeness as remarkable as someone else's squint. Whether everyone saw me as I saw myself is immaterial. The nagging feeling of discomfort at sharing the tub with a group of other men disappeared in the face of social support and cohesion.

Such issues led me to consider, in retrospect, three sources of discomfort for a non-Japanese that also have bearing on a cardinal methodological issue: the ability to comprehend the other. One issue has to do with physical comfort, a second has to do with social position, and a third with the definition of sexuality. Going to a public bath, where the rules were partly known if at all, also creates physical sensations that are not necessarily pleasant. Different stature, the need to touch and be touched by nude strangers, the discomfort of squatting before the washing taps (sometimes the number of stools was insufficient), and above all the temperature of the water make many cases of bathing a duty rather than a pleasure. For me, it was less than enjoyable for quite a while. Moreover, my physical features—pale skin and blond hair, taller stature, and artificial scarification—made me highly self-conscious. They also emphasized that foreignness to the Japanese with whom I came into contact, something they could ignore at least partially in daily, clothed interaction.

Sexual conduct in an average sento and even onsen is downplayed. Presumably it exists, particularly in onsen, but the hints and rules are often far too subtle for a stranger to be aware of the sets of signals and countersignals. That tended to make my sexual stance confusing. One way or another nudity is related to sex in my society of origin, and the cues in the bath were so ambiguous as to be useless as guides to behavior, either to encourage or diminish sexual messages. Instances of mixed public bathing exemplified that fact.

Mixed bathing presented a number of different issues. The first was the obvious social consequences of sexual attraction. I never asked what I was supposed to do if I had an erection in the bath. In any event, my first experience with mixed bathing proved as innocuous as a pavane. I was part of a large party, and the men and women entered through different dressing rooms. The decor was arranged to allow for a maximum of cover. Trees and artificial bushes were scattered throughout the bath, and by then I was aware of the towel rules. By the time we could make out who was who in the gloom and steam, all members of the party, about fifteen in all, were covered by water. The bathing rules also aided the formalization of the event. Women and men sat decorously apart, and there was no horseplay. After about fifteen minutes, each group moved to its side of the bath and climbed out. It was only while dressing that I recalled my earlier concern.

A subsequent visit to a mixed-bathing onsen was quite different in a number of respects. My wife, young son, and a good friend were with me in a small rural onsen in the midst of winter. We enjoyed ourselves as a family group and had time to observe other bathers. My wife pointed out examples of sexual byplay between individuals, and our little boy was a focus of attention. Social membership in a defined group provided a matrix that made the event contextual rather than personal. In subsequent visits even obvious sexual interplay between some female and male bathers provoked my intellectual curiosity rather than emotion.

## The Stranger as Stranger

In a naked Japanese crowd I stick out even more than in a dressed one. There were covert and not so covert looks in my direction. I was exposed, naked rather than nude, in Heinlein's felicitous distinction, in social ways I did not anticipate and could not control. Another source of my discomfort was that people around me knew one another. They saw and accepted one another's personae and physical and social blemishes in a way I could never comprehend. I overheard but was not privy to a surprising amount of information about the intimate doings of individuals and households. Finally, I was also discomfited by my social standing. Japan, for all the changes it has undergone, is a group-oriented society, and quite often I was not a member of a group. When I was, the discomfort was eased. My nervousness, such as it was, was focused on my group standing. In Japanese tradition, my seniors could make fun of me or haze me to the point of humiliation. So long as I wanted to remain a member of the group I would have to take it with good grace. They did nothing of the sort, but I was conscious while sliding into the hot water that they could. Because I was focused on them I largely ignored the other bathers.

The differences—social discomfort eased by social membership versus physical and sexual discomfort that I never fully shook off—have consequences for understanding what anthropologists do. That raised questions about how well anthropologists can understand their field of study. The Japanese indicate (Clark 1994:112) that the bathing experience is emotional and psychological, not only physical. It enhances intimacy, and the idea of sharing a bath relates to the idea of sharing a closeness that is otherwise partially unattainable. Although I learned to love Japanese baths, I never got to the point of missing them emotionally or psychologically. My varied discomforts with the situation likely prevented that, which implies that I would not be able to "enter the skin" of informants. It is true that the focus of anthropology has shifted from understanding to interpreting subjects. Nonetheless, either process requires an intimate understanding of the other. At least in this case, whatever understanding there was while naked was not intimate in a general sense.

My relations with informants in the bath helped shape my view of the Japanese. With few exceptions the other bathers were not informants with whom I worked but neighbors, friends, co-workers, or members of the same club. My bathing interactions were but a number of occurrences that linked me to the local community rather than to the focus of my research. Nevertheless, they were, if only by extension, members of culture I studied and part of the field setting. Being involved in an intimate although not erotic situation with them affected my perception of Japanese culture.

## Saunas in Vienna

I was first introduced to sauna bathing in Vienna in 1975 during my first field visit to that city. On each of the twenty visits I have made in ensuing years I have continued to participate in the baths. I have bathed in fifteen public and private baths throughout the city and in two suburbs, as well as in private clubs and apartment house facilities.[2]

Sauna bathing in Vienna fascinates me because it is an opportunity to come face to face with how metropolitan life writes itself upon the human body. This text is socially accessible only through the quasi-intimacy afforded by the baths. Just as makeup, jewelry, tattoos, and clothing communicate identity in the dry city of the streets, apartments, and offices, muscle tone, fat, hair, and skin color send messages about the self to others in the wet city of the baths. The Viennese are highly conscious of their relative status in a hierarchy that limits or facilitates life choices. The sauna affords a way of communicating that relative status—even without clothes.

### Background

As is the case in Japan, bathing has always been a part of Central European culture. It was commonly done in the open, and people were more or less modest about nudity in other contexts. Then came the nineteenth century and the rise of bourgeois modesty, and the Viennese hunkered into deeper and deeper body-masking. A natural process of linking social democracies culturally came with the economic stability that followed reconstruction after World War II. The Viennese began to imitate the Swedes, and the sauna tradition came to the city. Saunas were installed in public baths where families had bathed since the 1920s. The difference between sauna culture and non-sauna public bath culture in Vienna is behavioral. In bath culture, people's bodies are visible intermittently and can be masked by a towel. In sauna culture, bodies are on display for ten and twenty minutes at time. People shower instead of bathe and then lie around on beds to relax, showing full frontal nudity.

## The City in a Hot Box

Viennese sauna bathing is a complex social act in which multiple messages flow back and forth among bathers. To unpack all of these messages, to see the sauna as text, requires a discussion of several observations. The Viennese use public baths with enthusiasm. They use single-gender and mixed-bathing facilities and do so in multigenerational groups. Viennese bathing is considered part of a health regimen. It is also related to issues of identity and ideas of community and power.

The act of bathing takes between two and three hours, and most bathers set aside that time every week. I have sampled a number of public and private bathhouses in and around Vienna. All are open between 9 A.M. and 9 P.M. Random visits to large bathhouses reveal that the number and variety of bathers increase toward late afternoon and evening and toward the end of the week. At earlier hours and at the beginning of the week bathers tend to be retired persons who segregate themselves by gender. Bathing is therefore more like a recreation than an entertainment. It is one of a decreasing number of activities in the city that permits flexibility, and people time their visits to take account of competing needs.

Bathers, by the way in which they time visits to a bath, have the option of bathing only with members of their own gender, participating in mixed bathing with members of their own generation, or participating in multigenerational mixed bathing. All baths publicize schedules that include the categories of men only, women only, mixed bathing, and family bathing. The schedules are prominently displayed, and only an illiterate would be surprised by the characteristics of the group they discover in the sauna.

Vienna's residential precincts are stratified by real estate values, as they are in any city. Historically, some residential districts have held their real estate values at a very high level. Others have not been so fortunate. Every district has at least one public bath, and every bath has a sauna complex. Anyone can bathe at any sauna. Hence, if one wanted to bathe primarily with the wealthy, one would choose a modern, fully equipped sauna in a high-cost district. "Fully equipped" means the availability of a steam room, a whirlpool bath, a tanning booth, an outdoor rest area, and a plunging basin as well as the showers and sauna. Those who wish to bathe with working-class citizens can choose one of the beautifully restored art deco bathhouses of the 1920s that were originally built as public health amenities. By choosing the time of day and week and the site of the bath, one can construct an audience appropriate to messages about self.

The Viennese understand saunas as part of a wider health maintenance regimen that includes exercise and diet. Saunas cleanse the skin, exercise the circulatory system, especially the heart, and help the body eliminate waste. The public health virtues of sauna bathing are what persuaded the city to install saunas in public bathhouses after World War II. Previously, bathhouses had only showers, tubs, and swimming pools.

To maximize the health benefits of a sauna, bathers follow a specific regimen that is explained on a poster on the wall between the shower area and the sauna itself. They begin by taking a shower and washing their entire body with soap. The showers are open, and everyone is monitored by the other bathers to make certain that this step is fulfilled. The Viennese are highly conscious of hygiene. They wear sandals at all times in a sauna complex and sit on small towels when they are in the sauna room itself. Otherwise they are naked. Even those who carry robes into the sauna complex use them only to dry off after the various showers or plunges.

A sauna is a wooden box that can seat up to thirty people on three rows of benches built into its walls. At one end is a single door that provides access to the box. The box is lit by a low-watt bulb, and a stone box near the door is protected by a wooden rail. An electric element under the rocks heats them to provide overheated air. The electric element is controlled by a clock in the office of the bath master. A sign over the sauna signals when the element will be turned on, usually twice an hour for five minutes.

Bathers claim lounge chairs after their shower and enter the sauna box a few minutes before the heating begins. Everyone is encouraged to enter early to acclimate themselves. Air inside a sauna is always more than 100 degrees Fahrenheit and will climb to as high as 160 when the heating cycle is completed. The temperature rises very quickly. After a minute or two, a bather steps up to the stone box. Taking a long wooden ladle and wooden bucket full of water, he or she begins to drip ladles of water onto the hot rocks. The water immediately evaporates, and rising humidity causes sweat to increase rapidly. After ladling out half a bucket, the "dripper" (*giesser*) picks up a large towel. Carefully wrapping one end around his or her hand, he or she swings the towel in various ways, sending waves of very hot air over the others. People gasp, cover their eyes and nipples, and try to breathe. The dripper then uses the towel to give each bather an individual wave of hot air, after which each attempts a "thank you" while gasping. The bathers applaud the performance after the dripper finally sits down.

People are expected to stay in the sauna box for at least ten minutes. A light goes on when the cycle is finished. It is considered bad form to leave early, because opening the door admits cold air. There are a number of choices after leaving the box. Bathers can go outside into the fresh air and cool down, take a shower to wash away sweat, go swimming, or plunge into a basin of cold water. The latter option offers maximum stress on the heart. After cooling down, bathers reclaim lounge chairs for at least twenty minutes' rest before entering the box again. Many retreat to the snack bar to restore the fluids lost through sweating. Twenty minutes later they could theoretically return to the box. In practice, only those in a hurry do so. Others take only two saunas an hour. The pattern is repeated until each bather has ideally suffered through three stints in the box followed by the various methods for cooling the body. In better-equipped saunas other kinds of baths can be used to fill the time between. A full cycle of bathing takes about three hours.

The effect of all this on the body is unique. The skin is scalded by the hot air, and the mucous membranes of the nose, mouth, and throat are often affected also. The amount of moisture lost is considerable. After a sauna, individuals will weigh two to five pounds below their weight before the bath, but the loss is not entirely due to moisture. Regular sauna bathers swear that they are burning extra calories just as if they were exercising. I have no hard evidence for this. Muscles feel as if they have had a hour-long workout, however, the head is light, and one's mood is affected. The sauna has a calming affect. One goes through the rest of the day relaxed and better able to manage stress. These effects disappear after a night's sleep.

Even though saunas admit anyone who can pay the fee, not everyone feels comfortable in every sauna. Issues of cultural capital, gender, language, education, relative wealth, and age remain even when one is naked. All of these are mobilized in the sauna in one way or another. One informant, for example, advised going to the snack bar when bathing at a new sauna and telling the attendant that a telephone call is expected. Would the attendant please notify the visiter when it comes? The bather then hands the attendant a business card, which contains the bather's academic or bureaucratic title. From that point on, the attendant is obligated to call the bather by title. Thus, upon the next visit the bather will be greeted (e.g., "Good day, Frau Doctor"). In that way other bathers learn the newcomer's relative status without being informed overtly of it.

In Vienna, the aspects of identity that can be used to locate relative status in the social hierarchy are ordinarily mapped in space. The district in which someone was born and raised determines which elementary school they attended, which lifelong friends they have, and in which social network their parents participated. Those variables, in turn, determine how individual talents will be interpreted as people are tracked through the city's educational system. What results is an occupation from which the person can claim various metropolitan resources. That begins with a salary at a certain level of buying power and extends to the social networks they access, where they choose to live, and which entertainments and recreations they enjoy. Sauna bathing cuts across all of these relative statuses. Nevertheless, space continues to map the social hierarchy.

Everyone in a sauna speaks in Viennese dialect. Thus, those who are not Viennese are immediately cut out of any interaction unless they are prepared to announce their presence by making a comment in standard German. Because the dialect varies slightly from district to district, Viennese who are not locals also feel somewhat out of place. That would also the case if their dialect gave them away as having a working-class upbringing in a "good society" sauna.

Even though the sauna seems to celebrate the physical equality of men and women by bringing them together on equal terms, some bodies are more gendered than others. Thus, men and women whose bodies do not fit the cultural stereotype of what skin should look like or where hair should grow perhaps feel out of place. Surgical scars on breasts or faces are less tolerated than those on the abdomen, chest (if male), or joints. Some birthmarks are more acceptable than others. People who have such imperfections, as well as those whose bodies are out of proportion, tend to avoid mixed saunas. They can still bathe in a single-gender sauna but are ignored when they arrive at a mixed-gender sauna. Hence, just attending a mixed sauna constitutes a gender statement.

A similar situation exists for the family sauna. Mixed saunas are places for singles to meet, but many couples bathe there as well. At family saunas everyone must have a partner. A child is not required, but a partner is. The only time I was ever turned away from a sauna was when I did not have a partner; I had thought that the facility was a mixed rather than a family sauna. Family saunas have very different atmospheres than mixed saunas. Children as young as six are taken there by their parents. I have talked to people who first experienced saunas as children and then came weekly. One even met his spouse at a family sauna.

Regardless of the type of sauna, people talk to each other. Their topics of conversation and opinions reveal aspects of their occupation, education, and cultural literacy. For that reason when people find a compatible sauna group they stay with it for as long as possible. "Compatible" in this case means they have found people enough like themselves to acknowledge and appreciate their relative status and do not feel either threatened or condescended against. Sauna groups are self-selecting, and members may have no other interaction during the rest of the week. The groups are also open-ended, with many individuals around their fringes. Because they schedule saunas at the same time each week, fringe members likely feel some connection to the group, yet their relative status is not as well known and they are not members.

The Viennese are able to mobilize network ties to solve various problems, ranging from how to obtain a first passport to how to find a job or an apartment. Sauna groups provide one of the networks a citizen can use for such purposes. How much an individual can tax a network for a private problem depends on the strength of the group, which is determined by its longevity, the sum of the relative statuses of its members, and the affective intensity of the individual to the group. The relative status contributes to the group's relative power. "Affective intensity" refers to how much everyone likes each other. Thus, sauna group participation includes an instrumental component by which people trade information about relative status and create a potential pool of shared social power. The component has obvious costs as well as benefits to participants. All of these activities are tied to specific public and private baths. The query "where do you go for your saunas?" asks for a statement about the individual.

## Community

At least two communities use sauna bathing for the ends just described. The Viennese use the nineteenth-century terms *Arbeiterklasse* (working-class community) and *Bügerstand* (bourgeois community) for late-twentieth-century groupings whose sense of identity and class-consciousness originates in organizational structures within the metropolis. Although mobility between communities is possible on an individual basis, the communities remain separate and bounded. Sauna bathing has different implications for each community. These include ideological issues relating to the body and the embodiment of metropolitan life.

The Viennese are conscious of these issues and articulate their ideas about the body in advertising, photography, and other public graphic arts; in their choice of dress and other physical behaviors; and in their conversations about health, diet, and exercise. From these contemporaneous representations of the body, and from historical research and exhibitions, coherent differences between the two communities' understandings of the body emerge. Working-class attitudes begin with the recognition that the oppression of workers by capital is all-pervasive. Public modesty is an imposed constraint on the demonstration of the physical prowess of workers, whether in musculature, reproductive endowments, or the damage that capital wreaks on the body through disease and industrial accident. All of these strengths are hidden by the imposition of bourgeois modesty. To compensate, workers should seek ways of freeing their bodies and celebrating their physicality. Men and women should celebrate that physicality together, because reproductive strength is as important as muscular strength. The idealized body type in this community is the well-developed adult physique: broad shoulders in men and broad hips in women. Flat abdomens, tight buttocks, or a particular shape to the breasts or penis are alien to this ideal.

Based on an exhibition of photographs of working-class culture between 1918 and 1934, there were summer nudist camps composed entirely of hundreds of working-class young adults. Nudity had nothing to do with advertising sexual availability. It was often a necessity because all baths were public ones; mass housing for workers was necessarily built without baths in every apartment. Public bathing required people to relax whatever standards of modesty they may have picked up from the more prudish era of the late nineteenth century. Broadcasting a contrasting attitude toward the body that was more appropriate to the working class made a virtue of that necessity.

Bourgeois attitudes toward the body, on the other hand, celebrate sexuality through identification with media images linked to consumption power and property-ownership issues—the defining features of this community. Exhibiting a body like those that display expensive clothes in the media makes a statement about one's authenticity as a member of the bourgeoisie. In the working-class community, such a body would be considered a lovely accident. In the bourgeois community, the desired body is a product of a great deal of time, effort, and money spent on diet, exercise, and health care. Such bodies, regardless of gender, are thin and tight-skinned. Their muscles are well defined and toned, although muscle development is well below what might be considered strong. They possess fine body hair that has been sculptured and sometimes dyed to attract the eye to the reproductive organs. Flat stomachs, tight buttocks, firm breasts with well-shaped nipples, and long, flaccid penises are prized. In the dark it should be difficult to distinguish a person's gender from the outline of his or her body.

Evolving from a tradition of abject modesty, unveiling a perfect bourgeois body in a sauna is at once liberating and rebellious. The act is bound up first with the antimodern social movements of the turn of the century such as the Frei Korper Kultur movement and later with the bourgeois sexual revolution of the 1960s, the birth control pill, and relaxation of bourgeois constraints on sexuality outside marriage. Nudity is encountered less often within propertied families because their homes have private baths. Public bourgeois nudity, then, sends a message of sociosexual potency mixed with all the other messages about self explored previously. If a working-class bather's motto is something like "I am worker, see my strength," the motto of a bourgeois bather might be "I am rich, see my beauty."

These community tropes are rarely found in pure forms. The sociosexual messages of the bourgeois are apparent in some working-class saunas, and the bravura of working-class nudity appears in some bourgeois saunas. Class-consciousness in Vienna relies on historical experience for much of its content. In the case of saunas today, the content derives from the tradition of the working-class naturist culture in the 1920s and the sexual liberation of bourgeois culture in the 1960s. The extent to which individual bathers express one or the other of these community styles in a more or less pure form depends on family history, the location of the sauna, and a sense of self. Nevertheless, the differences in the community styles are known, referred to in conversation (often mockingly by the other community), and as real as other expressions of class-consciousness.

## Power

All of these considerations have implications for the micro management of social power in metropolitan Vienna. In this context, the kind of social power invoked is exclusively interpersonal, involving the negotiation of relative status, rank, and prestige. What is significant is that the context for the power being claimed, mobilized, and diffused is rarefied, momentary sauna space. Networks form there and pool the resources of knowledge and agency. Distinctions of class and wellness are constructed and deconstructed, and the self finds its point of social balance. One is surrounded by others who are simultaneously enough like the self to provide support and enough unlike the self to provide the discontinuity necessary for self-realization. At stake for an individual is the opportunity for a transition from the clothed anonymity of the everyday public world of the city to the naked identity of a semipublic sauna. Because such transitions are loaded with danger for everyone involved, the atmosphere of a sauna is charged with guardedness. Surveillance is the watchword. Everyone is looked at when they arrive. Are they alone? Are they known? Are they there for health, community, network, or self? All of that is revealed by the person's body and the way he or she moves through the sauna complex. Does the person address the showers with familiarity? Is a particular lounge chair sought out? Is the person properly attired (sandals, towel to sit on, robe, and soap)? Does the person greet anyone? Does the person have the group's kind of body and speak the group's language?

As the answers to all these questions unfold, the defenses of sauna bathers rise or fall. Because I visited a large number of saunas over the years I was usually cast as an outsider. As it turns out, my circumcision made that judgment immediate in all baths. Regardless of whether people thought I was an American or Turk, I was shunned. I can contrast such experiences of strangerhood to occasional experiences of community when I attended a sauna with a group of friends. The differences are extraordinary. While a stranger, I was given the space to take my bath and perform all the activities associated with it. Tolerance of my presence was perfunctory. No one spoke to me. The wave of the towel in my direction during the time in box was without energy or interest. People left the steam bath or whirlpool when I arrived rather than be drawn into conversation. The three hours were endless and socially unsatisfying. When I was a member of a group, however, time flew, and other regulars at that bath and other sauna groups became involved in animated conversation. My acceptance among strangers was immediate and trusting because I was already an accepted member of an acceptable group. The bath itself was physically less intense, and the auxiliary experiences of whirlpool, snack bar, and open-air areas were fun-filled and engaging.

The sauna is a space of such immanent power that it must be defended against encroachment by those who would diffuse its potency. Alone, I was a threat to the exchanges of signs of their identity and attendant qualities. As a member of an acceptable group meeting for the first time at a bourgeois sauna, I was entailed by this process. Those who saw the group as an attractive addition to the sauna's ensemble of constituent power networks worked through the members of the group to inventory its assets. As an American academic who spoke German I provided neither advantage nor threat, and people quickly moved on to engage other, more potent members of the group. Because the group met infrequently and rarely at the same time, that process was repeated on subsequent visits until I began to anticipate a pattern. Group encounters left me far more satisfied both physically and socially than had individual encounters.

## Discussion

Both Japan and Vienna share similarities as fieldwork sites. First, both authors were unsettled by crossing over into bath participation. The experience was uncomfortable, alienating, and bewildering until it was experienced as a member of a group. Before the group experience, we were present at the baths but could not find the thread of social meaning that our neighbors experienced. The group became the focus of the meaning of the bath experience. The social experience of public nudity was also similar in both cases. Both of us were physically identifiable as outsiders. That created a renewed self-consciousness of otherness that as researchers we had begun to leave behind with increasing language competence.

The class structure of Vienna is a historical fact. Japan has developed its asymmetries of power and knowledge along different lines. In Vienna, communication and interaction fall off at these internal boundaries; in Japan they do not. The same holds true for the position of the ethnographer-outsider. In Vienna, strangerhood is classified, and interaction can legitimately be withheld. In Japan, strangerhood was not a barrier to communication but no less a status because of that. In almost all cases, fieldworkers are middle class and educated. They may have some experience with working-class life, but their aspirations lie within the cultural framework defined by a bourgeoisie. Interaction with people in the working class, even in a bath where all parties are nude, is contrastive at best. Ethnographers cannot help but describe behavior in contrast to their personal norms. The issue is not resolved in the middle-class saunas of Vienna or the baths of Japan because the condition of an ethnographer's strangerhood initiates contrastive interactions from the local side. Although these conditions ordinarily apply in all ethnographic encounters, the absence of various shields exacerbates them in public bathing. In the sauna or ofuro there is no hiding behind a notebook ("I am really a busy professional") or sunglasses ("You have no idea who I really am").

Sexual awareness of gender also contributes to the strangeness of an anthropologist at the subjective level. The customary patterns of mating and sexual negotiation are often among the last domains of culture a fieldworker learns. Being naked in an environment in which such behaviors are common may accelerate the learning curve, but it is fraught with potential misunderstandings and embarrassment. Everyone else understands the rules except the fieldworker, whose very presence suggests sufficient knowledge to have found the way into this pristine sanctuary. The group knows when sex play is or is not appropriate. The fieldworker does not. Although both field sites provided different kinds of signs for us to decode, learning proceeded slowly enough to cause subjective difficulties.

The sexual issue is exacerbated in part because a role reversal is inherently related to the sexuality of the ethnographer. For both of us, an unacknowledged (at least until much later) feature of the baths was that we both associated them with sexuality. The "natives" did not define them in that way. True, a certain amount of sexual play occurred, but the overall local consensus appeared to be that public baths were not a sexual arena. For us, however little we were prepared to admit it, nudity in the presence of the opposite sex equated unconsciously with a sexual situation.

The issue of misunderstanding and embarrassment also affects anthropologists at their most primary level: the awareness of self and the confidence of controlling at least one's self-image if not the environment. But that is virtually impossible where one's objective image is exposed to the public glare in unmanageable ways. The issue of circumcision is an example. Being (mis-)identified in Vienna as a Turk (which has a laden meaning for the Viennese but less for an anthropologist) or as having been mutilated (a source of squeamishness for the Japanese and of ethnic awareness for an anthropologist) places the anthropologists in a category that is forced on them and one that almost no amount of presentation can entirely manage. The obvious explanation—I am a Jew and this is our custom—would have had perhaps undesirable consequences in Vienna, where anti-Semitism still lingers, and would have draw blank stares from most Japanese. The issue of being forced into a situation reversed the anthropologists' role. Being in the baths for both of us was a sexual experience that occurred among others who could, and did, define the situation asexually. More than anything else, that enhanced a feeling of helplessness. In a way that was definitive and that struck a major element of identity we were both forced to accept the local definition of a situation, and that definition made no concession to our sense of gender or sexuality.

Going naked into fieldwork provides a good example of the local contextualizing of meaning. Public adult nakedness is not tolerated in the societies we have described, except in the bath. There, men, women, children, old, young, infirm, handicapped, mutilated, and sculptured all converge. One is commanded to be naked—but not sexual. Bathing suits are never used. The social world is turned upside down. Nakedness is legitimated as a ritual of purification and accepted as actions in any other ritual might be, even by those who choose not to participate. An anthropologist-as-researcher is on firm ethical ground for choosing to participate. The action in question is not a deviant local act, even though many local actors might choose not to engage in it. Public bathhouses are regulated by a civil authority that ensures a clean bath and a level admission price. The action in question is transparently disinterested: One is ostensibly there in order to bathe. History, local knowledge, and our relationship to the people we studied made our decision to cross the boundary into public nakedness more appropriate and less fraught with danger than might be the case in other communities. Yet the overall definition, by the host societies, of the situation as asexual highlighted the fact that our societies consider nakedness to be inherently sexual.

Naked public bathing, even in single-gender and family groups, can be sexually charged. An anthropologist's genitalia will be on view, as are those of the bathers. Subtle signs of arousal among bathers of both genders are often evident. Nakedness is a marked action, the exceptional state. It is liminalized and treated as publicly acceptable and socially desirable in Japan and Austria only in public bathing. Thus, the decision by fieldworkers to cross over into a public bath partakes of the multivocality of nakedness, including its sexual valence. By bathing publicly with members of the community, anthropologists make their bodies available for the potentially prurient fantasies of others and makes others' bodies similarly available for themselves.

The bath exposes fieldworkers to encounters with informants in a potentially salacious context by the standards of the cultures from which we both came. Encounters are unavoidable. When most of the encounters in the bath are with strangers, research value declines. One can only learn so much from such observations. To understand what is going on, it is necessary to talk to people. At that moment, strangers become informants. Bathing naked with informants is not the same as engaging in intercourse, but the activities share commonalities. People reach a closer level of intimacy than would be the case in clothed conversation, even when the conversations are not about sexual matters.

How critical are bath encounters? Could a field project proceed without them? Because these were marked action domains for informants they offered glimpses of Victor Turner's antistructure—those moments usually contained by ritual and during which ordinary relationships of social life are alternately camouflaged and unmasked by symbolic inversions and behavioral transgressions. Our bath encounters were social dramas in which people ostensibly cleansed themselves both physically and socially, laying bare their bodies in both senses. We became more aware of what was important to them. We saw how people construct their bodies as they reveal them, exposing to neighbors how each interprets the physical self. Although the process goes on in every society through the interaction of the body with clothing, in the naked heat of the bath we saw a minimalist strategy for the physical construction of self. With few elements—posture, carriage, skin, towel, and movement—our informants were still able to maintain the identities of their clothed selves, which were so important that they could not be left in the locker room. Perhaps our field projects could have gone on without bath encounters, but our confidence in positing the priorities of informants in the social constructions of their identities would have never been as bold. We would also never have become aware of the degree to which our culturally derived sexualities affect our beings.

NOTES

This essay is a collaborative effort, and the authors' names are listed alphabetically.

   1. This description of sento is from the male perspective. Information about the women's section was provided by Jeanne Jacob-Ashkenazi.
   2. In Austria, there is one other context in which nudity is acceptable—swimming beaches specifically designated as clothing-optional. Like the scheduling of mixed bathing in the saunas, the special beaches are clearly signed. Only those who wish to be there partake of these opportunities. I [Rotenberg] consider them a special, warm-weather case of the same social dramas that are mounted in saunas throughout the year. As such, they represent the same sort of contrast as that between the sento and the onsen in Japan.

PART 3

# EXPECTATIONS AND CATEGORIZATIONS: WHEN SAME ≠ SAME AND DIFFERENT ≠ DIFFERENT

# 6

## Identity in Ethnography: Limits to Reflective Subjectivity

*Thomas K. Fitzgerald*

Little has been published on the effects of an ethnographer's sexual identity on specific research strategies while studying gay and lesbian formal organizations (D'Emilio and Freedman 1988; Paul 1982). Using the term *reflective subjectivity* (Warren 1977:104) to emphasize the central yet problematic nature of an investigator's self in a field setting, I will examine some of the limits of reflective subjectivity for ethnographers in terms of a specific study of gay self-help groups in Sweden and Finland (Fitzgerald 1981).

A consideration of identity in ethnography, the ethical issues involved in this study were those of self-disclosure, advocacy, and intervention. Nonetheless, in trying to ensure scientific excellence as well as social relevance for research, it became necessary to consider factors that transcended minority identity.[1] What were the effects of a gay identity on management of ethnographic interactions? Metaphors often help organize a debate and provide concreteness of imagery. Therefore, some current metaphors surrounding the complex issue of minority identity in the field need to be considered. How can this very personal process be phrased in terms of an ethnographer's changing metaphors of identity? Too, how did my identity as a gay person affect the way I ultimately viewed the field problem? Tracing that self-process back further, how had my sexual identity altered over the years? What were some of the changing "metaphors of identity" that accompanied such psychological shifts? Finally, how did these images and metaphors affect my evolving conceptualizations of such familiar anthropological abstractions as "culture" versus "society" and by extension my epistemological understanding of the notion of homosexual identity itself?

## Metaphors of Identity

I went to Sweden and Finland just before the AIDS crisis broke—a jubilant time of identity celebration for gays in the United States (Fitzgerald 1980). I had grown up in the rural South, where surely the most appropriate metaphor for homosexual was nonperson if "person" is defined as society's confirmation of self. Anthropology has reminded people that each culture has its own concept of "the person" that is determined by an individual's perceived place in the society. The self is an individual's awareness of a unique identity, but, as La Fontaine (1987:124) points out, the person is society's confirmation of identity that gives it the stamp of social and cultural legitimacy.

Homosexuals during the 1950s and 1960s, lacking such validation, paid a heavy price as far as identity was concerned. Younger persons (gay or nongay) may find it difficult to comprehend what it was like to be gay in the homophobic environment of the United States before the 1970s that virtually denied the existence of homosexuals as persons. Although there has been long-standing aversion to acceptance of gay citizens as persons in U.S. society, such harsh metaphorical imagery as "nonperson" strikes most people now as quaint or unreal, because—I suspect—its negative starkness offends liberal sensibilities. In the following text I use the concept of social stranger even though— as a pedagogical metaphor—it, too, has limitations (see Gudykunst [1991] for a discussion of the stranger metaphor in interpersonal communication encounters).

"Social stranger" in modern scientific discourse normally implies a status of social outsider rather than foreigner, one unacquainted with the culture (compare Gudykunst and Kim's [1984] concept of "cultural stranger"). Those who have been marginalized in significant ways by the society in which they grew up have described the feeling as being on the outside looking in. Caffrey (1989) uses the metaphor of stranger to characterize the difficulty Ruth Benedict had in reconciling her role as a professional writer and thinker with her sometimes tormented self-perceptions as a "stranger in this land." Caffrey argues that Benedict felt she was a stranger because she was lesbian, partially deaf, and a bright and sensitive female academic in a time when women were scarce in academia. Borrowing Bruce Bawer's (1993) especially apt metaphor for the same phenomenon, such individuals see themselves as having no "place at the table."

A social stranger, therefore, is someone who does not fit in socially because she or he is perceived to be different from the norm—not one unacquainted with the culture. With the emphasis on the social construction of personhood, certain individuals—by virtue of their place in society—will be excluded from the designation of "person." They remain, by cultural definition and social placement, outside society.

I grew up in the homophobic rural South of the 1950s and 1960s, a time when no room was made for a self-chosen identity as a gay person, especially one who wished to live a life of dignity and pride. Gays were essentially regarded as nonpersons, the ultimate existential insult of such a closeted existence. That was the personal imagery I had initially carried into the field, although it was severely challenged by the historical events of the preceding two decades.

## Gay and Lesbian Self-Help Groups

Kurt Hiller's 1921 United Front slogan, "The liberation of homosexuals can only be the work of homosexuals themselves," became a reality with the growth and expansion of gay and lesbian self-help groups during the 1970s and 1980s. Gay males and lesbians were beginning to find strength in the emerging self-help movement. By the 1970s, almost every sizable city in North America and Western Europe had witnessed some form of gay liberation (D'Emilio and Freedman 1988). If gays and lesbians did not have a shared place at the big table they were busily trying to create a smaller, albeit separate, table for themselves (Bawer 1993).

Since 1979 I have been concerned with the question of how gay groups provide help for people facing similar, difficult life situations. Specifically, I have compared gay and lesbian self-help groups in Sweden and Finland. The self-help, mutual-aid idea is an age-old concept of positive group association for dealing with social concerns and reflects the human need for affiliation and community (Lieberman and Borman 1976). How did these associations differ between Sweden, a country relatively tolerant and supportive of homosexuality, and Finland, where homosexuality was treated officially as an illness and, by implication, considered something not to be discussed in a positive way?

My investigation (Fitzgerald 1981) represented a somewhat different approach to the idea of support system, being about gays helping gays rather than the usual dependence on outside care-giving agencies. From a gay rights point of view, my study was a positive approach to the investigation of homosexual organizations. It also formed the basis for a fuller understanding of the social status of homosexuals in a comparative framework, suggesting alternative sources of support for this population.

Caught up in the liberation promise—it was a time of cultural transition toward more acceptance of sexual minorities—I assumed, incorrectly, that being gay would in itself assure easy acceptance and rapport in gay and lesbian formal organizations in Sweden and Finland. Many gay people at that time no doubt assumed a sort of mystical bond that supposedly united all gays everywhere. It is well known, for example, that such groups often refused to work with nongay researchers. I was gay and beginning to be proud of that label. Acceptance, then, seemed assured.

An "insider" ethnographer has many advantages, and it is often argued privately that she or he may be less ethnocentric than an ethnographer who originates outside the group. At the same time, it is possible to be subtly biased and misled by the comfort of that status. Gay identity can become problematic in a gay field situation. Despite the emotional need to belong to an exclusive group, pressing factors other than minority identity—age, sex, and professional status, for example—may be encountered (Fitzgerald 1981).

## Age, Sex, and Professional Status

### Male and Female

What first appeared to be a homogeneous population—a shared identity, mine and theirs—turned out to be firmly split between male and female interests. Despite any wishes of mine to the contrary, lesbians and gay males operated separately in Sweden (although not so much in Finland), making access to the women almost impossible for me. Lesbians and gay males clung together for psychic survival during the

1960s in the South. We did not think we had the luxury of separation based on imagined differences between male and female homosexual experiences. That separatism was the first challenge to my quest for an inclusive identity as gay.

Activities and interests differed less for the two groups in Finland than in Sweden. In Sweden there had always been separate self-help groups for women and men, both operating loosely under one umbrella structure. In Finland, however, gay males and lesbians attempted to work together on most issues. Finnish women, at least at the time of my study, were less involved in the international women's movement than were lesbians in Sweden and the United States (Fitzgerald 1979, 1980, 1981). When Finnish women were interviewed separately, they expressed slightly more interest in recreational aspects of the group and in personal development initiatives as opposed to political involvement. Lesbians in Sweden were decidedly more political.

## The Reality of Age

Much more serious than divided gender interests, however, was the factor of age. My metaphors of identity were largely inappropriate for these young Scandinavians. Even though I had begun to make significant contributions to gay and lesbian causes (for example, I was teaching the first officially recognized course on homosexuality in North Carolina and had started the only successful gay and lesbian professional group in Greensboro), I was still somewhat uncomfortable with the image-metaphor of gay people as "cultural outlaws," valiantly fighting against injustices in a presumably straight, homophobic environment (Butler 1990:87).

Although the vast majority of members of the self-help groups, both in Sweden and Finland, were what one informant amusingly called "Saturday night gays" (interested more in socializing than in participating in political activities), many younger gays during the late 1970s and early 1980s—in part because of pressures from the international gay liberation movement—began to press for more political activism, often alienating older members in the process. A definite and often unwholesome generational split began to surface.

The more radical minority (about 15 percent of the total), nevertheless, has helped bring about significant reforms in both countries. In Sweden, for example, their political accomplishments led to the legalization of homosexual activity between consenting adults (the age of consent being set at fifteen). Second, through a custom known as *sammanboende,* a kind of quasi-legal marriage, same-sex unions were placed on the same footing as common-law heterosexual ones, the privilege extending even to gay immigrants "married" to Swedes. Third, in October 1979 pressure from local and international psychiatric communities culminated in the removal of the hated "sickness label" that had previously been applied to all homosexuals in Sweden. After large numbers of Stockholm men and women—most from local self-help groups— telephoned employers to report being "too sick with homosexuality to come to work," the Swedish Health Board relented and ceased to classify homosexuality as an illness (Fitzgerald 1980, 1981).

The struggle over basic human rights has also extended to Finland. Although many Americans view Sweden and Finland as similar societies, attitudes toward gay people were quite different in the two countries. Finland was unique in the treatment of its homosexual minority. The Finnish Supreme Court had argued in 1969 that homosexuality was a "pathological deviation" that should not be given the status of a minority behavior. Homosexuals should be made to feel "sick" because that would encourage them to seek treatment for what was then still regarded as a disease (Fitzgerald 1979:4). By 1977 full censorship of homosexual topics became the unofficial policy for Finnish radio and television, a reactionary legal stand supported and justified by Finnish psychiatry. Article 20:9:2 of the Finnish Penal Code, which forbids public encouragement of homosexuality, is still on the books. However, Finnish radio and television censorship of homosexuality has eased up considerably, and Finland is in the midst of massive legal reforms, with all sex laws being looked at critically.

What was surprising was the almost complete refusal by both the Finnish government and scientific community to consider scientific evidence that contradicted the outmoded psychoanalytic view of homosexuality as a deviation, caused by presumed fears of the opposite sex, from the supposed biologic norm. Gay people offering contrary evidence sometimes found themselves charged with suffering from a defense mechanism that Finnish psychiatry called "querulous paranoia," defined as a type of paranoid reaction in which supposed or real injustices result in a "patient" carrying out an uncompromising fight against the injustices (Fitzgerald 1979, 1981). To complain became itself a form of mental illness.

One local injustice concerned the problem some gays encountered with nongay self-help switchboards, especially those run by religious organizations. Upon my initial arrival in Helsinki, I learned of a young woman who had been struggling with her identity as a lesbian and had, in a moment of crisis, telephoned a Christian hot line for help. Their moralizing response, in essence, was that she had better change or she would go straight to hell. She took an overdose of pills but luckily had the presence of mind to ring the gay hot line before she passed out. She had survived, and the local gay group was in the process of protesting the "go-home-and-pray" advice of the Christian group. Their defense, however, was predictable: What do you expect from people who are suffering from querulous paranoia?

Although I was fully in sympathy with the need for change and acutely aware of the suffering that resulted from Finland's archaic laws, I still was far from belonging to the same exclusive identity circle as these young Scandinavians. Age always remained a barrier to acceptance in this field situation, despite my advances in reflective subjectivity and accompanying positive changes in personal metaphorical imagery.

## Professional Status

Trust or distrust are important issues when the researcher and the researched share common ground. If age were not enough of a barrier, my professional status among these largely working-class, often Marxist-oriented, groups assured a definite social distance. Self-help groups, by definition, are essentially egalitarian. Although such associations are sometimes initiated and supported by gay and nongay professionals—albeit often behind the scenes—most groups operate outside professional agencies and are rarely legally recognized institutions. Thus, it is common to encounter a generalized distrust of professionals, especially those perceived as authorities who might stand in judgment of a group that had differing goals. I hope that was not the case with me, but undoubtedly there was some spillover in feeling about my professional status.

Some professionals working with gay groups have even been accused of using the sickness label for purposes of social control. Although these stories were usually impossible to substantiate, it was common in gay and lesbian circles to hear of professional abuses, for example, ethically questionable practices of aversion therapy (in which a gay "patient" would be given a picture of a loved one, followed by a drug that caused vomiting), or exorcism as a supposed "cure" for homosexual behavior (Ross and Stälström 1979). In more totalitarian states—Russia still had the infamous Code 20—concentration camps existed for sexual minorities that did not fit the prevailing political ideology. The attitude of many gay persons I encountered was one of extreme caution in regard to professionals, gay or nongay, and it was not difficult to appreciate why that was the case.

Polite cooperation characterized my encounters with these self-help groups but not much personal acceptance as a fellow gay person. So much for the myth of homogeneity. I had to use my "professor status" on numerous occasions to gain access to heads of educational and psychiatric organizations, but being accepted in these contexts cast a shadow over my other activities, as if I were no longer part of the gay group. They wanted concrete proof of my allegiance.

Even though my research orientation has always been to try to solve problems—my fieldwork concerned suicide prevention, for example—and my emotional commitment is to achieve humanitarian justice, I found myself torn between the roles of objective scientist and political activist (Fitzgerald 1981). That was especially true in Finland, where I briefly agreed to participate in a civic protest to the United Nations (then meeting in Geneva) about alleged violations of human rights of Finnish gays. An ethical issue of some personal proportions had raised its ugly head.

## The Ethics of Intervention

While doing my fieldwork on suicide prevention in the summer of 1979 I witnessed what amounted to a mild international scandal over the treatment of homosexuals in Finland. The United Nations met in July in Geneva to consider the issue of human rights and examined reports from six countries, including Finland. I agreed to help draft that report and also to write a supporting letter of protest. The Finnish government had characteristically overlooked its homosexual minority, but gay self-help groups in Helsinki quickly reminded the government, the press, and the international media that homosexual rights were being violated.

At the very least, the confrontation was an international embarrassment for the government. It also proved awkward for me. My letter of protest received a quick response from the Finnish equivalent of the CIA. Subsequently, all the books and papers that I had mailed home disappeared without trace. I began to wonder whether I had endangered any future permission to return to Finland. Yet many positive things have since happened to improve the social position of sexual minorities everywhere. On a recent return visit to Finland, for example, I was delighted to find that the subject of homosexuality, although not openly discussed, certainly was no longer hidden.

I now consider the protest gesture politically naive because the advocacy role involved too much personal and professional liability. I was wearing the cloak of cultural outlaw, but the fit was far from perfect. Those whom I studied, I began to feel, had unrealistic expectations of what I could and would do on their behalf. For one thing, I was seeking scientific significance for my work, but they were thinking in terms of its social relevance. The two were not always compatible. Problems of reflective subjectivity remained. In retrospect, I have to admit that there were serious limitations in trying to conduct research among a group of individuals with whom I only presumed to share a common identity.

I was also beginning to appreciate the subtleties of what has been called "ambigusexuality" (Mendes-Leite 1993:272). Appearances can be misleading when one holds too rigid an identity classification. The master status wears many disguises. Certainly, homosexuality in Scandinavia was not as likely as it was in the United States to be seen as a "thing." It was only a word that had different meanings in specific social contexts. That lesson became apparent in a rather dramatic fashion when I interviewed the head of a self-help group in southern Finland. "Marja" was a recent transsexual. Unfortunately, I was then largely ignorant of transsexualism and had some trouble sorting out identity and sexual orientation in this frame. When I asked who were her closest friends, gays or straights, she answered honestly but curtly: "Straights, of course, because I am straight!" The response emphasized the necessity of placing models of sexuality within a larger social universe rather than assuming the specificity of a minority context.

Nonetheless, I believe that I learned some important personal and professional lessons. Although I still believe strongly that the development and maintenance of personal identity cannot be divorced from the background of a largely repressive heterosexual world, that dialectic was more complex and more contradictory than my personal metaphors of identity allowed for at the time. Part of the problem is surely the tendency on the part of some minority members to use the rhetoric of cultural exclusiveness to express dissatisfaction with perceived social injustices. In fact, it is routine to encounter a huge gap between cultural rhetoric and social realities.

126    *Thomas K. Fitzgerald*

## Gay "Culture" or Gay Identities?

In a strange twist of events, homophobic societies may help create a quasi-cultural status for gay and lesbian persons where there would be no need for such if we were given full social equality. It is probably impossible to speak of a uniquely homosexual subculture. At any rate, the real danger is that identity centrality can become a defensive master status that is both exclusive and self-perpetuating and thus sometimes self-defeating. Any master status, as a central focus of self-definition, tends to inhibit an individual's creative capacity to fashion other identities (Johnson and Ferraro 1987:125).

Despite rhetoric (unsupported discourse) to the contrary, my association with these so-called cultural outlaws in Scandinavia led me to the conclusion that most gays and lesbians do not want to separate themselves from the rest of humanity but would prefer to communicate in the larger cultural arenas shared by gays and nongays alike. Too much emphasis on gay "culture" and exclusive sexual identity can translate negatively for sexual minorities seeking fundamental human rights. Sexual preference may be more analogous to ethnic markers that make collective identification similar to, but not exactly like, subcultural traits. Both straights and gays, however, are sometimes guilty of using the closet metaphor to symbolize and justify exclusion and exclusiveness.

When gay males and lesbians argue for a separate culture, they may inadvertently perpetuate a stranger role, the metaphor of social stranger being the most persistent and accurate metaphor for contemporary gays in the United States. By emphasizing differences, most of which do not actually exist, gays may be giving societal justification for more separation and hence more discrimination. Social scientists have a responsibility to clarify their positions on this still controversial matter of culture, which is so often confused with the need to assert identities. Gay identity may well have important functions that transcend culture as such (Fitzgerald 1993). At any rate, one must not fall into the trap of assuming that where there is an identity there is also a corresponding culture.

Unfortunately, the old models of culture change—with their not-so-oblique reference to a vulgarized cultural relativity—are still used to explain societal changes that take place in the area of same-sex behavior. Such models, and their accompanying metaphors of identity, may be inappropriate for groups that are not culturally distinctive

(Fitzgerald 1993). Identity politics can become an exercise in rhetorical contradiction. What really contributes to the stranger role for gays and lesbians in homophobic societies?

During the process of conducting my fieldwork, I discovered the limits of trying to share a common identity with those being researched. I also began to realize that my metaphors of identity were shifting in response to intellectual and personal growth. My first shift was from the stark and negative metaphor of nonperson, which I had inherited as a childhood legacy, to the more youthful rebel imagery typified by the metaphor of cultural outlaw, which had provided emotional fuel for conducting the fieldwork in the first place. My second shift was to the conservative and analytical metaphor of social stranger, which attempts to avoid the fervor of exclusiveness and separation while recognizing the realities of social complexity in the cultural construction of sexual identities.

NOTES

This chapter represents a much-expanded version of Fitzgerald (1991).

1. In a personal letter in 1979, Charles Lippy, who writes on southern religions, offered me the perfect rationale for why it is necessary to understand the inner self: "Effective professional performance requires that one acquire a deepened awareness of one's own inner self and come to grips with the struggle which confronts all people in the quest to affirm their own human integrity and creativity. The process of self-discovery and self-knowing has an important corollary: having undertaken the journey to discover one's own self leads to acceptance of the parallel journey of others to discover their own true-authentic selves."

7

# Performing like a *P'o* and Acting as a Big Sister: Reculturating into the Indigenous Lesbian Circle in Taiwan

*Y. Antonia Chao*

The terms *T* and *P'o*, which refer to the two mutually exclusive lesbian sexual roles in Taiwan, have been widely used by Taiwanese lesbians and are now even referred to in Taiwanese mass literature. According to many of my informants, the terms were first coined by the owner of a popular gay bar during the 1960s, a period when gay men and women mixed relatively freely at specific locales in major cities like Taipei and Kaohsiung. Originally derived from the English word *tomboy*, "T" refers to "masculine" lesbians. "We were seen as real men back then," a forty-nine-year-old T recalled in the spring of 1994, "and we were always respected and acknowledged as such by everyone there. As a matter of fact, at one point the owner of Round Table [a gay bar] jokingly claimed that it was not a bar for gay men anymore but rather for 'tomboys.' This is how the term *T* was created." P'o, a Mandarin word literally meaning "wife," was coined shortly thereafter by the same group to refer to a T's wife, or the "feminine lesbian." In the years that followed, P'o and T became terms, sex roles, and performative styles widely accepted by Taiwan's lesbians.

At first sight, these Taiwanese terms correspond to the Western butch-femme dichotomous model in the sense that T embodies full-blown masculinity and P'o overly theatrical femininity. Ts wear tuxedos, matching ties, masculine shoes, short hair ("tuxedo hair"), and talk loudly while drinking heavily. In contrast, P'os usually wear skirts, have long hair, and are constantly giggling instead of talking. The two seemingly heterosexualized roles need to be acted out often in a theatrical and even parabolic way, for in order to be considered a T or P'o an actor must "outdo" the heterosexual gender category by exaggerating and overacting it. Not only is a P'o feminine, for example, but she is also much more feminine than most other Taiwanese women, who would be considered silly, inappropriate, and even insane if they were to giggle all the time. Similarly, not only is a T masculine, but she is also much more so than most Taiwanese men because Ts are required to boast about their sexual expertise all the time, whereas a Taiwanese man would be considered strange, even idiotic, if he bragged as incessantly as does a T.

The T and P'o sex-gender identities could not have come fully into formation until the T-bar (a common term for exclusively lesbian bars in Taiwan) was founded. The first T-bar, Wang Yu Ku (Forgetting Sadness Valley), was opened by a T-P'o couple, A-pao and Ya-t'ou, in a red light district of Taipei in 1985.[1] Since then, more than thirty T-bars have opened in Taipei, Taichung, and Kaohsung, the three major cities of Taiwan. Since their inception, T-bars have provided a performative setting where lesbians can enact their sexuality and sex roles via distinctive activities such as drinking and participating in *hua-chiu-ch'uan* (a drinking game), performing Karaoke, and chatting and flirting with bar attendants and other patrons. Over the years, with the spread and standardization of T-bars, the T-P'o dichotomy became standardized as well.

Despite its widespread circulation in lesbians' daily lives, the T-P'o dichotomy is frequently called into question in grass-roots lesbian journals. The journals are sponsored by lesbians who have more advanced educational backgrounds (college and higher) than do regular T-bar patrons, who usually have an educational level of secondary school or lower and as a rule follow the North American feminist agenda they have adopted from Fu-Nu Hsin-Chih (Awakening), the organizational base for Taiwan's women's rights movement since the late 1970s.

Although acknowledging the existence of T-P'o sexual roles, *Nu-P'eng-Yu* (Girl Friends), an influential lesbian bimonthly during the 1990s, argues against the "heterosexualized" ideology inherent in a T-P'o relationship. That is not to say that North American feminist lesbianism is grounded in an essentialized conception of woman-man gender roles as a mirror image of female-male sex ones, yet that is how it was understood by Wo-Men Chih Chien (Between Us), Taiwan's first nationwide lesbian organization, which was founded in the spring of 1990. Indeed, back then the T-P'o relationship was conceived as a (usually adulterated) reproduction of heterosexuality and therefore antifeminist. That perspective is evident in, for example, *Nu-P'eng-Yu*'s response to a reader's question: "What's exactly the difference between T and P'o? I look like a P'o but my mind is like a T, so what should I identity myself with?"

> There is a noble term—"unclassified" [*pu-feng*]—that symbolizes your identity. You need not identify yourself with anything—no matter how devotedly you have been chasing fashion. Here is a great story (which actually is already common knowledge): The T-P'o classification was popular only in 1950s' America. Given the fact that American space shuttles have already made numerous trips to the Moon, their people certainly have evolved to the stage that T-P'o classification is no longer necessary to a love pursuit. So, look happily forward to your own love with a *pu-feng* mind! (Lei-szu-pien 1994:20)

I joined Wo-Men Chih Chien in May of 1990 as one of its earliest members. At that time, almost all of the members had recently come out as feminist lesbians. We identified ourselves as lesbians through our readings of feminist texts, predominantly North American ones produced in the late 1970s and early 1980s. It follows that lesbianism then was understood as a politically correct, self-constitutive way out of patriarchal domination. The form of same-sex love it conceptualized was coined in political terms in lieu of sexual or erotic ones. That is partly why, in the group's first encounter with T-bar people, who identify with the dichotomization of T and P'o, there was much discomfort.

On a more personal level, my first trip to a T-bar occurred two months later when the "sisters" of Wo-Men Chih Chien held a farewell party for me before I set off for Ph.D. study at Cornell University in the United States. Throughout the party I was amazed at, not to mention perplexed by, the sexual dynamics maintained at the bar. More precisely, I was shocked by the existence of lesbians whose body language and sexual codes I found incomprehensible. I had conceptualized and experienced same-sex love since high school days as derived from a desire for likes in lieu of opposites. But here in the T-bar there were only Ts and P'os, a lesbian dichotomy. By virtue of my long hair and feminine manner, I was identified by others at the bar as a P'o, a sexual role whose significance had completely lost me. As a result, I felt mostly disturbed and out of place, a self-confessed lesbian with no gender role that quite fit. Two days after the party I boarded the flight for New York City, my first trip abroad, and left behind the T-bar scene, never imagining that I would return to it as part of my doctoral research.

Then, at Cornell, a similar sense of disorientation overwhelmed me. I was out of place and, worse yet, had no referential system to even start conceptualizing my identity and foreignness. During our first telephone conversation the coordinator of a lesbian support group on campus cut off my self-introduction and asked in a scathingly condescending tone, "Are you sure that you are calling the right place? This is a group for gay people only. Are you sure that you are gay?" Shocked and mortified, I reassured her of my sexual identity. She then murmured to herself, "Really? So we do have dykes in Taiwan?" I saw white faces only at the two group meetings I attended. At the time, I knew literally nothing about racial politics in the United States. My only possible reflection was that no one looked like me.

In the classroom my sense of disorientation was even stronger. Most new students from overseas suffered from a profound feeling of cultural discontinuity, but my case was intensified because of my engagement with queer studies. My first year at Cornell, 1990, was the year that Sedgwick and Butler published their groundbreaking works on queer politics. Campus discussions of identity politics were in their heyday, yet I had misgivings about their implicit universalization of non-Western homosexual experiences. I began to ask myself a series of questions: If training in critical theory is supposed to aid one's investigation into humanity, why are its discourses unable to shed light satisfactorily on my subject positions as a Taiwanese and a Taiwanese lesbian? Can these two forms of discontinuity only be generated in a culturally alien or foreign setting? More important, can such a form of disorienting experience be constructive in understanding ethnographic encounters between a seemingly "decultured insider" like me and the presumably "cultured insiders" like my (future) Taiwanese informants?

My concern with all these questions finally led me back to Taiwan to work on the issue of T-bars, the prior "indigenous" cultural context that both shaped lesbian identity in Taiwan and also made me feel disoriented with my "Taiwanese-ness" and lesbianness. Over the next four years I would conduct two sessions of research that differed markedly from each other in terms of ethnographic experience and theoretical considerations. The first session, from February to June 1992, marked my initiation into the T-bar community as an "amateur" P'o. During this period I learned to act out the role available to me and was tentatively but not happily accepted by my informants as a P'o. The second period, from May 1993 to July 1994, marked my recognition as a "big sister" and acceptance as a true insider by the community. In the sections that follow, I shall trace my increasingly strong identification with and performance as a P'o and the evolution of this identity into that of big sister as I analyze the meanings and implications of Taiwanese gender categories—a topic I had never expected to pursue as a scholarly interest, certainly not for my Ph.D.

## The First Phase: Performing like a P'o

I had not planned to become emotionally or sexually involved with anyone when I took my first trip back to Taiwan. Nonetheless, I met my current girlfriend, Wen-tsai, at the very beginning of my fieldwork. Unmistakably T by T-bar standards, her accompanying me to a bar opened the possibility that I could be seen both as a P'o and a *ch'uan-nei-jen* (those who are within the circle). T-bar people use that term to refer to the lesbians who frequent the T-bar scene. To those who do not look familiar or, more usually, to those who obviously do not fit in, both regular customers and waiters immediately ask, "Are you within the circle?" With that question, a distinction is simultaneously drawn between insider and outsider. Despite Wen-tsai's presence, during my first week at the bar I was bombarded with the question all the time. The reason was simple: I did not act correctly.

My identity as P'o was tentatively assumed instead of well accepted because I had not learned the distinct rules of performance that all insiders must abide. I had not yet internalized the order of things in the T-bar or the roles of all performers. For example, immediately after patrons are seated at the bar, either a T attendant called a *shao-yeh* (young lord) or a *kung-kuan* (public relations) P'o attendant will come and sit with them. Because the T-bar is "sex-role divided" in terms of interactions between employees and patrons, the kung-kuan will usually cater exclusively to T patrons and the shao-yeh to P'o ones. For a kung-kuan, service begins by initiating friendly conversation with patrons, and they always wear thick makeup, long hair, and fashionable women's outfits, in particular miniskirts that reveal legs, arms, and the curve of their bodies. They are highly playful and flirt constantly with patrons. Their standard greeting is immediate: "You have not been around for quite a while. How've you been?" (to long-term patrons) or (to newcomers), "You look very familiar. I know you must have been around, but I'm terrible with names. How may I call you (*tze mo ch'eng-hu*)?"

The name one goes by at a T-bar is both social and contextual. By "social," I emphasize the fact that the social networks toward which one's T-bar name is directed are ordinarily suggestive of the circle one identifies for herself. One uses a T-bar name only in the contexts and under the conditions related to one's practices in a circle. For example, a seventeen-year-old T who had recently *ch'u-tao* (become out on the road—that is, recently entered the circle) had a T-bar name of Hsiao-I. It had been provided by her *ta-ko* (big brother), a more experienced but not necessarily older T who introduces one into the circle. Almost as soon as she received that name, Hsaio-I abandoned her former nickname, Pien-pien (Flat-flat), a euphemism for her figure. Pien-pien is not an appropriate name for a self-respecting T, and to show the extent of her identification with her T identity Hsiao-I used her new name at her workplace, a video-game arcade owned by a thirty-ish T. That is significant, because only those who have established a secure T-bar identity go by their T-bar names in other daily activities.

If Hsaio-I provides a good example of the social nature of the T-bar name, my experience shows how it is contextual. By contextual, I emphasize the name's performative quality. A T-bar name is required for social interaction but need not convey one's identity in the larger society. Significantly, under most circumstances one's "real" name is not at all expected at the bar. At the very beginning of fieldwork I made a mistake by giving a shao-yeh my Chinese name, Chao Yen-ning. For five minutes she ridiculed me by repeatedly asking for its correct pronunciation and stress pattern.[2] Finally, she laughed, "I got it—that *ning* of *Ning Wei Nu-Jeng* [would rather be a woman]!" The term comes from the then-popular television talk show of the same name. Aimed at housewives and pink-collar professional women, the show addressed such issues as husbands' extramarital relationships and new "feminine products" on the market (cosmetics and diet pills, for example). In Taiwan, television programs geared to women are generally considered less serious than "men's programs" such as news and sports, and the women who watch them are usually assumed to be dull and silly. Therefore, the T meant to mock me. I blushed immediately and did not know how to react. Making a perfunctorily polite gesture, she said, "All right, all right. The *ning* of Chao Ning."

In Mandarin Chinese the two *ning*s are represented by the same character yet connote totally different meanings. Chao Ning is a popular male writer and was a legislator at the time of our conversation. The substitution, however, was still problematic because, coincidentally or not, he was a host of that very talk show. Since that encounter I have gone by my English name, Antonia, whose attributes have never been called into question because more than a few ch'uan-nei-jen go by English names as well, such as Joseph for a T or Lulu for a P'o.

The anecdote illustrates the fact that without an appropriate name one is denied recognition. Benveniste (1971:224) argues that "it is in and through language that man constitutes himself as a subject, because language alone establishes the concept of 'ego' in reality, in its reality which is that of the being. The 'subjectivity' we are discussing here is the capacity of the speaker to posit himself as 'subject.'" In the bar context, however, it is clear that the discursive or linguistic subject—in my case, the new patron—cannot be constituted or recognized as such simply by establishing a dialogue with an other or, more precisely, by positing herself as a linguistic being. Instead, what constitutes her as a legitimate subject is not language or discourse per se but rather the contextual regulations by which one needs to abide. My inability to follow such a set of regulations explains my failure to recognize that the other—ch'uan-nei-jen in general and the shao-yeh in particular—is the only legitimate producer of discourse.

One regulation I had failed to follow was to provide an appropriate name. Dumont (1978) provides an intriguing story about being named by Panare informants. The naming transformed him from a socially nonexistent being into an acceptable outsider—not yet an authentic Panare social subject but rather someone that the Panare would be able and willing to come to imagine as differentially distinct from a well-defined insider. Dumont had at first been rejected, or at best ignored, by the Panare because of his inability to provide any referent relevant to their symbolic system so they could identify him. By contrast, after he showed them pictures of Western bearded men such as himself he was first ridiculed, but then the Panare named him The Bearded One. Afterward, they began to tell him their own real names and, more important, the kinship relations embedded in those names. He was being allowed to participate in real speech acts.

The newcomer to a T-bar faces a situation similar to that confronting anthropologists such as Dumont in spite of one significant difference between the two cases: At a T-bar a consciously fictitious name is required. It is precisely because the bar context is a performative one that constructing a new self, which is in part realized through acting out in the semantic domain of a pseudo-name, is expected. In my case, Antonia is acceptable because of its foreignness—in other words, it was "false" enough. More important, the fact that it is not a Taiwanese name entails a broad enough semantic domain for me to act out my foreignness in both cultural and ch'uan-nei-jen terms.

The fictive reality of the bar context is also evident in the fact that despite the seemingly friendly atmosphere maintained, friendliness is made possible only because of a split between one's everyday social identity and the ch'uan-nei-jen role, especially for newcomers. People freely refer to their love-lives, other ch'uan-nei-jen, and—occasionally—their jobs. They rarely mention any other aspects of their everyday lives, however, especially their family. One night right after my father's funeral in March 1992 my girlfriend and I went to a T-bar, where she immediately announced that we had lately become "engaged." Right away, everyone came to congratulate us and propose toasts in our honor. Later, several people questioned me about how long we had been together. When I mentioned that I had come back to Taiwan this time for my father's funeral, they dismissed that piece of information. At first I thought they did not hear me—T-bars are always noisy, partly because of the Karaoke-singing—because it is unusual for Taiwanese not to offer at least perfunctory consolation in response to others' family crises. As a result, I repeated myself several times, but people started to drift away. Finally, I realized that they did not want to hear about my family at all.

Taiwan is a society in which homosexuality is at fundamental odds with what are considered to be family values, which include "compulsory" heterosexuality.[3] Because the family of origin collides directly with unconventional sexualities, it follows that, in a T-bar, family life is relegated to the category of *ch'uan-wai* (outside the circle). It is intrusive to the performative setting and does not belong.

The performative fictiveness of the bar context manifests itself in another significant case—that of T-P'o dynamics, which are normally carried out through drinking together and telling stories. In order to initiate social connections, patrons—mostly T—begin by proposing toasts to each other. An ability to consume is expected, and failure to display a high tolerance for alcohol is nearly unacceptable for those in the circle. A thirty-four-year-old T in the fall of 1993 recalled a mortifying experience: "It happened a couple of years ago. I had an upset stomach for three weeks and was able to consume nothing stim-

ulating. One night I went to a T-bar with several old T friends I had
not seen for years. Of course they ordered liquor. By contrast, I could
not even take a drop of beer! That really was a most humiliating night!
I literally shrunk into the corner of my seat for the whole night and
did not dare look at anyone."

After proposing toasts, a much more intimate relationship is established, and previous strangers may converse in more familiar tones. A
T would immediately identify herself as a T by first either praising the
other Ts or P'os or expressing perfunctory envy for her "good luck":
"You got so lucky having such a good wife (*lao-p'o*)! Now I shall give
you another toast!" After more toasts are exchanged, the first T will
begin to tell her own love stories, characteristically failed ones. These
stories share a similar narrative. She used to have a P'o as pretty and
as sweet as the one in front of her right now (at this point the latter
should express modesty and appreciation by toasting the T), yet she
made certain mistakes fatal to the love relationship (for example, she
invested too much time in business or showed more loyalty to her T
brothers than to her P'o, or took on certain bad habits such as heavy
drinking). Finally the frustrated P'o left her for someone else.

Storytelling presents a specific ch'uan-nei-jen way for both T sto-
rytellers and P'o listeners to constitute and negotiate their sexual roles.
In a bar context storytelling plays a central role in maintaining both
performative fictiveness and an expected T-P'o interaction, a decisive
feature I failed to see for most of this stage of fieldwork. As an indication of my failure, the first T love story I ever heard was recounted by
a shao-yeh during the first month of my fieldwork.

"Before I came to Taipei, I had lived in Chia-I for all my life," the
story began. At the time, she was nineteen, an age that by Taiwanese
standards is between social immaturity and maturity. Therefore, it
seemed somewhat bizarre that she said "for all my life." I realized only
later that it was a common strategy T employ to dramatize their lives—
in particular to P'o. In my case, by demonstrating her "full-blown" T-
ness to a much older P'o (I was ten years her senior and would normally have been called "big sister" by T of her age) and by implying
that she had led a socially sophisticated life, she would be able to initiate a quasi-erotic exchange with a P'o. Such an exchange is critical
to building relationships between Ts and P'os at the bar.

"Back then," she continued, "I had a lao-p'o who was as pretty and
sweet as you are. We lived together for three years. Last year I decided
to carry out my husband's duty of making money for her. You know,

we men are always into business; it's just part of our nature. So I opened up a teahouse in Chia-yi." By equating me with her lao-p'o she also equated me with "woman" as opposed to "man," a subject position she took on while telling the story. "Certainly I invested all my time and energy in my business because we men are just like this," she added. "As a result, I did not have enough time to be with her. She got very upset. She is a woman, and you know how they women are."

Suddenly, I was no longer being equated with "woman." My subject position was moved from the absent lao-p'o and generic woman to that of a good P'o listener. Previously, the former lao-p'o had functioned as a third person by mediating between the present interlocutors' subject positions, thereby helping in their establishment. By contrast, now she was being subsumed under a generic "woman" and thus losing her original referential status. By positing her as one of "those women," the T was creating a binarism of "they" and "you," the latter being non-ordinary and therefore better women, including me. Such a transformation in discursive subject positions represents a typical quasi-flirtatious play between T and P'o in ch'uan-nei-jen. The fact that the T addresses the P'o as such indicates her recognition of the latter as at once sexual and sexually different from both herself (as a T) and other women (as discursively nonresponsive).

In taking on that role, the P'o acknowledges the T's sexuality and her own willingness to participate in their erotic exchange. "She simply could not understand why I ignored her," the T said. "She started to pick fights with me. I tried to explain, but she didn't want to hear about it. Oh, women! We had lots of fights. Finally she left me for somebody else. I was heartbroken. As a result, I closed down my business and came to Taipei. For half a year I have been working here. Every night I get to know a lot of pretty women but I just am not interested in them. The only woman I love in the whole world is her."

The genre of the story recalls popular masculine love songs in which a male protagonist swears eternal love for a former lover who fails to recognize his true heart and then deserts him. Usually, he has recently moved from his hometown in rural Taiwan to an urban area to seek a more profitable future. As a consequence, he experiences two forms of disorientation: geographical and sociological. Conventionally, these are condensed into a lost love—a woman unresponsive to his life-pursuit. Those features are evident in "Hsing-shih Shei Jen Chih" (Nobody Knows of My Heart), first released in 1982 by Shen Wen-ch'eng and one of the most popular songs of this genre:

If I still refuse to let out what is on my mind
Nobody will ever understand me
Once in a while I am to speak out
All the sorrow contained in my stomach
It is all my fault
To ever get involved in hoodlum connections
Now I am regretting it
But nobody would ever believe me
My love
Spare me just a little understanding
Please be patient
Men are not without tears
But dare not to shed them.

The second part of the T's story followed the outline of this sort of love song. Both posit the subject position of the first-person narrator in opposition to a resistant other, the woman.

By the time I came to comprehend the discursive significance of this storytelling act I had heard the same type of story five times. In the meantime, I failed to realize the fact that its merit does not lie in its authenticity and, therefore, I was wondering if all the T-bars in Taipei had conspired to circulate such stories. It seemed impossible that all Ts shared the same kind of love-life. As a consequence, I decided to challenge the fifth T. After she had finished, we had the following conversation:

I: You told me that your lao-p'o left for somebody else.
She: So I did.
I: Then tell me, is that person a man or woman?
(She stared at me, stunned. I repeated the question.)
She (reluctantly and smiling uneasily): Well, it's a man.
I: A man? Are you talking about a real man?
She: Well, yes. You know how women are. (She became even more uneasy.)
I (sarcastically): Oh, yes, women are like that. They always go for men, isn't that what you are saying?

We toasted each other one more time. Shortly afterward, she left my table and never returned that night. I realized then that I had jeopardized my already-tenuous P'o status in the bar. Storytelling is one of the acts a T performs so as to produce her T-ness. Likewise, it is a performative act for a P'o to act out her P'o-ness by posing as a sympathetic and responsive listener. The quasi-erotic exchange in this case is both perfunctory and constitutive. It is perfunctory because no sexual desire is necessarily involved. It is nonetheless constitutive because through such a seemingly eroticized discursive act the subject position of both T and P'o can be constructed vicariously and secured. My failure to do so disrupted the flow of the performance and thereby deconstructed the mutually constitutive relationship between us. Even worse, my questioning of the T's self-claimed maleness discredited her T-ness. Pronouns that traditionally carry heterosexual meanings are among the culturally available codes Ts draw upon to build a T subjectivity instead of a male subjectivity.

In this phase of ethnographic investigation my failure to fully comprehend the significance of T-P'o performativity was largely owing to my unconscious resistance to acting like—not to mention acting as— a sexual being (that is, a good P'o) in the field. The resistance was caused by two conditions. First, my consciousness was taking on the subject position of an ethnographer, which detached me from physically and discursively participating in the almost imperative T-P'o erotic play. In other words, the anthropological other (to my mind) was a conceptual one rather than a sexual one, which rendered me as asexual. Second, although from time to time I did attempt the erotic play in question, I found myself freezing because I have never been comfortable performing *sa-chiao* (flirting in an overly feminine way). I am not sexualized in that way.

The doubly asexualized aspect of my ethnographic performance in the field thus greatly undermined the effectiveness of my research. In principle, only when one is recognized as a ch'uan-nei-jen can she gain access to the heart of the bar scene. In turn, that requires one to be sexualized in the proper way. I needed to occupy a P'o subject position that most suits my own character. But at the time I was at a complete loss about how to do so. I had to wait for another year.

## The Second Phase: Acting as a Big Sister

I returned to the bar scene in the summer of 1993. For the first two months I still found myself being considerably awkward. In addition, I had not been able to engage in ch'uan-nei-jen daily activities outside of the bar. I wondered whether there was a node connecting the bar scene and daily life.

The answer came to me one day when an eighteen-year-old T called me *chieh-chieh* (big sister). She had come to my table in the middle of the night, asked to be seated with me, proposed a toast, and then claimed that she had found most P'o there "boring, immature, and too young." She continued, "I prefer women of sixty-three or sixty-two 'year ranges' [*nien-t'zu*, nineteen or twenty in 1993]." Then she asked me, "What's your year range?"

During the preceding two years, owing to the appearance of teen-aged customers, a new question—"What's your age range?"—had been addressed to all new patrons. The majority of my informants during the second stage of my fieldwork were primarily in the category of "six-headed" (*liu tzu t'ou*). They were born in the 1960s of the Republic calendar, which dates from 1912. Put another way, they were between fourteen and twenty-three in 1994. Those who were jokingly termed "uncles" or "big sisters" occupied the category of "five-headed" and above. Accordingly, bars geared toward them are called "uncle bars." Age had recently become a designator of identity, and relationships would be expected to grow between bar patrons in accordance with their relative ages. That relationship is usually encouraged when an attendant makes typical statements such as, "Another six-headed! Exactly sixty what? Sixty-five?[4] Student? Good, we've got a lot of sixty-fives tonight. See the one wearing a white jacket over there? She is a sixty-five as well, and her name is A-Cheng." Or perhaps the attendant would say, "Wow! A five-headed! Then I should call you uncle! Tonight we have only kids—they are all six-headed."

My reply, "fifty-three" (twenty-nine), to the T who had claimed to take a strong interest in "mature" women so stunned her that she sank into complete silence. Participating in any erotic exchange with a woman of my age must have been beyond her imagination. Shortly after she came back to herself, she asked permission to call me "chieh-chieh" and has since acted as such toward me. Immediately, her friends of all age ranges heard of the fact that she had a new chieh-chieh and would stop by my apartment to chat. Soon I found that chieh-chieh is a conventional ch'uan-nei-jen term that a T uses to address a much older P'o. The response would be *ti-ti* (little brother). By addressing someone as "chieh-chieh," a fictive kinship relationship is constituted that would then govern one's behavior. For example, because ortho-

dox kinship regulation and incest taboos prohibit amorous relationships with one's siblings, one is likewise expected to refrain from having sexual relationships with ch'uan-nei-jen counterparts. An emotionally intimate relationship between chieh-chieh and ti-ti, however, is
expected. As a result, all my ti-ti—I would have thirty—frequently visited my apartment in Taipei, had long telephone conversations with
me, and consulted me about their personal affairs, in particular their
love-lives and family obligations. As a chieh-chieh I was expected to be
doting, nurturing, socially sophisticated, and, most important, available whenever they sought support. P'o usually do not call each other
by kinship-related terms, but prefer nicknames. Normally, sexual ten-
sion does not exist among P'o, whereas it is considered natural between
T and P'o. Therefore, the T-P'o kinship reveals a fear (and even desire) for the sort of erotic exchange it attempts to nullify.

In any case, it was much more comforting to act as a chieh-chieh
than a P'o. The previously distinct boundary between insider and
outsider and between emotional involvement and conceptual aloof-
ness began to fade. Not only did ch'uan-nei-jen began to show increasing interest in my life, but they also familiarized my inconsistencies and
incorporated them into their own lives. The most conspicuous was my
ignorance of ch'uan-nei-jen values, which they attributed to the fact
that I had lived too many years in the United States and were glad to
correct.

The fact that my Americanness was not equated with ch'uan-wai was
due to the nearly fantasmic reputation of North America among the
younger generation of Taiwan. Its features are also often associated
with a commodity culture. Teenagers have considered frequenting
McDonald's, smoking American cigarettes (Marlboro and Virginia
Slims in particular), wearing Giordano, listening to pop music, and
hanging out at "American bars" such as Friday's and Roxy, among other
activities, as prime signs of youthfulness, even progressiveness, since
the mid-1980s.[5]

Take smoking as example. The combination of Americanness, styl-
ishness, and subversion implicit in that act is evident in the following
case. Hsiao-wu is a T who, she said, was devoted to upgrading the
ch'uan-nei-jen life-style and spent a lot of time researching the proper ways of acquiring taste and good reputation—that is, she followed
the consumption advice of foreign fashion magazines such as *Cosmopolitan* and *Esquire*. Her P'o, Hung-mao, was even more serious in terms

of dressing and acting properly. In the spring of 1994 she was planning to open a boutique selling "those fashionable outfits in the magazine." At one point she even asked me to teach her English. She told me that she had always wanted to make American friends. "There are so many Americans on the street," she said, "I really want to speak with them, but my English is too poor."

Hsiao-wu was very proud of Hung-mao for her knowledge of the fashion world. Once, however, they had an argument about the proper ways of smoking. It began when Hung-mao criticized Hsiao-wu's habit of smoking while riding her motorcycle or walking on the street. Hsiao-wu argued that she had done so since high school days and that it was considered cool by all her T friends. Hung-mao contemptuously pointed out that most of these friends "had no taste" and that "only high school kids would consider it cool." Finally, Hsiao-wu contended that Hung-mao also sometimes smoked while walking. "I do this only in T'ien-mu," Hung-mao replied matter-of-factly. "T'ien-mu is different. It's so Americanized that you cannot help but have to smoke on the street—those Americans do so as well."

From the 1950s to the late 1970s T'ien-mu was a district on the outskirts of the city of Taipei where U.S. Army officers resided. Since then it has been considered an "American neighborhood" where "authentic" American products can be purchased, such as "correctly flavored" ham and steak. There is also an American school open to both foreigners and Taiwanese, a Japanese elementary school, and numerous American-style bars and restaurants. What Hung-mao was arguing was that the authenticity of American cigarettes is most evident while they are being consumed metonymically, in a physical sense, with "genuine" Americans. In addition, the persona of a "real" American-style smoker is most authentically assumed through smoking the right kind of cigarettes in the right place—T'ien-mu.

Even though my knowledge about American products was scanty compared to that of most of my informants, they still considered me an expert in American culture. Few questioned me about the United States, though. The only question they asked constantly was, "Are there people like us in the U.S.?" By "us" they meant ch'uan-nei-jen: T and P'o. Therefore, they showed profound surprise—occasionally even doubt—when I replied that butch-femme roleplay is not exclusively practiced in the United States. Once a ti-ti asked how American ch'uan-nei-jen make love. All my informants practiced penetration, and the T would have been called a "stone butch" in the United States. When

I replied that, as far as I knew, people do a variety of things and that vaginal penetration is not universal, she sighed, "Oh my, these American T are really too lazy!"

## Conclusion

Although I am presumably a doubly indigenous ethnographer, my original Taiwanese-ness and lesbianness did not necessarily guarantee my being considered a true insider of the circle. In order to conduct my fieldwork successfully, I had to at first sexualize myself into a P'o and then asexualize my P'o-ness to big-sister-ness. That process needed to be initiated by my informants before I could take it up, in accord with the behavioral rules regulated by the circle. At least two sets of rules were involved. The first concerned the implicitly erotic discursive exchange between Ts and P'os in the bar. The second concerns the conventional Chinese patrilineal kinship regulations and strategies on which my informants drew to construct their *Ch'uan Nei* connections and construe mutual relationships on a daily life basis. The de facto kinship relationships are usually first initiated in the T-bar context and then transferred to other sociocultural spaces, where they are actualized. They embody the specific way in which the performative bar context and personal life context intersect. Only after being incorporated into this de facto T-bar kinship structure was I able to gain access to the circle and, finally, be considered by both *Ch'uan Nei-Jen*s and myself as "one within the circle."

## NOTES

I gratefully acknowledge the financial support of the Joint Committee on China Studies of the American Council of Learned Societies and the Social Science Research Center. I also express my gratitude to the teachers, colleagues, and friends who have so generously helped me, especially to P. Steven Sangren for his advice throughout my fieldwork and to Geoffrey Waite for his insight into ethnographic self-reflexivity. Thanks, too, to Fran Markowitz for assistance in structuring this chapter. My biggest debt is to Wen-Tsai Hsiao, who contributed so much intellectually and emotionally to my research. This chapter is dedicated to Shao-Te, my beloved "little brother," who has shared emotional ups and downs with me and called from Taiwan frequently since my departure in the summer of 1994, always yelling "chieh-chieh!" at whomever answers the telephone.

1. I give pseudonyms to all the informants mentioned in this essay except for those who have been already noted in other texts. A-pao and Ya-t'ou are

quoted in *Chung-kuo-Jen Te T'ung-Hsing-Lien,* the first sympathetic sociological report on homosexuality published in Taiwan (Chuang, ed. 1993:135–42).

2. Spoken Chinese languages have a large number of homophones. All are tonal and lend themselves to varied puns and plays on word meaning. Taiwanese and Mandarin, the two Chinese languages commonly used in Taiwan, use different intonations and stress patterns, which adds to the potential confusion and intentional wordplay.

3. Here I am borrowing Rich's (1980) classic term.

4. The attendant means, that is, eighteen years old in 1994.

5. Giordano is a Hong Kong brand. Because it is characterized by traits associated with Americanness, such as bright colors and simple but comfortable design, Taiwanese teenagers have perceived it to be quintessentially American, however.

# 8

# Deconstructing and Reconstructing
# My Desexualized Identity

*Éva V. Huseby-Darvas*

On the tail end of a bad marriage, I was forty-two when I arrived
in Hungary during the hot summer of 1982, alone and intending to conduct fieldwork for my doctoral dissertation. My three children, two daughters and a son, were in their early twenties and went
to school and worked in the United States. I had chosen Cserépfalu, a
lovely, predominantly Calvinist, northern village of 1,394 at the foot
of Bükk Mountain, from fifty-two other potential research sites in the
region.

It took weeks to secure research and other permissions, but in early August I visited Cserépfalu again, this time with Tamás Hofer, my
Hungarian mentor and academic sponsor, with the intention of finding and moving in with a native family. As was (and likely still is) the
custom among most of my colleagues before and since the socialist
period in Hungary and elsewhere, Hofer and I paid protocol calls to
the village elite and their families, told them of my plans and desire
to live with a native family for a year, and asked for their help. Among
other papers in my sizable portfolio I showed everyone an official note
written on the letterhead of the Hungarian Academy of Sciences—a
stamped, signed permission to conduct research in the village.

The two most important figures among the local elite were both non-
natives. The first (and, in more ways than one, first in the socialist pow-

er echelon) had resided in the village for almost two decades and was the local Communist Party secretary (PS) and principal of the eight-form elementary school. He also taught Russian. The second, the Calvinist pastor, was a relatively recent arrival in Cserépfalu. The two men and their families lived in the middle of the village, just across the street from one another, and all the while I lived there neither they nor their wives ever spoke to or greeted each other.[1] I also visited and told my intentions to the village's council president, the Young Communists' secretary, and a number of other "lesser elite" who were all natives of the historical and in many respects still closed traditional community. They, as well as the Calvinist pastor and his family, warmly welcomed me and were helpful and kind throughout and beyond my stay.

It was the PS, however, who on one of my initial visits helped me find room and board in a native household. From the time of our first meeting, he and his wife were helpful and nice to me. In fact, the PS was too nice; he was outright flirtatious. Ernestine Friedl (1994:833) is correct in suggesting that human coitus conducted privately is a near-universal, but she does not mention that specific, general or universal, overt public flirting often precedes coitus. In East Central Europe in general, and Hungary in particular, it is not considered unusual for men to flirt with and proposition women. Yet there was a curious angle to the PS's approach. The pattern of his ardor could be called "predictable alternation." In public, he was always romancing me verbally, looking at me in a certain way, kissing my hand, or holding my arms or shoulder too long.[2] In private, however, he was definitely shy and never suggestive.

The flirting made my stay in the village difficult for a number of reasons. Clearly, it was both actually and potentially damaging for my status. Too, I often felt that I had to, at least to some degree, play along in order to accomplish my work. On a decidedly different level, the particular pattern of the flirtation also meant an additional quandary that concerned what from the moment of my arrival in Cserépfalu I perceived to be desexualization by the villagers. In this essay I will discuss that quandary and probe (but never answer) the question of what a female anthropologist is to do while in the field, alone in a culture in which "actual privacy cannot be managed" (Friedl 1994:834) but where talk about or relating to sexuality is treated—at least ideally— as "dirty" and done neither outside marriage nor for other than purposes of reproduction.[3]

### How I Was Categorized, Addressed, and Desexualized in Cserépfalu

For the villagers, my children's unmarried status at their "advanced ages" was one of the greatest, most often voiced objections about me. I had not fulfilled my parental duty because I had allowed them, particularly my daughters, to enter their twenties and had not married them off (Huseby-Darvas 1987). The villagers were concerned about and interested in my marital status and parental roles, but they did not know about the quality of my marriage. After reading Golde (1986; Golde, ed. 1986) and others concerning the problems women encounter while doing fieldwork alone, I conspicuously displayed photographs of all my family members in my room, which, according to the norms of the village, was open for all visitors at all times. They would come in, most often without knocking, and be ready to visit and talk at all times of the day. I also regularly sent mail to the States and received it in return.

Because I have written this essay more than a decade after my experience, I am trying to deconstruct the identity the villagers constructed for me—no doubt with my help. I was in a multiply ambiguous position in Cserépfalu. In a sense, I had what Goffman (1959:141–66) calls a "discrepant" role. I was a native Hungarian and yet I was an American. I was fluent in the language yet not in the regional terms and spoke with a different dialect. Although I was able to create an excellent rapport with the villagers, I was also suspected as being a spy. I lived in the village, but it was obvious that I was urban-born and there only temporarily. I tried to dress and act properly and listen to the women in my household, but I made glaring mistakes, particularly at the beginning of my fieldwork.[4]

Reference and address terms were also signs of my incalculable status. How villagers referred to me in my absence—*az amerikai asszony* (the American woman) or *a kém asszony* (the spy woman)—and how they addressed me in person also indicated my ambiguous role. In the village, even five years' difference in age means that a younger person must call someone older *néni* or *bácsi* (aunt or uncle) and use formal terms and pronouns. Older people, however, call younger ones by first name and use informal terms and pronouns. Most women and some men, even those in their eighties and nineties, addressed me as Éva Néni (Aunt Éva) and always used formal terms.

That indicated not only the respect and distance the term *néni* implies but also that they did not think I could be called by first name, although I asked them to do just that and, to respect their age, addressed them as néni, a reciprocity or mutuality that was not only unusual but also bizarre. Some men addressed me either as Éva Néni or *tanár néni* ("aunt teacher," which at the time I was not) or Éva *Asszony* (which literally, and awkwardly, translates as "married woman Éva" or "Madam Éva"). Children had the least trouble. It was proper for them to call me Éva néni and use formal terms in conversations, whereas I called them by their first names and used the informal terms. My cohorts, both men and women, either used the formal terms and avoided calling me anything or, after I had repeatedly asked them to call me by my first name, continued the formal terms but called me Évike, which in this context was a polite yet endearing nickname. Only the adults in my adopted village household used informal pronouns and called me Éva from the first.

For all practical purposes, the villagers desexualized me. Although in many ways I considered that a blessing, I cannot say it did not bother me. In my heart of hearts, I was annoyed whenever the often agonizingly direct villagers declared me unfeminine and unwomanly. It was obvious that I did not fit their ideal. In too many ways I was glaringly different. Being five feet, eight inches in height, I was much taller than any other woman and some of the men in Cserépfalu. Also, as I was told many times, I did not "walk right." They told me repeatedly, for example, that my stride was "too sure," my steps too big, and I did not move my hips the way "real women" in the village should and did. These and other physical and behavioral differences made me an other—both unapproachable and unalluring to approach.

There were, of course, other reasons why the natives did not perceive me or treat me as a woman, a sexual being, and a potential sexual partner. My age was one. Age is perceived and treated very differently in rural Hungary than in the urban spheres there or most of the West:

> According to traditional rural standards, "a woman is considered . . . young . . . for ten years [after her wedding], during which period she may sit in the young wives' pew in church. . . . [however], if her health is broken down by the birth of numerous children and the rigors of work, she leaves that pew sooner . . . and takes a seat with the older women" (Fél and Hofer 1969:209). After the age of forty

she may cook, clean, prepare and keep on eye on the reveling young at wedding and other celebrations, but she must behave with dignity, she may not dance at these celebrations; "henceforth [she] wears a rather dark dress and no longer takes communion on the day of the church festival [with the young], but rather on the following day, along with the elders" (Fél and Hofer 1969:203). . . . It appears that [in Cserépfalu] there is no native concept of middle age for either gender. According to traditional notions, which are expressed clearly by local dress codes, and by kinship, address and reference terms. . . . [a woman is] generally considered young until about twenty-eight or thirty. While the period between thirty and forty is undefined, the public conduct of a woman in that age group, as well as the local address and reference terms used by younger villagers, already indicate that she is no longer considered young. After forty a village woman refers to herself as old. Past sixty she frequently may say about herself "well, I am on my way home" or "I am already homeward bound," signifying that she is on her way to the grave. (Huseby-Darvas 1987:19)

Second, in spite of being Hungarian-born I was an urban person and a stranger (which alone would have been bad enough in this particular village) who arrived from America. There were several families who were, I was told after 1989, officially given the role of keeping an eye on me and reporting on my activities. Partly because of that, and partly because of the nature of anthropological endeavors in a socioculturally closed community in which I was the first outsider to conduct research, some villagers considered me a spy. Nearly a year after I initially moved to the village, a Hungarian colleague, Tamás Mohay, came from Budapest to visit for a couple of days. He lived in the household of the pastor and visited around, collecting bits and pieces of information about me. The villagers told him that I was interested in everything and knew more about them and the village "than any other stranger, even the one who is living among us for over eighteen years [the PS]." Within some families there was disagreement, but in others there was total consensus that I was an American spy on a mission. One of the most amusing explanations for why the U.S. would send a spy to Cserépfalu was that Ronald Reagan had "sent her to find out how we live here and learn from our frugality and economy." It was testimony about the ever-positive self-image of Cserépfalu's natives. How notions about sexuality were articulated in the community was more complicated and less amusing.

## Sexuality in the Villagers' and Ethnographers' Ideal Culture

Repression of sexual matters is not only typical to Cserépfalu, a Calvinist and in many respects closed and traditional village, but also to
rural Hungary in general. As Mária Vajda (1982, 1:60) notes, "It was
not the actual sexual act that was taboo, but the acknowledgement of
sexuality, and any evasion or circumvention of society's moral codes."
Sexual behavior and talk are claimed to be dirty. The fact that men
attack actively and women receive passively is implied on the occasions
when intercourse is explicitly mentioned. Both women and men use
the word *kihasználni* (to use and exploit women).[5] A closely related
issue is privacy, which I found from the beginning of my stay did not
exist. On the contrary, as the villagers rightly and frequently claimed,
"A falu szemi mindég rajtunk van és mindent lát" (the village has
omnipresent probing and all-seeing eyes)—and ears. Those omnipresent eyes and ears help in the extensive denial and repression of most
matters relating to sexuality, which, as villagers say censoriously, "only
Gypsies talk about."

Thus the treatment of sexuality in general was minimal. Gyula
Ortutay (1935) cautioned that "Hungarian ethnographers who want
to explore and understand folk culture, and the structure, motivational
forces, and innermost tendencies of folk society, must not shun any
longer the detailed examination of our peasantry's love life and sexuality" (cited in Vajda 1982:58). Yet there is still little published in
Hungarian ethnography on sex and sexuality, not because it is not an
immensely important issue but most likely, as Vajda (1982:59) summa-
rizes, because of the prudish and hypocritical nature of Hungarian
ethnography and its practitioners, the prevailing zeitgeist, public opinion, the methods and forum of the ethnographers, the personalities
of researchers, and the lack of adequate contact and proximity between
researchers and informants. A number of Western-trained anthropologists have also explored various aspects of Hungarian rural society.[6]
They cannot, however, claim to have made progress in the study of
sexuality, sexual expressions, or reflection of how, either as women
alone or men alone in the field, they were "sexed" or "desexed."[7] Of
course, as Okami and Pendelton (1994) show, there is also need in the
West for new cross-disciplinary endeavors in this important area of
study and self-reflection.

Although talk and some behavioral expressions of sexuality are
taboo among Hungarian rural people, great discrepancies exist be-

tween the ideal and practice, although much of the discrepancy emerges indirectly. In Cserépfalu, for example, local parlance is bountiful with sexually explicit swearing. Villagers often mentioned intercourse not only between Homo sapiens sapiens and their parents but also between existing and invented species, between supreme beings and these species, between Homo sapiens, and between real and fanciful kinds of animals and selected supreme beings. There are even some hitherto unexplored and impossible options, positions, and configurations.

As there are also other indications of the repression among those who use such expressions, so is there repression among ethnographers, anthropologists, and practitioners of related disciplines. One edited volume, for example, devotes only 7½ of its 266 pages to a discussion of "Sexuality in Contemporary Hungary" (Buda 1986). Sexuality emerges, either vividly or more subtly, in numerous expressions in folk art (Hoppál n.d.), agrarian and other folk plays and customs (Ujváry 1978), and folk tales (Róheim 1925).

## Fieldwork among American Hungarian and Canadian Hungarian Immigrants

I recall very different, earlier fieldwork experiences that I had assumed would prepare me for my major work in Cserépfalu. They did not. In previous research projects between 1979 and 1982 among Hungarians in America and Canada I had dealt with other male informants who apparently considered themselves close to me—and wanted to get closer—after we had worked together on several occasions. Many flirted openly, which I did not consider a problem because I had been born and raised in urban Hungary and knew how to handle flirting in a Hungarian immigrant setting. A few informants either unambiguously propositioned me or physically attacked me, episodes that were without exception upsetting and unattractive. Verbal propositions were not as problematic as physical and clearly sexual attacks. I would reply with an often successful "let us stay friends and not complicate matters between us."

Some incidents were sad, others were bizarre. They all left a bitter imprint. I felt vulnerable, exposed, and unable to handle the situations as well as I had thought. None of the maudlin advances had attracted me and not only because of ethical considerations. One recently widowed, still grieving man, for example, an outstanding, exceptionally intelligent, and sensitive informant with whom I just finished a three-part, open-ended interview that had gone very well, lunged from his chair onto the sofa where I was sitting. He was annoyed by my statement about not complicating matters. The most bizarre approach involved an eighty-six-year-old man who grabbed my backside with both hands while following me upstairs after he had politely beckoned me toward his waiting wife, who was talking to us while preparing tea and food upstairs in the kitchen. While I answered the wife and tried to balance my tape-recorder, notes, and bag with one hand, I was trying—without success—to push away his hands with the other.

These and similar episodes did not and could not have prepared me for what I experienced in Cserépfalu. In the 1979 and 1982 fieldwork in North America, informants had felt close to me and I was approachable to them. As an American-Hungarian myself, I was and remain one of them, regardless of gender, class, educational, occupational, and other differences. Also, in America, where "the president is called mister and so am I" as one informant—an unskilled Ford factory laborer—pointed out, I could clearly be approached and abused. In the rural Hungarian setting, however, regardless of good rapport and the fact I was not just visiting but living there for more than a year, I was and remained a stranger—and a strangely desexualized other at that.

Because I was a desexualized being (although one who, as the villagers said, "will write a book about us and our beautiful village"), a key power figure was seemingly interested in me. I had no idea at the time that the public flirting of the PS was a power play, but in retrospect I am convinced that was the case. It was a performance to prove his status and identity as well as those of his wife and family. Regardless of my unceasing otherness and desexualized status, the flirting evoked a strange kind of competition from a man from one of the village's most prominent families during a wedding. It also created a jealousy among the village's women that I had to face on several occasions, particularly after an episode of *pincézés* (congregating and drinking at a wine cellar)—usually an exclusively male activity. Even after more than a decade, these episodes still cause me to cringe.

During one wedding, a prominent villager, while slightly drunk, asked me to dance with him. I replied, "No thanks, I don't dance." Indeed, aside from the facts that I had never danced in the village and was doing my best to dress and act with proper local decorum, I had never really learned how to dance and was self-conscious. Nevertheless, after insisting for a while longer he grabbed my hands, yanked me from my chair, and began to drag me around the dance floor. It was one of many occasions where the eyes of the village were indeed upon me. Well over four hundred people were staring, and I felt and was clumsier than usual. But the real problem was that my decidedly unwelcome dancing partner was pushing his lower body and obvious erection toward me. To say that I was uncomfortable is an understatement. First, I tried to push his entire body away but did not succeed. Then I pulled the lower part of my body away and after what seemed to be an eternity was able to escape from him completely. It was a bizarre and painfully humiliating scene. No one had come to my rescue while our "dance" lasted. The PS, who was away from the village at the time of the wedding, heard about the tawdry incident and later referred to it repeatedly—and always in public. While shaking his head and grinning, he would say, "Évike, Évike, hát mi történt magával?" (Évike, Évike, what happened with you?).

The other incident, not nearly as awful but potentially even more damaging, happened during pincézés. Although I realized the great importance of this male institution, I was also aware that after sunset no village woman entered the areas of the village where the wine cellars were located. Most informants, both men and women, insisted that after dark "a decent woman from our village would not even look toward the wine-cellar rows, not to mention going there." Thus a *pince* (wine cellar) is male territory, and pincézés are a man's activity. During the day a woman may run out to a family wine cellar, but most would rather ask their male kin to bring home wine or, in cases where produce is stored in or near these cellars, potatoes or vegetables.[8]

Yet once again there is inconsistency between ideal and reality, and there are many indications that the pincézés are not exclusively male activities. For example, I found several notations in the local church archives dating back to the eighteenth and nineteenth centuries about local village women and men "having to pay public penitence for illicit intercourse in the Berezd pince." Too, everyone in earshot heard an angry exchange of words between two village women in the fall of 1982. One yelled, "You got knocked up with all your kids in the pince and *you* dare call *me* a whore?" The oldest village man, ninety-one-year-old András Barkó, told me, "The old men way back told me that on Saturday nights some non-village women—mind you not from our

Cserép[falu]—walked through the wine cellar rows and yelled three times to each wine cellar: *'cserényi'* [exchange, barter, swap]. Some men asked them in and *megkamóták* [village slang expression for coitus]. The next day or the following Saturday these women came back with a wheelbarrow to collect their pay in grain or wine" (Huseby 1984:266).

Yet the wine cellar is still, as the men often say, the place to "get away from our women folk." In some sense the traditional concept still prevails, yet there are generational differences. For example, younger men and sometimes those who have returned to the village take their fiancées, wives, and families to a wine cellar in late afternoons or early evenings to fry bacon, drink wine, and perhaps even talk and sing, although older people disapprove of them doing so. Then the young men walk the women back to the village and return for what they call *real* pincézés.

The tradition that decent women do not go to the wine-cellar row after dark made my study of pincézés in Cserépfalu challenging and for a while impossible. Yet I was convinced that somehow, without compromising myself in the process in the ever-present "eyes of the village," I must have at least a glimpse of such events. When I was invited to one late in the afternoon of the name-day of the PS and there was talk of his wife also being there, I could not pass up the opportunity to observe and participate as much as possible.[10] I knew it would not be a truly local event because too many elites from and outside the village would attend, but I was convinced that even that would be better than not going at all.

The PS's wife came for five minutes to bring food for the eighteen men and myself who were present, had a small glass of wine, and left immediately. I seated myself between two barrels and tried not to worry as I watched the drinking, singing, and talking men. In about an hour, when the drinking started to get out of hand, I got ready to leave. I was uncomfortable and also realized that my presence in the wine cellar made the men immensely uncomfortable and changed their behavior.[11] The PS, who was the host, did the proper thing when he first offered and then insisted (in public, of course) that he would walk me from wine-cellar row to my car. I responded that there was no need, I would find my way. When that did not convince him, I asked two more revelers to walk with us, not because I was afraid of the PS but because I wanted to protect my reputation in front of the men.

Immediately after I got in my car, I drove to four houses. First I paid a visit at the home of PS, talking with his wife for a while, and then I stopped in with three more families and chatted about the next day's market plans and such. I was desexualized by the villagers. In a sense I was even masculinized by the PS's invitation to join an all-male activity that might have had homosexual overtones in a culture where homophobia is rampant and homosexuality likely to be the greatest of all taboos.[12] Yet I still felt I had to protect my reputation and make certain that not only would nothing "unbefitting" happen to me on wine-cellar row but that everyone would also know that nothing had happened. The visits were intended to make certain that the village's women in particular knew that I had left wine-cellar row, my clothes were not wrinkled, my hair was neat, and I was heading home at a decent hour.

## Sequel: The Happily Ever after . . .

It was six months after I returned from Cserépfalu that I met my present husband while conducting fieldwork among American-Hungarians in southeastern Michigan. Although he was not an informant I did meet him during research. We were both waiting for Sen. Carl Levin, who was more than an hour late arriving at the grand opening of the Hungarian American Cultural Center in Taylor, Michigan. From the moment of our meeting he looked at me in a certain way that I much needed after my experiences in Cserépfalu. With his attention and my slow readaptation to life in Michigan, I have been able to deconstruct, reconstruct, and mend my desexualized identity.

NOTES

Without the generous support of the International Research and Exchanges Board (IREX), Fulbright-Hays, and the Hungarian Academy of Sciences, my research in Cserépfalu would not have been possible. I am most appreciative of my good friends and colleagues György Csepeli, Norma Diamond, and Fran Markowitz for stimulating discussions and constructive counsel during the often difficult and painful gestation of the present endeavor.

1. In some respects, the relationship between the party secretary and the Calvinist pastor symbolized earlier relationships between the Communist Party and the church. Not only had the men had a personal altercation over the pastor preparing twelve- and thirteen-year-olds for the annual confirmation in the Calvinist Church, but the PS had also slapped children who were preparing for this important ritual and in school gave them unsatisfactory marks in conduct. The villagers, in an uncharacteristic action, signed a petition

against the PS and in favor of the pastor—a potentially dangerous act in a small community where the PS was all-powerful. Yet illustrating the softening of the regime by the time of the early 1980s, the powerful Kádár Committee examined the issues and decided in favor of the pastor, that is, in favor of the church.

2. Hand-kissing, although not common or prescribed behavior for Communist Party secretaries, was and is not unusual in that part of the world. Some middle-aged and older, middle-class men kiss hands on certain occasions, whether from respect toward the person whose hand is being kissed or as a mimicry of pre-socialist gentry and middle-class behavior.

3. In reality, however, that was not the case. There was much gossip about women who did not dress modestly and perhaps wore see-through blouses or inappropriate colors for their ages or statuses. Often these women were called *baszhatnékok* (those who want to fuck), in a similar vein to *latrok* (men who are active womenizers). According to the marriage and birth records of the village church and the village council archives, sexual intercourse did occur outside of marriage. There were cases of first children being born considerably before nine months after weddings and also to widows and unmarried women during and before the time of my fieldwork.

4. The worst mistake I made was dressing for the funeral of a villager. I was wrapped in the proper dark attire and tying on a proper dark kerchief—knowing I was doing everything correctly as I had been taught by my landlady/sister/friend/key informant/cultural mediator—only to see her in tears. She told me that evening that I had brought shame upon the household because my black kerchief was hanging down my back in the wrong way. I had not folded and tied it properly, but "like Gypsy [Roma] women tie their kerchiefs when going to steal chickens."

5. Numerous other terms are used as well, such as *megkamóni*, which I never heard outside Cserépfalu. Although I cannot locate the etymology of the word, it also connotes active male and passive female roles in the sexual act.

6. See, for example, the work of Bell (1984), Gal (1978), Györi (1975), Hann (1980), Hollós (1983), Kürti (1991), Lampland (1990), Morvay (1981), Nagy (1977), Sozan (1985), Vásáry (1991), and Vöô (1969), as well as Huseby-Darvas (1983a,b, 1987, 1988).

7. Although Gal (1978), Lampland (1990), Kürti (1991), and I (1983a,b, 1988, 1987, 1990a,b) deal with gender relations, and Vásáry (1991) discusses the one-child system in a specific Hungarian region, no one focuses on the subject of sexuality per se.

8. During and after wars, as several informants told me, that was not the case. World War II and subsequent social and economic changes not only affected but also in some ways totally transformed the social institution of pincézés. Sándor Bodrog, a villager born in 1937, recalled that "the proper order of the world was all topsy-turvy [during the war], so it was no problem for me and my pals to steal the wine-cellar key from under the head of my great-grandfather where he kept it [the key] in [a] straw sack. . . . my age group and I stole out to the pincézés regularly from the ages of seven or eight." Aunt Lenke Dankó, born in 1911, recalled that "in the forties none of us had our men; all of them were away, on the front. My man fell at the Don when I was

thirty-two. The same year I buried my father-in-law. There we were, women and children. We would have made wine, but did not have enough grapes and did not really know how. . . . Well, we ended up making beer from barley. It was good but different. But everything was different [in those years] and nothing ever became the same as before ever since. . . . After my man died I had to go to the pince, then soon after my sons were confirmed they went to the city to study and then to work."

Since World War II three parallel and mutually reinforcing processes have altered all aspects of village life, including pincézés. First, forced industrialization brought about large-scale mass commuting between villages and industrial and mining centers, and permanent out-migration resulted; approximately six hundred people moved away from Cserépfalu permanently between 1949 and 1960. Second, from the early 1950s the drastic reorganization of agriculture and its branch industries radically changed traditional relationships and hierarchy within and among families. One result was that most households of extended families broke into nuclear families after being forced to join the cooperatives. As one consequence, atomization is evident in all generations and all strata of village society. Third, expanding mass communications since the war have strongly influenced the villagers' views, values, and aspirations and accelerated the complex processes of embourgeoisement in rural communities.

These processes changed the traditional order, practice, and meaning of pincézés in the village. Now, wine-cellar activity has a strong attraction, particularly for village men who regularly commute and those who live in cities and visit their former home, as well as for teenagers and old men. Rather than being more or less seasonal, now pincézés are year-round activities. Friday and Saturday evenings, Sunday afternoons, the evenings of all holidays, the village's patron saint's day, and various male name-days all provide key occasions. According to most accounts, it is much easier now for young men to get a key to the family cellar than it used to be. It is generally held by middle-aged and older villagers that everything is more effortless and available for young people now than it used to be for previous generations of Cserépfalu natives. "These kids simply get it if they ask for it. . . . for us it was not so easy," a village man born in 1921 remarked.

9. Although elsewhere in the Carpathian Basin there were separate and clandestine pincézés for women on certain occasions when roles were reversed, like at *farsang* (time of winter carnival) (Szendrey 1938; Ujváry 1978). In Cserépfalu, however, I only heard of one isolated incident. An elderly woman told me that when she was a young married woman, she and a group of women friends had disguised themselves and gone to a pince at night.

10. I rarely drink alcohol, and when I do it is in small quantities because I have difficulty tolerating it. Therefore, even beyond the main issue of women not going to wine cellars, this activity was not for me.

11. Later, rather than go in person, I would ask visiting male friends and colleagues to accept the villagers' invitations to wine cellars on such occasions and study what went on there. Although I am certain that their presence also altered events, their visits were less intrusive than mine. I particularly must

acknowledge the kind help of Tamás Mohay, a sociologist-ethnographer from the Museum of Ethnography and the University of ELTE, Budapest; Peter Skeie, who in 1982 was a student of anthropology at the University of Minnesota; and the late Michael Sozan.

12. The men hug, kiss, and joke with one another in this exclusively male gathering. I thank György Csepeli for pointing out this aspect of pincézés.

# PART 4
## SEX AS PRAXIS

9

# Sexing the Anthropologist: Implications for Ethnography

*Fran Markowitz*

Until very recently, sexuality, although certainly a topic that generates much emotion, debate, and controversy throughout the world, was a non-issue among anthropologists. Anthropological methods courses in the strongest and most influential of departments completely ignored the topic (Conaway 1986:53; Dubisch 1995:30; Newton 1993:4), and even passing mention of an ethnographer's sexual urges or sexual vulnerability was absent from virtually all ethnographies and from the pages of field manuals.[1] For all any student or novice ethnographer knew, the "field" was an arena of androgyny and gender-blindness.

Many have had rude awakenings. Sexuality frequently explodes onto the forefront of human interactions, and anthropological fieldwork is no exception. Sometimes the avowal of sexual attraction causes one or the other person involved shame, disgust, even self-blame, whereas at other times, even when least expected, it may pique positive feelings and lead to the formation of an intimate relationship.

Ignoring the place of sexuality in field situations therefore strikes me as surprising if not obtuse, especially in light of the stunning developments that have occurred in anthropological inquiry since the 1970s. Gender studies has moved from the periphery of the discipline into its very center, and reams of articles have been and continue to be written that explore and often celebrate the "personal" or "intersubjective" dimensions of interaction between anthropologists and informants. Why is it then, given these two parallel revolutions in anthropology, that a heavy silence continues to veil the sexuality—or sexlessness as the case may be—of ethnographers among their informants?

What I would like to do in this essay is expand the hushed discussion begun in the early 1980s by Manda Cesara (1982) and continued by Esther Newton (1993), Diane Bell, Pat Caplan and Wazir Jahan Karim (1993), and Don Kulick and Margaret Willson (1995) that not only may there be "No Hiding Place" for the sexed anthropologist but perhaps no reason for hiding. In 1984 I had entered the field assuming the asexual pose I thought necessary to anthropological inquiry (cf. Probyn 1993:2, 60–64), but neighbors, acquaintances, informants, and friends found that stance ridiculous. Ultimately, I concurred with them and allowed myself to be sexed.

I hope to draw some general conclusions from my personal experience of conducting sexed ethnography, that is, incorporating into anthropological research and its resulting texts the recognition that ethnographers are viewed as sexual beings and placed into gender categories—male, female, homosexual, heterosexual, bisexual, neuter, androgynous, and more—by the people studied. It is important to note as well that such categories often do battle with the sexual selves researchers bring along, or attempt to leave behind, as they plunge into the field. By acknowledging this paradox, my wish is not to turn the genre of ethnography into sexual autobiography but to continue the trend of situating ethnographers in a real place, among a real group of people, as physical as well as intellectual persons (cf. Abu-Lughod 1991) striving to create an ethnographic tale as self-meets-other in its making.

## Why Gender Neutrality?

Having established—as if they did not know—that sexual behavior is part of the cultural repertoire of every human group, it makes good theoretical sense for anthropologists to experience native practices of sexuality as part of their holistic approach to gaining knowledge via participant observation (Dubisch 1995). But when anthropologists do reveal lustful thoughts or flirtatious behavior toward informants, to say nothing of all-out sexual relations, they risk professional censure. Erotic nuances, signs of affection, and sexual relationships are deemed illicit means of gaining information and acquiring power or protection and are subject to condemnation—not informant fees, dispensation of medicine, or the giveaways of tools, tobacco, and other prized goods, which can be just as disruptive (if not more so) to normal social relations within a group. Where does this order of things come from and is it appropriate to the ultimate ethical and practical aims of anthropology?

Much of the silence surrounding anthropologists' sexuality, coupled with an official morality that bars sexual involvement from anthropological practice, derives from the Victorian heritage of the discipline (Stocking 1987). This ban on sexuality was later upheld by a postcolonial concern for establishing and enforcing a code of ethics to protect the people of anthropological investigation from exploitation and to differentiate ethnographers from their co-nationals, who are usually in a position of economic and cultural dominance over those being studied. Even the expansion of anthropological inquiry into notions of gender and cross-cultural sexual practices could not break the ban on including sexual play in the scheme of participant observation. Instead, ethnographers remained professional voyeurs and persistent interviewers, sometimes causing hilarity among informants (Gregor 1985; Shostak 1983:349–50).

Indeed, sexual abstinence during research is an important mark of the discipline of anthropology, proudly brandished as a badge of commitment to the welfare of those being studied. Thus in the rare instances that ethnographers publicly discuss their sexuality in the field it is usually to show the lengths to which they have gone to ensure their sexlessness or how they have avoided involvement in courtships or romances (Fischer 1986; Giovannini 1986; Golde 1986:6–7; Strasser and Kronsteiner 1993; Whitehead 1986).

When the taboo against sex in the field is broken—either wishfully or physically—the anthropological community rallies to distance itself from the incursion, claim the occurrence is an isolated incident, and deny that it has wider implications for the endeavor of fieldwork. Witness the shocked reactions to the posthumous publication of Malinowski's personal diaries (1967). Hsu (1979) called him, and only him, ethnocentric; Wengle (1988) took pity on him for being on the verge of losing his "self"; and Geertz (1967) hearkened back to classic Western dualism as he congratulated Malinowski for overcoming his carnal side by writing superb ethnography. Paul Rabinow (1977) was also subjected to criticism after writing that he slept with a prostitute procured for him by informants—which was, incidentally, the "culturally correct" way to have behaved. Then there was the scandalized statement reportedly made by a distinguished professor from the University of Chicago, who claimed, after reading Esther Newton's article (1993) that Newton advocates sleeping with informants (personal communication from Newton). To maintain professional legitimacy and avoid censure anthropologists would do well to conform to the convention of asexual fieldwork by assuming a position of gender-neutrality with informants and making that position clear when they write (Conaway 1986; Probyn 1993:2, 60–64; cf. Wade 1993).

I, too, prepared for the field intending to separate my sexuality from the empathetic, objective persona I would present to my new neighbors and friends. In fact, I looked forward to it, because for almost as long as I could remember sexuality was problematic, even scary, as it hovered unseen over the realm of academia and professionalism. From the time I was a teenager and my father let me know in no uncertain terms that I was not to accept a photographer's offer to shoot my portfolio (after all, he explained, the photographer was interested in only one thing, sex), I was forced to acknowledge the irony that people, especially females, can be sexually exploited by those in power and that it is disgraceful for those not in power to allow that to happen. In college I changed my major to anthropology when a philosophy of religion professor was too enthusiastic about a midterm essay I had written and suggested that we work long evening hours together. As I considered going on to graduate school, I heard a group of male Ph.D. candidates snidely attribute the success of a female classmate to having done her coursework and examinations "on her back." The message was clear: I had always to act with sexual circumspection. Under no condition would I have a romance with any of my professors or, when the time came, in the field with informants.[2]

As I looked ahead toward fieldwork I thought longingly of Margaret Mead's (1961 [1929]) experience in Samoa. Because she was definitely not male she had access to the women and girls of the village, and because she was so different in appearance and character from Samoan females she was also afforded the opportunity to interview chiefs, partake of their rituals, and participate in a wide range of male activities (see also Caplan 1993:170–71). No one, male or female, made sexual advances to her, because in the eyes of the Samoans Margaret Mead was asexual. For her part, Mead reported no longings for an erotic relationship with anyone in the village she was studying. What an ideal situation.

Everything seemed to be going along with my plans to present myself in a neutral light—except for one thing. A matter of months before I was to move to New York City to conduct a study of Soviet immigrants, a new professor at my university, himself a native of that group, warned me, "I hope you're not going to Brighton Beach alone! Russian men consider American women 'fair game' [for sexual conquests]." That statement jolted me a bit, but if for some reason I would not receive the same treatment as Margaret Mead had in Samoa I still had the situation under control: I was going into the field with a husband who, among other things, would be my protection against unwanted sexual advances. But, I repeated to myself, there wouldn't be any. I was well read, well trained, and eager to begin my research as an anthropologist—a genderless being like all other anthropologists. My agenda was to do a study of identity change and community-building among recent immigrants; I neither wanted nor anticipated sexual adventures.

## Gender Neutrality Thwarted: The Anthropologist Gets Sexed

Although Soviet immigrants recognize nuanced cultural differences between themselves and Americans, they point to many similarities as well. Unlike Margaret Mead among the Samoans and many other anthropologists who study people quite different from themselves, my physical appearance, mannerisms, educational level, and ethnic background did not demarcate me from my hosts in the field. Consequently, men had no problem recognizing me as a woman, and females, from young girls to grandmothers, urged me to join their celebration of femininity by throwing my baggy clothes in the trash, having my hair styled, and wearing more makeup. My informants did not find my gender-neutral stance convincing.

Just as perplexing, as my research went into full swing my husband also challenged my assumption of sexlessness. He became jealous of the time I was spending with male informants and claimed that these men viewed me as an attractive young woman interested in them rather than as a curious, asexual anthropologist. Accusing me of naivete in not recognizing the importance of sexuality in encounters between men and women, he forced an issue I was unprepared or unwilling to consider.

The men I encountered, for the most part, were not nearly as interested in me as my husband suspected. Almost all of them were married to women they loved, and they respected the fact that I too was married. Every so often someone would comment about my exotic or "sexy" way of speaking Russian, but it was easy to laugh off such remarks by asking the men involved if they were told the same thing about their English. Once, well over a year into fieldwork, a married man several years my senior who was just as friendly with my husband as with me thrust himself on top of me and slobbered me with kisses. I immediately threw him off, shouting, "Ty soshol suma?!" (Have you gone crazy?!).

But that incident, although bothersome, was not problematic; I knew what to do with unwanted advances. The real problems arose when informant relationships developed into friendships, and those friendships became tinged with erotic attraction. Perhaps because anthropologists have been trained so well not to think of informants as sexual partners, or because of a general consensus that "sexual relationships in the field are going to be disastrous" ("Cathy" in Wengle 1988:61–62), or simply due to fear of professional censure, I had known of no anthropologist who became romantically involved with an informant.[3] I certainly did not expect to find myself attracted to any of the men I met during the course of my research.[4] But it did happen.

During my first period of fieldwork, as soon as I had an inkling of more than casual interest on the part of male informants I immediately rebuffed their declarations of affection and denied their attraction. Perhaps over-eager to nip developing relationships in the bud— I was, after all, married as well as an ethnographer—I depersonalized myself and the situation, refusing to believe that I was the object of affection. Paraphrasing Lévi-Strauss, I insisted that only in my role as an anthropologist, where I displayed intense interest in the life histories and current experiences of my informants and became privy to intimate information, was I "good to think." Moreover, from the informants' point of view, an empathetic and energetic anthropologist who is here today, gone tomorrow provides a perfect opportunity for a fleeting romance.

Yet I was too afraid to embark on romantic adventures. As I strove to maintain a platonic relationship with two men who expressed their attraction to me and for whom I felt affection, I emphasized my genderless persona as an anthropologist and downplayed, almost to the point of denying, my sexuality.[5] Perhaps even more telling was that I did not write one word about my feelings in either a field journal or personal diary, and I edited out—consciously or unconsciously—flirtatious remarks from my records of interviews and field notes. As a fledgling anthropologist I wanted to follow the rules, all of them, and despite the insistence of the men closest to me that I was an attractive female I fought unrelentingly to deny that fact.

In Jerusalem three years later I entered the field with a different status than I had held in New York. I was a new Ph.D. and divorced, without the protective shield of a husband. And I was indeed fair game. Several times, during interviews or outings, married men would lavish me with exaggerated compliments, stand too close, and reach over to kiss me. It was my responsibility to inform them that such behavior was inappropriate because they were married and to come up with answers to their ingenuous question: "What does that have to do with anything?" I found my earlier explanation, that as a here-today-gone-tomorrow anthropologist I was "good to think," confirmed many times when men recounted their fantasies about me, knowing full well that even were they to fulfill them I would be around for a limited period and therefore posed no threat to the stability of their marriages.

But amid what became a tragi-comic routine of rebuffing propositions I became fond of two male informants. One was married, so despite my affection for him and his promises of mountain getaways and Mediterranean cruises our interviews and activities together included nothing more carnal than an occasional—and culturally appropriate—embrace. The other man, however, was divorced. One evening, as we finished supper and a long session of interviews and conversations, he asked me to spend the night. I explained that while I was conducting field research it was ethically incumbent on me to refrain from sexual relationships with the men involved (cf. Wengle 1988:25, 91). "What?!" he exclaimed with incredulity as he was looking up the word *celibacy* in his Russian-English dictionary, "Aren't you a human being?!"

That declaratory statement made me wonder—was I? Does being an anthropologist automatically preclude humanness as researchers conduct fieldwork in a liminal period of voluntary sexlessness? Or was I confused by his definition of what constitutes a human being? Is sexuality always a part of personhood? Must it be? Aren't sexuality and personhood separable categories? Can sexuality be put on hold for professional reasons, for callings, and disengaged from human beingness? Was I discovering something critical about being a person in the society I was researching? Were my Western ideas about the separability of sexuality and personhood different from those of the Russians? Could I, as a celibate anthropologist, enter into this cultural knowledge and come to understand it? If not, would it be possible to have a sexual relationship with a person in the researched group and maintain the necessary posture of detached involvement, to say nothing of avoiding censure? Finally, I wondered whether I was using the ethics of anthropology as a convenient excuse to avoid the personal feelings of vulnerability (Wengle 1988) that an amorous relationship entails.

As I pondered such questions I began to consider that the cost of skirting confrontation with sexuality would be greater than the personal and professional risks involved in facing the issue. Unlike the loud silences about flirtation, sexual innuendoes, and erotic encounters in my first fieldwork, I now recorded thoughts and feelings about sex in the field and diligently included in my field journal all the come-ons and propositions of male acquaintances and informants.[6] I also decided that relationships in the field do not necessarily have to be disastrous (Cesara 1982). In fact, I came up with a slew of reasons why a romance with an informant could only help my work. It would certainly improve my knowledge of the language and open doors to little-known facets of the culture (i.e., sexual practices, ideas of love, male-female courtship, and matters of hygiene).[7] Intimacy is what all anthropologists desire in the field and also what they fear most—that nebulous line between being "in" and going native, retaining objectivity and an autonomous sense of self versus doing and feeling as informants do and thereby losing part of the self in the process (Markowitz 1988; Wengle 1988, esp. p. 8).

Dropping my celibacy—something my informants viewed as ridiculous bordering on crazy—and engaging in what they and I thought was a perfectly normal relationship brought with it a great deal of advantages that last into the present. My biggest problem, however, remained the nagging thought that I was doing something wrong that went against the ethical foundations of the discipline. To this day, I remain uncomfortable and ambivalent about that problem but have come to understand that assuming a pose of gender neutrality is not the way to deal with this discomfort.

If I had been sexed as a heterosexually attractive, interesting, exotic, and pleasant, "good to think" woman by male informants, they were generally more subtle than the women. The women I encountered during fieldwork, first in New York and then in Israel, rejected my self-imposed genderlessness by commenting, from the start, on my appearance, advised me on how to be "more of a woman," and actively made me over. I was not treated much differently from anyone else;

hairstyles, clothing, and choice of cosmetics are open to public review and criticism. From these comments and actions—and the use of me as an example—I learned much about female informants' views on femininity, family, aesthetics, and male-female relationships. I also discovered along the way that there is no Russian word for privacy. My generic, genderless pose was out of the question for these formerly Soviet women who took such joy in recapturing and embellishing upon their femininity.

My female informants, from eight-year-old girls to women well into their sixties, were unremittingly concerned with doing to me what they did to themselves: enhancing their beauty. Ostensibly, their reasons for doing so were to retain their husbands if they were married and, if not, to attract a husband. When I challenged these reasons during their unsolicited advice—"Change your hairstyle. You'll look more beautiful and your husband will love you more"—they further explained, amazed that I did not know, that women by nature want to be beautiful. Several informants portrayed in vivid detail the privations that the Soviet state had foisted on them to thwart their efforts to be soft and lovely. In the United States and in Israel, these women did their utmost to throw off whatever remained of a dowdy, Bolshevik-woman pose and instead embraced eye-catching clothing and cosmetics that best expressed their feminine ideals (Markowitz 1993:178, 183, 187; Markowitz 1995). My voluntary assumption of the look they wished to leave behind seemed to them senseless, counterproductive, and stupid "for a woman as intelligent as you."

But even more important than my appearance was the fact that I was childless. I was asked several times, in New York and Israel, how many abortions I had had. My reply—"none"—led to discussions of birth control and the widespread use of abortion in the USSR. The women took pity on me as they asked confidentially if there was "anything [physically] wrong" (i.e., to have prevented a pregnancy). They told me again and again about the importance of motherhood in making a woman's life meaningful, and because they were unable to classify me as sexless or unready to accept me as a woman whose life has no meaning they urged me incessantly to have a child, offering babysitting services as an incentive. When it appeared to them that my marriage was in trouble, or later when I was single and in a steady but uncertain relationship, several advised me to "accidentally get pregnant" so I could keep or get my man and fulfill my womanly destiny. My sexuality, something I had always considered to be unquestioningly private, had become an issue of public debate and concern. As it provided a bond between me and these formerly Soviet women they became increasingly close friends and told me more and more about vital issues in their lives.

The fact that I was sexed as an anthropologist was critical in making me aware that personhood, at least within the group I studied, does not transcend sexuality. There is no tradition of sexual abstinence in either Judaism or Russian Orthodoxy, and Russians view celibacy as absurd and unhealthy. "Sexless personhood" is a contradiction in terms. One may be heterosexual, homosexual, or bisexual, but no one can or should be asexual. Sex and sexuality are considered so critical to the normal mental and physical health of each individual as to warrant a list of ailments and a semi-slang linguistic term to describe someone who fails to engage regularly in sexual activities (Markowitz 1993:186). As a result, sex and sexuality also play a sizable part in sociability, and it is not unusual for soft-core porno videos to be shown at get-togethers and ribald jokes to be told in mixed company.[8]

Seeing now that sex plays such an important and obvious role in shaping the personhood of the former Soviets (cf. Kon and Riordan, eds. 1993), I am certain that I never would have been invited to participate in so many activities, and make so many friends and join them in their family and friendship circles, had I persisted in maintaining a sexless, gender-neutral stance. I may even have been diagnosed as abnormal, sick, and threatening. Contrarily, my engendered, sexed self provided a key to unlocking many cultural enigmas I could not have anticipated: the legitimate use of trickery and deception to reach desired ends, the heartfelt appreciation by men and women alike of femininity, the centrality of motherhood in women's lives, and the fundamental link between sexuality and personhood.

Although at times I felt invaded and threatened when informants' foisted their gender-concepts on me, my data became all the more rich as a result. More important, because I allowed myself to be sexed, those I set out to know could experience me as a person and I could also know them better. Almost certainly the understanding I gained would have been different had I entered the group as a heterosexual male or a homosexual male or female. But I contend that denial of one's own sexuality and an attached refusal to conform at least somewhat to society's gender expectations are counterproductive to anthropologists' endeavors.[9] The generic, genderless ethnographer is more likely to draw dry, colorless portraits of the people she or he studies than to gain the multidimensional, holistic understanding sought in the first place.

## The Sexed Anthropologist: Implications for Ethnography

Sexuality in the field provides a cogent example for examining and critiquing some of the basic tenets of anthropological research strategies and their effects on those being studied. As aware as ethnographers ought to be that the categories that structure fieldwork are their own creations, anthropologists are routinely jolted when the personal boundaries they experience as steadfast and real are challenged or rejected by field partners. They must recognize that implicit in the strategy of gender-neutrality is a requirement that informants also be de-sexed. That balance in role relationships works well when they view anthropologists as too different to fit into their sexual scheme of things and then relegate them to a sexless category unto itself. In such situations the host community concurs with the anthropologist's self-other division and all goes well. But the balance of sexual power does not hold when "the natives" view visiting anthropologists not as asexual sub- or super-humans but as mature, sexually active, receptive, and more alike than different from themselves.

Jill Dubisch (1995:35; see also Herzfeld 1987:17) has noted that anthropological fieldwork is predicated on a hierarchical structure skewed in favor of the ethnographer simply by defining "one person as researcher ('superior') and the other as the object of research (by definition somehow 'inferior')." The fact that it is the anthropologists who set the rules without the complicity of their informants helps confirm that hierarchy, and that is a powerful side of the story of ethnographer-informant relationships.

The other side is that field ethnographers are by nature anything but superior. While conducting research they rely on informants for everything, food and shelter, language instruction, and guidance in rules of etiquette to say nothing of obtaining the prized "data" that make a field trip a success. It is humbling to stumble and bumble through an unfamiliar language, make egregious linguistic mistakes, and become the butt of laughter in going from person to person to request bits and pieces of cultural knowledge.[10] I know that I smile more, hesitate more when I speak, and end up looking "cute." I am, consequently, more approachable, weaker, and more feminine in the field than in my regular life. It is no coincidence that I am propositioned more often by Yugoslavs, Russians, and Israelis than by Americans. It is only when I return to the sanctuary of my desk and the omnipotence of my computer to analyze "my data" that I can turn the relationship around according to the conventions of the discipline—or at least balance it out.

Fieldworkers need to negotiate their sexuality in order to fit their expectations to those of their hosts, avoid and cope with harassment, express affection and attraction, and even convey sexlessness. I do not suggest that every anthropologist must, at some point, engage in a sexual relationship with an informant in order to have the complete participant-observation experience. If anthropologists acknowledge not only in cocktail party conversations but also in professional writings that their sexuality is problematic and negotiable in interactions with field partners, their ethnographic representations will be more balanced, richer, and more authentic if perhaps less objective.

Lila Abu-Lughod (1991) has convincingly shown that the privilege of being a "halfie" anthropologist enables her to cross, dissolve, and rebuild the presumed boundary between researcher and researched, thereby allowing her to "write against culture." All anthropologists, even heterosexual white males, those icons of convention, are somehow halfies in that their sex can provide a natural link to informants. By overtly identifying with a salient gender category that makes sense to both ethnographer and informants—male, female, two-spirit, *xanith,* warrior woman, and others—hosts can classify ethnographers in their scheme of things as they are in turn being classified.[11] As sexual beings researchers become more approachable, more human, more real, and less removed and powerful or pathetic than as genderless anthropologists. We are then on our way to combating arrogance (cf. Narayan 1993). But this is not a simplistic solution to the complexities of the researcher-researched relationship. Anthropologists and their hosts will be required to rethink lines of inclusion and exclusion each time their fieldwork takes an intimate turn.

In the beginning of the discipline, when the goal of anthropology was to document the variety of human culture by discovering and chronicling every people on earth—the more exotic the better—the scientific stance of objectivity was taken as a necessity. One route toward that objective stance was to de-sex the anthropologist as he-she-it went about getting data from those under study. As the thrust of anthropology has changed from reportage to interpretation, anthropologists now attempt to minimize the distance and reduce the hierarchy that separates investigator from investigated. Indeed, they call informants "consultants," "hosts," and "teachers" and treat them as such. Perhaps "lovers" should also be added to the list.

Gender makes a fundamental difference in each society, and anthropologists' personal blinding to that point is no longer warranted. The fact is that sex matters, not only in its connection with gender but also as a physical act, subject of conversation, leisure activity, and important factor in defining each individual as human, and needs to be apparent in ethnographies. When it is, anthropologists will be one step closer to putting the crisis of confidence in their endeavors behind them.

## NOTES

I am grateful to Susan P. Pattie, Yishai Tobin, Niza Yanai, and Éva Huseby-Darvas for having read and commented on an earlier version of this chapter. Their comments helped me streamline and sharpen my argument, but all responsibility for the information and ideas presented rests with me. I wish also to express my gratitude to Manda Cesara/Karla Poewe, Esther Newton, and Jill Dubisch, whose pioneering work paved the way for me to bring my thoughts on sexuality in the field into the public arena of anthropological discourse.

1. In preparation for writing this essay, I explored five field manuals published between 1980 and 1988 for mention of ethnographers' personal encounters with sex. None of the volumes' indexes listed sex or sexuality, and only one chapter in one of the books discussed "romance," treating it as a curiosity or "funny incident" (Weibust 1983). Several chapters in more recent collections (del Valle, ed. 1993; Golde, ed. 1986; Whitehead and Conaway, eds. 1986) offer hints on how to ward off sexually interested informants and avoid falling prey to natives' gender stereotypes, but not one piece explores the ethnographer's feelings of sexual attraction.

2. I was subsequently taught a humbling lesson: Others' opinions cannot always be controlled through one's own behavior. I was hurt, bewildered, and frustrated when during my second year of graduate school a friend in my class told me that three fellow female students were whispering to everyone within earshot that I was carrying on a sexual liaison with a married male professor. Nothing could have been further from the truth. I decided, however, to ignore the fact that this information had been passed onto me and never confronted the rumormongers.

I was not the only object of such false allegations. One day another female student told me that a close friend of mine was sleeping with her foreign-language teaching assistant. I knew that was a barefaced lie and told her so. But that was not the point. What was the point is that women students were attempting to sully the reputations of their peers. These incidents burst my bubble of female solidarity and the feminist message (see also Bell 1993:33).

3. I did not read Manda Cesara's *Reflections of a Woman Anthropologist* (1982) until 1987.

4. I do not exclude women from this sentence because I am homophobic, but rather, in the words of a lesbian friend, because I am "hopelessly heterosexual."

5. Even at the time, I was aware that in order to do my study I had at least once a month to don a dress, high-heeled shoes, and makeup to dance at birthday, wedding, and anniversary parties at Russian restaurants.

6. I have never been propositioned by female ones.

7. In fact, I found out that many more Soviet Jewish males had been circumcised during Stalin's regime than had been thought (Rozenblum 1982: 96–97), confirming ideas I had earlier developed about the persistence of Jewish practice as well as identity in the Soviet Union (Markowitz 1993).

8. In this day of political correctness and somber feminism, I was at first (and remain at times) offended by many of the jokes that illustrate the abnormality of sexual abstinence, especially those in which solitary middle-aged women are gang-raped and at the end of the ordeal express their gratitude and delight.

9. It has been brought to my attention that gay men and women have a difficult time both in their home and field societies when they wish to establish consistency between their public and private sexual selves. In rethinking this statement, perhaps what I am calling for is a self-aware process of negotiation regarding anthropologists' presentation of gendered selves. It may be more appropriate, or at least less uncomfortable, in some instances to display asexuality rather than a lesbian or gay identity or a hetero-male or female one at that. What I am calling for is an overt recognition that gender categories and sexuality have an impact not only on social relations among individuals in the societies being studied but also between the researcher and the researched.

10. I once used the word *zajebavati se* in place of *zabavati se* at an evening gathering in Zagreb, proclaiming to the group that we "fucked a lot" instead of "we had a very good time."

11. "Two-spirit" is used to include contemporary Native American gays and lesbians, as well as people who have been referred to as "berdache" by anthropologists and other scholars (Jacobs, Thomas, and Lang, eds. 1997:2). The Omani Arabic term *xanith* designates a third gender role for persons who are anatomically male yet who speak of themselves as "women" and are classified with women with respect to the rules of sexual segregation (Wikan 1982:168).

# 10

# Life on Mars: Love and Sex in Fieldwork on Sexuality and Gender in Urban Japan

*Wim Lunsing*

This essay focuses on two problems related to sex in the field. The first concerns having sex with informants and the ethical questions that doing so may produce. The second concerns openly becoming a sexual persona and how that may influence the field. I carried out field-work in urban Japan from 1991 to 1993 on a research topic that stemmed from personal experience.[1] On earlier visits to Japan as a student of the Japanese language and culture many people had asked me whether I was married. It was a question that I, being gay and living in the Netherlands, was unused to. Therefore I wondered how people whose life-styles, ideas, or feelings vary from Japanese ideas about life cope with the socially prevalent idea that everyone should marry in order to be a fully adult person (*ichininmae no shakaijin*).

My research categories consisted of gay men, lesbian women, single men and women, and women's and men's liberationists, categories that include most of my friends in the Netherlands. In addition, I wished to investigate whether it was possible in Japan to live more or less as I did in the Netherlands and find whether there are Japanese who live similarly. I thought the topic would be of interest in establishing not so much the details of the general social organization in Japan but the extent to which it limits people's freedom. If it were possible to live as I did at home, than perhaps the scope for individual variation might not be that much smaller than in the Netherlands. That would undermine the prevalent depiction of Japanese social organization as extremely rigid.[2]

## On Sex, Scholars, and Participant Observation

When reading material on experiences of love and sex in the field, two features come to the foreground. One tends to romanticize them (Bolton 1995; Cesara 1982), and the other tends to be a justification of individual actions (Bolton 1995; Cesara 1982; Wade 1993). Although the romanticization of field experiences is common throughout reflective descriptions (Mead 1977), it is likely more pronounced in issues of love and sex than in friendship (Hendry 1992). Friendships in the field appear to be regarded as commonplace, but sexual relationships may be seen as unethical, an idea that seems to stem from a line of thinking that equates anthropologists with physicians, psychiatrists, and the like and suggests that anthropologists possess more power than others to induce informants to have sex with them (Abramson 1993; Wade 1993).

Anthropological ethics are generally seen as a "system of moral principles" employed to avoid harming informants (Siebers 1993). Morals in Western countries are generally based on Christian ideas, which, even if people do not adhere to Christianity, strongly influence ideas concerning sexual behavior. That makes it understandable that sexual activity in the field is controversial, and it is logical to pose the question of whether it is ethical. Most discussions of sexual relationships of fieldworkers concern the spouses who accompanied them (Oboler 1986; Schrijvers 1985, 1993). In such cases the structural position of a fieldworker as part of a family enhances her or his credibility. That is of great importance in research in traditional settings where single individuals are seen as prostitutes, threats, or anomalies and may have difficulty gaining the confidence of informants (Angrosino 1986; Conaway 1986; Hamabata 1990; Killick 1995; Warren 1988). In work on gender, sex, and fieldworkers, it is often stressed that there is a difference in the way people react to men and to women (Whitehead and Brown 1986). Work on the difference of experience among men and women in the field (Warren 1988) invariably fails to take account of the fact that sex and gender are not the same. Female gender is taken as an attribute of the female sex only, and male gender as an attribute of the male sex.

Less has been written on a subject that came to play a major role in my field experience: having sex and love relationships with informants (Warren 1988). There are, however, ample indications that sexual relationships with informants are not that uncommon. Malinowski's diary (1989) contained sections concerning his sexual desire in the field, making clear that anthropologists are not immune to them. In Japanese studies the large number of male Westerners married to Japanese women may indicate the widespread nature of sexual relationships in the field.

Anthropologists may discuss sexual experiences in the field informally, as do other scholars, and some go into the field and have sex with people there while posing as monogamously married at home. That makes it plausible that many people prefer to avoid the topic when acting in a scholarly capacity. Secrecy seems to be the norm, and ethical questions concerning sex in the field are not dealt with. The secrecy lacks a professional basis, however, and seems to stem from a general uneasiness about sex and sexuality. Anthropologists' reluctance to conduct such research and discuss sexual experiences in the field formally is based on the fact that such matters are seen as unimportant and often not presented with a serious professional attitude. According to James Wafer (1996), in American culture there is a strong boundary between the private and the professional, and sex is assumed to be part of the private sphere. Ignoring that distinction and including sexual experience in academic writing might mean that one's work could be dismissed as unprofessional. Therefore, Wafer is circumspect about his relationship with a man who remained his steady partner after the fieldwork and writes about the relationship as if it concerned other people. Ralph Bolton (1995) writes of having sexual contacts with men in Belgium while conducting AIDS research there but denies using information from those with whom he had sex, although he does not explain why and how that worked. Stephen Murray (1996), however, describes learning from sexual experiences in the field.

Clifford Geertz (1988:77) describes the importance of Malinowski's dairy as lying in the fact that it confronts readers with the problem of living a "multiplex life" that characterizes fieldwork. If fieldwork is living a life, it follows that fieldworkers may have sexual relationships that influence their fieldsites. If living in different worlds simultaneously constitutes a major problem concerning participant observation, that may not be very special for some categories of people. The fact that the academic world is dominated by white men has forced women and black men to develop at least two comprehensive outlooks on the world: one of their own and one to communicate with the establishment (Whitehead and Price 1986). Lesbian and gay people have been overlooked. One reasons why I as a child hoped to become gay was my awareness that being gay and viewing that in a positive manner means coping with conflicting worldviews, which seemed an interesting prospect. Matters that may be received knowledge in some gay circles may be alien to heterosexuals, and because few heterosexuals study gay matters it may be impossible to discuss certain matters with them without adjusting to their worldview. Gay people have no choice but to deal with heterosexual people, but heterosexual people can choose whether to show interest in homosexuality or ignore it.

Being well educated in the mechanisms of repression of homosexuality in Western contexts, much of which amounts to a social demand to remain silent about any sexual experience on penalty of being regarded as a sex maniac, I feel affinity with Whitehead's description (1986:232) of how he was viewed by supervisors who appeared to think that black men always chase women. He went through much trouble to avoid having sex in the field, but a supervisor commented upon the description of his efforts by saying, "I don't understand the problem, everybody gets laid in the field." Such lightheartedness seems to be the prerogative of men who do not take seriously the impact that sexual relationships in the field, and their implications for ethical behavior, might have on research results.

Unlike Whitehead, I did not endeavor to avoid having love and sex relationships in the field, and when writing reports I do not endeavor to hide what I see as relevant facts that are bound to arise concerning them, including questions concerning ethics (Wade 1993). In my life the distinction between friends and lovers is often unclear. People who are friends could be occasional lovers, and many lovers later became friends. Part of that may be due to the fact that I have never attached much important to sex as such and usually find satisfactory emotional and intellectual relationships more important. Sex may have a place and function in the love that binds me to others, but it is seldom of central importance although I have few inhibitions about enjoying it.

The distinction between female sex and male sex in analogy to female gender and male gender may be important, but it is trivial when discussing the cases of individual fieldworkers like myself. Although I am mostly seen as a man, when discussing intimate matters with women and men alike that hardly plays a role. Once a discussion begins, it is quickly established that I am not a man in the sense of being wholly characterized by male gender. After our interview, even a woman from the women's group against sexual harassment in Osaka remarked that she had never talked so openly with anyone about her sexuality. Although I have male genitals, there is no reason to be bound to ideas concerning male gender if they hamper me. For the development of confidentiality it was advantageous for me to be anomalous in relation to gender, especially with female and undecided informants and also with quite a few male informants. Fitting into a generally accepted role in Japanese society was not germane to my research goals because I wanted to interview lesbian, gay, single, and feminist people—people who are generally seen as anomalies. In that context it was beneficial to present myself as queer.[3]

In the colonial period, research with practical aims went hand in hand with research for the development of theory. Opposition between the two developed only later, as did a critical stance toward local governments and concern about the ethical problems relating to research (Nas, Prins, and Shadid 1987). Moving toward combining the practical and the theoretical stances, feminist anthropologists have pleaded for consciously siding with informants and considering how research may influence their lives (Kennedy-Bergen 1993; Mies 1983; Reinharz 1983).

The advantages, disadvantages, and contents of my relationships and sexual activities in the field and the ethical questions concerning them will be a focus of this essay, as will the specific case of my Japanese lover, Onitsuka Tetsurō (Oni), who asked me to come out with him as a gay couple in the Japanese mass media. In doing so, I acquired a public sexual persona, which had implications for my fieldwork. The major ethical problem concerned the possibility that informants could be hurt by being associated with me. Although I never intended to conduct action research or applied research, I did some things that seem close to such types of fieldwork. It is equally important to consider the extent to which informants changed and influenced me and my research.

I do not believe it to be useful to hide criticism. Doing so only works to prevent progress, which in the case of anthropology "is marked less by perfection of consensus than by a refinement of debate" (Geertz 1993:29). As there is, if anything, a lack of debate concerning sex in the field as well as a lack of debate on homosexuality among scholars,

I feel the need to take some liberty in assuming an attitude that the feminist lesbian scholar Elspeth Probyn (1993:163) deems necessary "to stretch ourselves to the limit."

## Preparations, Looks, and Sexual Harassment

My two previous visits to Japan had familiarized me to some extent with that country's gay and feminist circles. I knew that I would be likely to encounter men who would want to have sex with me and with whom I would want to have sex. Given that situation, it seemed that resistance would only complicate matters.[4] I usually engage in sex and love relationships wherever I am, and conducting my fieldwork would make me, to rephrase a Dutch saying, as a cat bound to bacon (in English, a fox left with the geese). I would interact on a daily basis with people who fall into categories that select me (and that I select) for sex and love relationships, and I saw no reason to abandon my usual behavior. What influence that would have on my research remained, however, to be seen.

Deciding that it would be best if I adapted myself to an ideal many Japanese have of interesting, likable, and sexy men, I bought new clothes such as a leather jacket and a pair of jeans. For summer I brought my shortest cutoffs and revealing tops; more were sent later by friends. In Japan I regularly went to a hairdresser, which I had not done for more than ten years. Many Japanese find cleanliness in appearance appealing and important. For that reason I shaved more often than usual and went to the public bath regularly, which, apart from its cleansing effect, also confronted me with obviously gay couples and men who showed interest in me. Two high school boys stared and smiled at me constantly, and a few gay men showed similar behavior, obviously noting that the person who accompanied me was more than "just a friend."

My self-presentations in Japan varied from what a friend called *burikkoburi* (play-acting the ingénue) to someone who has much experience and knowledge to draw upon when discussing personal matters. My looks and efforts at cleanliness worked out well, and many people called me *kakkōii* (handsome). That also made me a focus of harassment. In one case I ran into a man on a train who claimed to be a *yakuza* (a Japanese mafioso) and insisted that I, who he thought looked like Alain Delon's son, join him for a drink. He showed me that he had money and physically restrained me from changing trains while he started to fondle me. I managed to shake him off in the crowd at the railway station where we got off. On other occasions I was harassed by men who insisted on fellating me, having a drink, going to a public bath together (and invading my crotch and other parts of my body when I refused), or fondling me wordlessly.

Such experiences are similar to those of many young Japanese men. Young gay informants often were afraid to visit gay areas for fear of harassment by *henna ossan* (dirty [lit. weird] old men), and one had been raped in his youth. Sexual harassment is also experienced by Japanese women. For them, age makes less difference. One informant had been raped when she was seven, and another was raped by her husband when she was forty-two. Sexual harassment experiences among female informants were so commonplace that I still wonder how all books on Japanese women could have failed to mention them (e.g., Lebra 1984). One reason may lie in the fact that it was the norm for women, as for victims of environmental pollution (Kawamura 1994), to "cry themselves to sleep (*nakineiri*)" rather than talk about their experiences. Talking was regarded as shameful, and women were usually blamed for causing the abuse.

An indigenous term relating to sexual abuse is *chikan*, which typically refers to a strange man who harasses women or children although men are not free from their assaults either. Potential victims are supposed to be alert against their attacks. A newer term is *sekuhara*, a contraction of *sekushuaru harasumento*—Anglo-Japanese for "sexual harassment." I found the nature of harassment in Japan to be sometimes different from that in Europe, where, in my experience, it is more aggressive and aimed at having sex. In Japan, harassment may be for the sake of harassment itself. Following the dissemination of the term *sekuhara, sekuhara bā* (bars offering patrons the possibility to sexually harass hostesses and waitresses) were established.[5] I have no way of knowing whether sexual harassment and rape are as common in Japan as in Western countries, but it is evident that more takes place than many scholars acknowledge. For example, not many countries have train carriages set aside exclusively for women and children during rush hours, such as the Keihan Line in the Kansai area.

Having similar experiences to many informants' not only made it easier for me to understand their stories but also for them to understand mine. An important method I used in interviewing was to tell of my experiences. After that, informants usually became eager to tell me theirs. Having experienced harassment myself, I could empathize with my informants, understand how they reacted toward it, and in some cases help them voice experiences they had never before discussed. The prevalent view in Japan is that the only way to understand something properly is to experience it, although I do not believe that to be true. I did not blatantly seek to be harassed in order to experience what informants might experience, I merely adapted my looks in order to be an attractive conversation partner for them, which also made some people feel free to harass me.

My position in the field had everything in common with what has been described as "experiential analysis" (Reinharz 1983) and with feminist ideas about ethics. Although I learned from my informants, I also gave them what knowledge I had for their use. Usually I went along as far as I could with what they proposed, which, given that most participant observation centered on leisure activities, consisted in large part of attending meetings, visiting places, eating, drinking, and sometimes having sex. If asked, I introduced people to lesbian, gay, feminist, and singles' organizations, and by liberally sharing my telephone number I tried to make sure they felt free to contact me. Because two of my first interviewees had recently attempted suicide, one on the day before I met her, I dreaded losing anyone in that manner and thought that the least I could do was to make people feel free to contact me whenever they wanted. Fortunately, none of my informants attempted suicide after I met them, although they told about cases of suicide among their friends.

### Friendship, Love, and Sex

Many individuals participating in my research became very good friends, and some became lovers. All knew what I was doing and supported my research to the extent that they often bared their souls for me, something I did in return for them. Most knew one or more of my lovers and my ideas about Japan and the rest of the world. I felt that to be necessary in order to build the confidential kind of relationships I thought necessary.

An academic friend advised me not to fall in love with informants because doing so might bias me toward those persons. I thought about that and concluded it was not a problem. I am partial toward many people, and having a love relationship with someone does not make me less critical of them. On the contrary, by having a love relationship one is most likely to be confronted with less desirable aspects of a partner's character. Nevertheless, the advice was interesting because it points out widely held ideas about love. Love is supposed to make one blind and thereby vulnerable. I do not see that as a problem for myself; except during the first days of a new romance I am usually quite stable emotionally.

The question of whether having sex with informants is ethically acceptable is significant. Gay sex in Japan can be a casual activity that is not necessarily supposed to result in a relationship. As such, there is no reason to avoid it as long as one makes clear where one stands. I always made clear that I would leave Japan in April 1993 and that it was unclear when I would be back. Further, I made it understood that I could not be monopolized by one relationship because I already had a lover in the Netherlands. People who love me may believe they can make me love them enough in return to relinquish my plans and adapt my life to be with them. I thought my activities should have made it clear that this would not be. My research consistently came first, and apart from having lovers I was busy interviewing people and attending meetings.

I discussed my ethical stance with Tsutamori Tatsuru, a male interviewee well known for his gender-crossing activities (Tsutamori 1993). He thought I was being too cautious and considerate of the feelings of lovers and suggested that I should not be afraid of hurting them. That critique, backed by other informants who said similar things, changed my views. The gist of their advice was that I took too much responsibility for other people's lives and should not worry about how lovers dealt with personal issues as long as I was honest and open about my feelings. Such worries, to them, were paternalistic and showed that I didn't take lovers seriously as independent human beings.

Increasingly, therefore, I took a lighthearted view of the ethical matters relating to love relationships in the field and gradually abandoned the idea that a researcher's ethics prescribe avoiding hurting informants. Pain is part of life, and relationships may produce pain. Some informants were hurt when our relationships did not develop as they wished, which was also the case with some friendships. I also refused to become friends and lovers with some informants, not because I did not like them but because I lacked the time.

If participant observation means participating in all aspects of the lives of those with whom one conducts research, that should include love and sex. Just like eating, which may be taken for granted as a usual part of participant observation, love and sex are important aspects of culture. Participation in sexual activities contributes to understanding, especially if the research is on a theme in which love and sex play a major role. A researcher's feelings may produce problems, but that only happened to me when I had to leave Japan after completing my fieldwork. As it turned out, it was possible to continue relationships with many of those who became friends and lovers in Japan, which made our separation less painful.

Sex constituted the major portion of my relationships with only few of my lovers in Japan. Although I enjoy courting and being courted, the fun often wears off once a relationship starts. I usually enjoy sleeping together and the physical closeness of touching and kissing, but in longer-lasting relationships having sex to orgasm is not a frequent event. Love relationships were important because they allowed me to enter the most private spheres of people's lives and understand the problems of maintaining relationships. In other cases, most of which occurred after my change in philosophy, sex was a major binding factor. Such cases tended to be short-lived or infrequent. From them I could also learn about the problems caused by secretiveness, which often was the cause of their short duration.

No doubt because I was overt about myself and my research from the start and most friends understood they were of interest because of that, I did not have problems such as those described by Joy Hendry (1992). A friend of Hendry's had been shocked when she found that Hendry was using her as part of her participant observation experience. She did not like being a subject in Hendry's research, and the friendship was upset because of her discovery. In my fieldwork a similar case occurred only once. When I told Oni that I wrote fieldnotes after parties he was shocked. *"Kowai"* (frightening), he said. I explained my point of view, which was that being frightened or not depended on how I would present my findings. He found that fully acceptable, and his trust in me was sufficient enough that my note-taking had no influence on our relationship.

Having a Japanese lover was almost imperative in order to keep sexual advances at bay. My research was not particularly focused on sexual behavior, although that gradually became more important because informants brought it up. I found it necessary to place limits on the number of relationships in which I was engaged. Having a lover on the other side of the world was, in many gay scenes, considered irrelevant. The usual question concerned whether I had a lover in Japan. People generally quit courting me when I said I did. My primary reason for having lovers, however, was the only acceptable one: love. In total I had amorous contacts with ten men during my fieldwork period. They were from nineteen to forty and from various walks of life; one even thanked me for being chosen as part of my research sample after we had sex. We had not discussed anything much, and I had certainly not interviewed him, yet he seemed to think that having sex was my research method, and by that time it may have been so more than I realized.

After sex became a major theme of my research it seemed sensible to participate more in sexual activity. One feature that directly concerned sex and perceptions thereof and played a major role in furthering my work was the Japanese perception of the meaning of kissing. It is generally perceived as an activity carried out between lovers. The act of kissing helped me discover reactions toward explicit homosexual behavior; my kissing a man in a public situation confronted people with homosexuality. I have kissed men publicly many times before and since my work in Japan—at predominantly heterosexual parties in the Netherlands, an open-air disco in communist Hungary, in many situations in Vienna, and at many airports throughout the world. What made Japan different, however, was that I paid attention to eventual reactions to a kiss there; before then, I usually did not give much consideration to how that act might be seen.

In Japan, Oni and I usually kissed goodbye whenever we took leave of each other, and it became evident that people hardly paid attention or feigned not to pay attention, except on one occasion. When we kissed goodbye after having breakfast in a coffee shop in Kyoto, the owner of the adjacent shop started to make odd sounds ("uuuuu"), which suggests that he did not know how to deal with what we were doing. On another occasion a young lover and I kissed for nearly an hour on an underground platform in Tokyo. Eventually, we drew a reaction from an early commuter who said, *"Ohayō gozaimasu"* (good morning), an uncommon thing for Japanese commuters to do. The remark was possibly an attempt to draw us back into the world around us, to which we were largely oblivious. Never did I meet with any aggression in Japan, which differs from my experiences in Europe, including supposedly liberal countries such as the Netherlands and Denmark.

On another occasion a lovely young man and I spent most of the night kissing in a club in Osaka. The setting was predominantly heterosexual but positive toward homosexuality, and any reactions were

of an admiring character. The result, however, was that my relationship with Oni became a matter of concern to some people. Although
he was also present in the club and we eventually left together, as had
been agreed the day before, a mutual friend who saw me kissing the
third man concluded that my relationship with Oni must have ended.
That news arrived at Oni's place in Kyoto two days later via two friends,
one of whom asked Oni whether the news was true. The incident confirmed the speed of gossip and the fact that few Japanese, like most
people, understand the idea of open relationships.

The other feature that directly concerned my work was the connection many Japanese, like people elsewhere, make between homosexuality, promiscuity, and AIDS. Before going to Japan I had not engaged
in anal intercourse for nearly ten years because I felt discontent with
the impersonal humping that may characterize it and because I was
afraid of AIDS. While conducting research on AIDS activities, however, I became interested in AIDS prevention and thought that it might
be useful to experience how it is dealt with. In two cases partners set
out to have unprotected anal intercourse with me. Both times I prevented them from doing so by picking up one of the condoms lying
about my room, which I had collected in settings such as the International AIDS Day or had been sent to me on request by my Dutch lover, and either made my partner wear it or used it myself.

Such events underscored what I knew from discussions in groups
and from interviews: Japanese gay men did not see AIDS as much of a
threat. One of my partners even went as far as to praise foreigners for
their awareness of AIDS and the need for safer sex before setting out
to "rape" me without a condom. Although he agreed that AIDS was
something to take into account in general, he did not apply that knowledge to himself even though he found condoms lying about my room.
Later, when he visited me in Oxford, however, there was no question
that we would have safer sex. Another man, with whom I had no relationship in Japan except for dancing and kissing in a club in Kyoto and
chatting at parties, also insisted that we have safer sex before he came
to visit me in Oxford.

Sexual activities provided some additional information, usually of
the sort that underscores other findings. More important than the
sexual activities were the data that resulted from engaging in relationships of love, wherein sex may or may not play a role. Constraints posed
to gay relationships, and what people seek in and expect from those
relationships, became clear.

## Going Public: Participating in a Process of Change

Coming out as gay or lesbian is often divided into three parts. The first concerns coming out to the self and recognizing and accepting feelings of being homosexual. The second is coming out in gay and lesbian context, and the third is coming out to significant others (Edwards 1994:26). Here, however, I am concerned with something that is one step beyond—coming out in the media. Oni and I appeared in *Couple (Kappuru)*, a collection of photos of unmarried couples in Japan (Hashiguchi 1992). At my request, Oni had also written a brief essay discussing not only our relationship but also my other lovers. He had asked me to appear in the collection with him because he was happy that we were together. Although he was apprehensive about possible negative reactions, my unhesitating positive reply made his hesitation vanish.

After the photos appeared we were asked for an interview that would appear in a lesbian and gay special issue of *Takarajima,* a trendy youth magazine that increasingly dealt with themes related to sex. The article led to instantaneous recognition among many young lesbian and gay people. The effect of the book was longer-lasting. Even two years after its publication, Oni said, friends and acquaintances still contacted him about it, and even in 1998 a Japanese friend wrote me that the picture had been shown as part of a television documentary on the photographer's work. In August 1994 in Copenhagen a Japanese student who conducted research on gay and lesbian issues in Denmark said he recognized me from *Takarajima*. Others, such as my Japanese supervisor Ueno Chizuko, remained unaware, however. She found out only because a student told her when I visited her the year after I left Japan.

For Oni to come out in the media was a novel event in Japan at that time. Those who had done so before were primarily students or freelance writers who wrote about homosexuality, not people who had a regular job. Oni was an assistant professor at a relatively highly ranked university. My easy-going reaction was the result of experience I had gained after appearing in a television documentary on Hirano Hiroaki, a gay high school teacher. I had been warned that doing so might endanger the anonymity of informants and hamper my research because informants might not want to be seen with me. Although the appearance lasted only a few seconds and the program was aired at the impossible time of 5 A.M. on Sunday, some informants did see it. They invariably reacted positively, including the most closeted ones. Therefore, and because I knew the book would not be published until most of my research in gay bars had been carried out, I felt no anxiety. Gay men who frequent bars had been described as people who might not like to associate with gay men who are out (Fushimi 1991).

*Couple (Kappuru)* was published in the autumn of 1992 when my fieldwork had about half a year to go. That timing offered the opportunity to experience being a publicly out gay man in Japan, which seemed to be a sensible step in the light of a growing movement of gay and lesbian people coming out in the media. The most remarkable change I noticed during my fieldwork was that, when I began, lesbians found it unthinkable and impossible to come out. When I left Japan many had come out on television and in magazines following the unproblematic coming out of Kakefuda Hiroko, who published a book about being lesbian in Japan (Kakefuda 1992). One informant reported that her parents had been upset when she decided to stop being a homemaker and began paid employment outside her home. Although she continued to share a house with her legal husband, they did not maintain a sexual relationship. When she came out as a lesbian mother in *Asahi Shinbun*, a national newspaper, her mother appeared to be proud of her and appeared to see the media coverage as something chic (Hayamizu 1994).

Problems in the form of negative reactions did not occur, and Oni assumes that was because people who find homosexuality *kimochiwarui* (sickening) would rather bite off their tongues than talk about it to him. Furthermore, he works at a university, and, as in most other countries, people who work at universities in Japan are relatively well educated in political correctness. They have learned to act as if they were liberal even if they are bigoted. In my case, I was surprised that a member of the office staff of my university, who on our first meeting had shocked me by referring to a mutual acquaintance as *okama*, a term for homosexual that he used in a derogative manner, now told me smilingly that he read *Takarajima*.

### Changes: Who Influences Whom?

In his essay Oni wrote that my presence was a condition for his coming out, but I believe that he would have taken that step sooner or later anyway. It was only because he had been busy that he did not appear in the documentary on Hirano Hiroaki and, given the media attention for gay issues, it is likely that his activities in gay contexts would have led to his exposure.[6] My presence merely made it happen at that precise time and in that manner. Before meeting me, Oni had come out in several circumstances and with many of his friends, including colleagues and students of his university. He had much influence on developments in my fieldwork. Had he not been there, I would not have been in *Couple (Kappuru)* nor met many of his friends who became important informants.

The idea, prevalent among feminist anthropologists, that informants should benefit from a researcher's knowledge and a researcher should take informants' wishes into account related to improving their situation by developing visions from the ideas of those concerned (Mies 1983; Schrijvers 1985) does not seem to have been useful in my work. I answered requests for information but could offer informants little else apart from talking with and writing about them, which for many were major motives for participating in the research. Most people were able to help themselves and each other and did not need foreigners to advise them and support their goals. I have come to believe that the assumption that foreign researchers can have an impact on the lives of Japanese informants, let alone Japanese society, is erroneous. Those who seem to have influence only happen to say or write what the Japanese want to hear or read, which precludes the idea of an independent agent changing a field.

My image as someone who had many sexual relationships gradually became a major topic of discussion in two of the social networks in which I participated. Especially after I had come out with Oni, many people who knew I also had other relationships began to question matters such as promiscuity and jealousy. They asked for information about lesbian and gay meetings, a phenomenon Fushimi Noriaki and Kakefuda Hiroko also experienced. For me, it meant that the scope of my research had been broadened to include a discussion of sexuality and promiscuity in many different settings. Some informants even vied among one another to be interviewed. People who were unused to talking much about such matters were evidently changed by these events, but that change was occurring all over Japan, not only where I was. I merely participated in it, which was useful for my research.

Now, Oni advocates *rankōgata*, which used to be a derogatory term for promiscuity but has come to be used in a positive sense by some AIDS activists. Although he had written that being confronted by my promiscuity had influenced his ideas (for example, my Dutch lover came to visit), he had earlier said that he liked the way I talked about having more than one lover. He had come to understand how promiscuity may work by experiencing it. His ideas were also related to his AIDS prevention activism.[7] Long before I arrived he had criticized Japan's AIDS Protection Law proposal because it appeared to be primarily directed at harassing prostitutes. The compiler of that proposal, Ōhama Hōei (1988), defended it and justified limiting the freedom of HIV carriers by writing about a prostitute who works while being HIV-positive.

In a left-wing network of people in Osaka, most of whom lived near my apartment, my love-life became a major topic at a party shortly before I left. One of the women present, whom I had interviewed, told the others that I had ten lovers, which was an exaggeration because I never had ten at the same time. Nevertheless, people were interested in how all this worked and how the lovers and I dealt with jealousy. Because I have never believed in jealousy, I could only say that it was not a problem. I also repeated what my lovers had told me: Oni liked me in the first place because I was not possessive or monogamous, and my Dutch lover, who most of them had met, also had no jealous feelings. That made a lasting impression, and when I visited Japan a year later a woman who had not been at the party the year before but had heard about me invited me to discuss such matters over dinner.

Among Oni's friends in Kyoto, coming out has become a major trend. In March 1993 the multi-media performance group Dumb Type asked us to appear in their performance, in which they, for the first time, wanted to show more of themselves and make sexuality and AIDS the themes. Furuhashi Teiji, a central figure of the group, had developed AIDS-related illnesses. In the same series of performances Matsuo Megumi came out as a divorced woman who has lovers, and later a lesbian friend joined the discussion from the audience. She was asked to come forward and discuss her sexuality.

There was also a theatrical event simulating gay sex acts. The performance was developed further after my departure from Japan, and when I saw it in Luxembourg in 1995 I felt that many of the ideas I had proposed during nocturnal discussions in Kyoto had found their way onstage. The audience, for example, was asked about themselves after three male performers, one black, one deaf, and one HIV-positive, said that they were gay. It was the only suggestion I made that led to resistance at meetings about the performance. The only American participant thought the group should be cautious and not upset the audience by being too confrontational. Ironically, in the production itself he addressed the audience with this question.

My influence on the performance was limited, however, and I merely participated in the process of development. That I recognized many of my ideas is because of a convergence of thought that is often attributed to Japanese decision-making processes (Rohlen 1974). Our ideas converged, which is what happened with most of the informants with whom I was closely involved. At meetings of other groups my voice was usually only taken into account in cases where central figures or many people agreed with what I said. I was not heeded when I said something no one the group had considered. Often I felt like an instrument in the hands of my informants, who asked me to do things that I, in turn, although selectively and in my own way, did. Oni asked me to appear with him in *Couple (Kappuru)*, likewise Dumb Type asked me to appear in their performance. The Japanese molded me to their image, and I answered positively when what they requested agreed with my research goals, which was increasingly the case.

With Oni, I went to discuss homosexuality with a group of young volunteers. They were primarily engaged in matters related to disabilities and thought it would be useful to know more about homosexuality in case they would have clients who were gay or lesbian. I was also involved with a small group of gay men in criticizing the Osaka prefectural government for its AIDS policy, and I appeared in a video about International AIDS Day in Tokyo. After I left Japan I wrote an article on growing up gay in the Netherlands and the Dutch lesbian and gay movement, and the piece was published in *Fujin Kōron,* a women's magazine (Lunsing 1994). I have continued along the lines set out, keeping contact with my Japanese friends and lovers and writing about their lives and mine in an academic context. This work is furthered by my being out in Japan as gay and as a sexual being.

## Discussion

Whether sexual relationships in the field are important in fieldwork, whether particular fields allow for the exposure of such relationships, and how these relationships are brought into agreement with ethical demands are questions that should be asked rather than whether it would be right or wrong to engage in sexual relationships in the field. It all depends on the situation. It is apparent that different situations require different measures. In my case, having sexual relationships in the field proved pleasant as well as useful. In other situations, and conducting research on other matters, it may be advisable to be more circumspect. In a village in Greece, for example, a young woman was thrown out of her aunt's house for talking with me on the village square. In urban Japan, privacy is much better preserved, and if informants were closeted it was hardly a problem to keep our relationship from becoming known to others.

Until the end of my fieldwork period the public presentation of my research theme remained without direct mention of homosexuality. It was presented as being concerned with problems related to people who do not agree with or fit into the marriage system. Homosexuals are obviously a foremost group among those people, but that point is not grasped by most, either in Japan or in Western academic contexts. That fact may have contributed to the absence of anxiety among informants, who seemed to think that associating with someone who is openly gay did not endanger their position. The nature of our contacts, the fact that they were interviewees partaking in research concerning sexuality and gender, was not public. Most people were unable to understand that homosexuality might be a serious research topic.

If conducting participant observation means leading multiple lives, it is not surprising that fieldworkers have personal relationships in both, or all, of these different lives. Some could be sexual, because sex happens to be part of people's lives in most worlds. Conducting participant observation is living a life. That happens through interaction with others. Interaction allows people to define themselves and each other; therefore, participant observation necessarily involves changing the self and the other. Some situations demand close interaction with informants who do not necessarily see the researcher as other, which was the case with my fieldwork.

In the end, some people decided that I was more Japanese than most Japanese. When speaking on the telephone, people assumed that I was Japanese until I mentioned my name or something else that gave away my foreign status. Some who did not know me asked whether my father was Japanese. I had not endeavored to become Japanized. On the contrary, on previous visits to Japan I had tried to behave in accordance with Japanese patterns of behavior and was exhausted by doing so. I set out for my fieldwork thinking that I should stick to my "own self"; only afterward did I realize that my own self is constantly changing. I went through major changes while in Japan. Informants taught me how to let go of certainties without fearing consequences. They taught me the freedom of chaos, of acting without reflection, which may be related to what is called *muga* (non-self) (Lebra 1992), which in turn can be related to the Sanskrit Buddhist term *anatta* (non-soul) (Morris 1994). A more down-to-earth phrasing is that I became sexually liberated and discovered pleasure I had not known to exist inside me. Being amoral, without values, may result in anything from total passivity to indulging in murder. Amorality and the lack of values increasingly marked my activities, which were checked only by avoiding hurting people deliberately except when they wanted me to do so, as in sadomasochistic play.

Although I was aware that many scholars think that having sex with informants in a fieldwork situation is ethically problematic, I increasingly took little heed. Christian morals tend to find all sex apart from that between husband and wife ethically problematic. Some forms of sex I had in the field are illegal in American Bible Belt states, and others are widely believed to be morally wrong or sinful by orthodox Christians but not by many Japanese. Allen Abramson (1993) wrote that the ethics of sexual relationships in the field are the same as the ethics of all sexual relationships. In Japan, my ideas about ethics of relationships progressed, and I quit trying to foresee how partners might feel about developments in our relationships.

The only ethic to which I persistently adhered was honesty; I tried to be honest about my feelings and activities so partners could decide how to deal with me. That my feelings and activities did not always agree with what they desired hurt some. People have a tendency to ascribe images to others without checking whether those images are correct. I could not take responsibility for the fantasies of others. Seen from the concept of *muga*, there is little against the positions of scholars who deceive their wives; they likely act without reflection all the time. If relations are part of research they need to be balanced and checked by reflection. There is some difference between a research relationship and any other relationship.

It has been argued in several discussions that my position in the field changed it. That view is derived from the idea that fieldworkers have power over informants. It is an idea that does not relate well to my field—a highly developed environment in which informants are often well educated. In the interaction called participant observation the fieldworker influences the situation and vice versa. The opposition between research oriented at practical aims and research aimed at theoretical development seems artificial to me. Both should be combined, albeit in a way different from the practice in the beginning of anthropological fieldwork. I fail to see how fieldwork can be only practical or theoretical. In research oriented at practical aims, fieldwork would be something like social work; in research aimed at theoretical development, it would have to be void of personal interaction with informants. That may be common in sociology and even psychology, but it does not agree with what anthropological fieldwork really is: research by sharing one's life.

The major problem with sex and love relationships in the field was the one I encountered after I left Japan. When I began to write my reports, I was confronted by those who said I should not write so much about my "personal sex and love life" because doing so might make me appear childish and slight. There are two ways of looking at this. One is that proposed by Hashimoto Osamu, a prolific gay writer who compares adults to children (Hashimoto 1988). Adults in this context are people who are married and *ichininmae no shakaijin* (fully adult social beings). They exist in a limbo, doing what they are supposed to do until they retire and must think of something else to fill their time. Homosexuals are, if they remain unmarried, children. They fail to become adult. Hashimoto regards that as positive. They must make decisions about their lives continually. No clear path is laid out for them, which prevents them from entering the limbo of adulthood and promotes creativity. From that viewpoint, scholars who think it childish to write about sex are right, but being childish is superior to being adult.

Another view holds that it is childish to treat the subject of sex any differently from others. Given the fact that the English language dominates most scholarship and definitely anthropology, I do not find it surprising that the area of sex is treated with circumspection. That leads to positions such as Bolton's (1995). Yet Bolton also used information gained from informants, even if in a reflective paper rather than a research report. It seems a waste that he otherwise dismisses possibly valuable information on the basis of what must be common-sense notions concerning the problematic nature of sex.

What all that circumspection proves is that not enough account is taken of the influence of the social, political, cultural, and personal background of anthropologists' visions of the societies they investigate and the subjects they choose. I believe that discussion of these matters is important not because they are necessarily very problematic but because many scholars think they are. I also feel compelled to take a strong attitude in order to present my findings. Doing so may make me seem vulnerable, but there precisely is where I find strength.

## NOTES

Research relating to this essay was supported by the Austrian Ministry of Research and Science, the Japanese Ministry of Education, the Japan Foundation Endowment Committee in Britain, and the Erasmus Fund.

1. Japanese names in this essay will be given in the Japanese order—first the surname and then the given name.

2. The results of this project are presented in Lunsing (1998).

3. This presentation is characterized by appropriating and discarding male and female gender attributes in a constantly changing prism of combinations.

4. Although I am aware that sexual harassment actually is supposed to refer to harassment in situations where power relations play a role, such as at work or school, I share this awareness with very few people, in Japan as well as in Europe. Therefore, I use the term here as it is popularly being used, inclusive of undesired sexual advances in contexts where power relationships are absent.

5. Sexually harassing hostesses, however, ranging from making remarks about their physical features to touching in intimate places and kissing, are integral parts of what happens at most hostess bars in Japan. It seems that the whole point of hostess bars is that customers can abuse hostesses. See, for example, Allison (1994).

6. The phenomenon of media and gay issues is discussed in Lunsing (1997).

7. With the advent of AIDS there has been a move toward monogamy among gay people throughout the world. This has, however, been criticized because it could be a false search for security. Monogamy in reality often means serial monogamy, which takes away much of the perceived security. More important, however, is the idea that one can never be sure whether one's partner is really monogamous. Therefore, promiscuity can be seen as a solution: If one is promiscuous, it is clear that one should always protect oneself and the other when having sex.

# No Hiding Place: Reflections on the Confessions of Manda Cesara

*Karla Poewe*

Give me chastity and self-control but not yet.
—Augustine

I did not vow chastity, neither did I plan to fall in love.
—Karla Poewe

On my first field trip I fell in love. He was a magistrate. He was root-ed. He was rooted in the valley, his beliefs, and his people. Al-though his motherland was poor, he loved her. He carried the key to my ethnic past and I the key to his academic future. I was a fledgling anthropologist. I was German, Lutheran, and married. My husband was an American whom I wronged.

I was also a Cinderella. I protested against my ethnicity, Christiani-ty, and marriage. I protested against my stepmother, North America. And when I wrote the Cesara book I also protested against the profession.

Our love for one another opened us to a new experience of the valley. We saw it, smelt it, heard it, felt it, and tasted of it the way one can only do once, when mind and body are young, receptive, and free of fear, when we are surrendered for "the love of the catch, of under-standing, conceiving, considering so that others can be told what has occurred" (Wolff 1976:23). I wore my golden shoes and together we embarked on a journey of discovery.

The discoveries and disclosures that came with participating in a way of life as a full human being I constructed as a book under the pseudonym of Manda Cesara (1982). But if I gave myself that name because I wanted to stand up tall, as a Cinderella must, and confess myself to all those things of which I was previously ashamed, especial-ly my being German, I soon lost heart and returned to my ashes.

## Facts and Things

> If St. Augustine, who was a devout Bishop and church father, could write his Confessions, why can't we?
>
> —Karla Poewe

*No Hiding Place* was written under my real name. I started work on it in 1979. When it went to press I was in the field in Namibia. There was no chance, therefore, to correct several small but significant errors. The pseudonym had nothing to do with hiding. My publisher had insisted upon a pseudonym for various reasons, among them that they had never published this type of book before. Because I was uneasy with their decision they compromised and put my real name on the back of the title page. As for the rest, I had to change names throughout—in those days manually, hence the slip on page 200 that Wengle (1988) thought was "Freudian."

The very method of participant observation invites writing in more than one ethnographic genre (Poewe 1996). That is precisely what anthropologists still do. But in the Cesara book I was not so much concerned to experiment with writing in a different ethnographic genre as I was with the meaning of fieldwork and the need for leaving a personal record for the sake of the history of the discipline. In other words, I thought that the time had come for anthropologists to do what philosophers have done for decades, even centuries: write academic works for the sake of increasing the knowledge of the discipline, then write an autobiography, a memoir of fieldwork, or simply a confession for the sake of increasing the knowledge of colleagues and history (Leiris 1980 [1934]). Finally, like Sartre, among others, I thought that the discipline was mature enough and humanistic enough to permit the writing of anthropological novels (Bowen 1954; Jackson 1986).

## The Ethics of Fieldwork: Cultural and Ethical Relativism

One of the problems that haunts anthropologists and fieldworkers is the issue of cultural relativism and, since Herskovits (1951, 1972), its correlative—ethical relativism. Cultural relativism refers to "the principle that other societies must be understood through their own cultural values, beliefs, norms, and behaviors" (Scupin 1992:409). Ethical relativism essentially requires that anthropologists in the field evaluate people's doings only according to local "standards of right and wrong" (Keesing 1976:179). In practice, these principles are not very helpful. First, they fail, or can be used to justify hardened indifference, when the ethnographer is confronted with violence. Second, the principles were formulated from the perspective of empiricists who looked objectively at facts; they were not formulated to refer also to the behavior of participant observers (Herskovits 1951:22, 23).

If I cannot judge "them" in terms of my ethical standards, then I also cannot judge my own behavior, to the extent that I am a participant in their way of life, in terms of my ethical standards. That means I either drop my ethical standards entirely or I judge my behavior as participant in their way of life in terms of their ethical standards. But judging my behavior by their standards tends to justify going native, which the profession dislikes. Dropping all ethical standards leaves a vacuum, which is filled by something. Instead of continuing to talk about generalities, I will discuss what I did and what happened to me in the field as I described it in the Cesara book.

Wengle (1988:164) argues that the Cesara book is "the most psychologically open and revealing account of fieldwork yet written." No colleague has yet observed, however, that the Cesara book is possibly also the most ethically transparent and revealing account of fieldwork. Furthermore, no colleague who has disliked the book has yet argued that Cesara shows most clearly the failure of a cultural and ethical relativism.

Without of course intending to, North American anthropologists put the fledgling anthropologist that I then was into an ethical bind. I was born in Germany in 1941. Since age fourteen I was raised in Canada and the United States. As a German, I felt deeply guilty, not only about the concentration camps but about being German period. Cultural relativism taught, of course, that any society must be judged in terms of its own values, norms, and history. So why, then, were all things German—not only Nazism—judged negatively by most North Americans, including anthropologists? Why did cultural relativism apply to all and every culture except to Germans? Were not American anthropologists hypocritical in their seeming adherence to cultural and ethical relativism? Should not their hypocrisy be shown to them in such a way that they might experience it? The Cesara book, precisely because of its intimacy, is a kind of uncomfortable mirror that did just that.

I was raised a German and a Christian, the latter even during the Nazi era in Germany. Because that upbringing was highly suspect in the North American world, it seemed safest to adopt a cultural and ethical relativism in the field. I trusted my basic sense of humanity, and, given my nation's history, I trusted too that I would go overboard to avoid harming or denigrating people who were other than myself. Finally, I believed deeply that given this trust I could safely immerse myself into the world of the ethnographic other and observe what would happen. There could be no "color-bar" where my behavior was concerned.

But chucking my cultural standards left a vacuum that was filled by the habit of examining every experience. I came close to what Keesing called "wandering in a desert of relativism" (1976:179), so that the whole fieldwork experience became a kind of "vision quest" (1976:179) in which each happening, each experience, was carefully examined for the motives and memories it contained and the conscience it revealed (1976:179).

All this was recorded in my diaries and personal letters. A student saw some of this material and suggested I publish it. I knew that if an experientially honest work were to be produced and be of value it would have to mirror anthropological and North American hypocrisy. You might say I indulged in a justice of the desert, an archetypal justice, which is never free of moralism nor of protest or revenge, even when the latter is repressed and passive. The Cesara book, therefore, lays bare an existential ethic. It does so not by saying what this ethic is but by showing it at work. It is an ethic I now reject but that then filled the vacuum of the abandoned Judeo-Christian tradition (Cesara 1982:25–26).

If the first reaction of some colleagues, upon being told that the contributors to this volume want to discuss sexuality and fieldwork, is to say "don't," the second reaction is to demand explicit ethical statements. And yet, if the essays herein teach us anything, it is that concession to either of the above inclinations would have been unwise. An implicit ethics pervades all the essays. Were it not so, then the authors would not have been compelled to start their chapters with disclaimers, explanations, and humor; nor would readers be provoked to think, squirm, and shed some presumptions. Because sexuality has frequently to do with things other than sexuality (for example, with ethnicity, religion, love, alternative consciousness, and insight [Kulick 1995]), it is important to suspend prescription and let the values and ethics of readers enter into an open-ended discourse.

Explicit ethical statements can not protect a profession based on participant-observation, relativism, and openness from criticism. Looking at the cognate field of missions, nor can signed oaths promising celibacy protect a profession from transgressions. But professions can permit the publication of documents and works in some or other desired form wherein practitioners examine their thoughts and actions and thereby shed light on both anthropologists' implied ethics and the profession's hidden inauthenticities.

## Authenticity

Neither Malinowski, nor Rabinow, nor even Margaret Mead were asexual in the field. Whether sex was fantasy, worded visual images, conventional repression, repression for a higher goal, prostitution, or a change of husbands it was present. Indeed, we now know, that Mead's ethnography on Samoa illuminates more about her personal struggle with her own and America's sexual predilections than it does about the sexual practices of Samoan youths (Bateson 1984; Freeman 1983; Howard 1984; Mead 1972).

Controversies and controversial topics tell much about the state of being of, and the changes occurring in, the discipline (Koepping 1987). They, like these essays, describe what anthropologists continue to value: the methods of participant observation. They make researchers aware of what they fear in the field: isolation, limitation, fragmentation, and incompleteness. They tell what they expect and desire: personal and professional fulfillment. Finally, they tell something about the changes in the profession's priorities. For example, simultaneous understanding of self and other has been an explicitly recognized but hotly contested goal of the profession for decades (Cesara 1982; Landes 1970; Leiris 1934; Mead 1972). The contributions to this volume show in the tiny details of everyday research just how this simultaneous understanding is not only possible but also natural. The same may be said for authenticity. In fact, some would argue that aiming for authenticity in fieldwork and ethnographies is a more realistic goal than aiming for objectivity and verifiability (Koepping 1987). At least when the endeavor is authentic its ethics and humanity are put on display.

Fran Markowitz's essay best exemplifies these points. Her fieldwork activities show themselves to be as authentic as her definition of authenticity is accurate. To paraphrase, authenticity has to do with situating a specific ethnographer in a real place, among a real group of people. As such and in this context of dialogue and encounter with people as well as their historical documents, the ethnographer discovers and constructs an ethnographic story about a specific aspect of a shared humanity.

## Full-Bodied Experience

Every encounter of any significance for an ethnographic work involves both full-bodied experiences as well as edited thought. What will I experience; what personal, familial, or group memories will be stirred; what insights might surface; what clouds descend when I, a circumcised Jew, enter naked a well-attended Austrian sauna (Ashkenazi and Rotenberg)? Does Austria's unacknowledged Nazi past crowd my observations? Does it influence my description of their nakedness? Does my memory of things gone-by guide and edit my thoughts? Must I as a reader edit out or factor in the ethnographer's historical specificity?

Having full-bodied experiences has something to do with the fact that fieldwork temporarily uproots or unmoors the researcher. Climo's discussion shows most vividly how this unmooring may bring with it an exhilarating sense of freedom, a preparedness to take calculated risks, and a deep sense of inner peace. Sensory perceptions sharpen, until each new sight, smell, sound, taste, and touch opens yet another gate to the past. Climo points out that the experience of fieldwork bridged his past to the present and did so "through an otherwise 'inappropriate' or 'censored' love relationship."

If American or Israeli Jewishness is an important dimension in the fieldwork experiences of Markowitz, Ashkenazi and Rotenberg, and Climo, then an Italian American Catholicism is surely the motive force behind Salamone's picaresque anthropological adventures. His humorous account is the obverse of Jones's serious one. If Salamone is the picaresque hero whose adventures are staged in the brothels and missions of Nigeria, then Rose Jones is the stage on which the picaresque fantasies of Lucians are tried out.

## Sexuality and Spirituality

Sexuality differs from society to society, from one specific context to another, from person to person. It is one thread both in the tapestry of human existence as a whole and in the tapestries of lives lived in different communities. Almost inevitably, in some form or fashion ethnographers, as participant observers, are drawn into it or have their attention drawn to it.

All of the essays in this volume demonstrate that participant observers become entangled in three major threads: sexuality, ethnicity, and religion. These are what they research as well as what they live. Field-workers who immerse themselves in their work, as these authors have done, become aware of those special (experiential) moments when an aspect of one's personal life illuminates a research problem and vice versa. All significant diaries, journals, autobiographies, and other experiential accounts engage in this sort of reciprocal illumination (Poewe 1996). This reciprocal illumination is there in Markowitz's Jerusalem encounter; it is there in Jones's *zameze* encounter; it is found in the companionships of Salamone and the almost mythical relationship between a "rebelling" Zionist Jewish boy and a Christian, German anti-Semitic maiden who "together" work out analogous incestuous sibling hostilities without the repetition of a holocaust; and it is there in Ashkenazi's and Rotenberg's encounters with nudity in Japan and Austria.

I cannot help but notice, however, that the main issue of some chapters is not sexuality but something often seen as its opposite: spirituality. That is not surprising, for as an Anglican priest once pointed out to me, they are two sides of the same coin. It is particularly obvious in the essays of Salamone and Climo, but it is there in all the rest, too. It is also present in Malinowski's diary and in my Cesara book.

Because Wengle's (1988) thoughts are mentioned in several discussions, I want to contrast what I see as matters of spirituality and empathy with what Wengle sees as matters of identity maintenance. Wengle's basic assumption is that an anthropologist's personality structure or self-representation affects how he or she experiences the field. From that follows a further assumption which goes as follows: If the researcher has an "extreme" experience, it has to do with the researcher's personality structure. The culture and people she or he studies are without power to persuade or affect; they are innocent until the researcher despoils them (Lévi-Strauss 1975). Cultural others do not even have the power to attract, as they did seventeenth- and eighteenth-century explorers (Kohl 1987). It follows that empathy means projecting the anthropologist's personality structure onto the people, culture, or nature she or he studies (Geertz 1983). Works that explore happenings, including sexual happenings. are mere confessionals. They are matters of embarrassment rather than illumination.

That is not, however, what I see in these accounts. The work in this volume, Malinowski's diary, the diary of Michel Leiris, and my Cesara book start with the opposite assumption, that conducting research affects the researcher. They show anthropologists open enough to

being affected by experiences to such a degree that old assumptions
are questioned and—sometimes at least—their own cultures, disciplines, and personal pasts are newly illuminated or rethought in terms
of this experience. After all, experiences are useless to the anthropological enterprise unless approached with an inquisitive mind. While
anthropologists usually gather, interpret, and explain their data, something else is done with experiences. Where the latter are concerned,
researchers are much more likely to discover something unexpected
and uncover or disclose hidden background assumptions, personal
memories, and human existentials. The existential Markowitz uncov-
ers, for example, is love, "cognitive love," not only in the sense of being thrown back on that which she "shares with (hu)mankind" but also
for the sake of the "catch," by which Wolff (1976:40, 20) means the
cognitive or existential yield. The existential brushed over in most
essays, which requires deeper archaeological work, is spirituality. But
the ironical humor and heroic innocence in the close-combat play that
Salamone describes are already "signals of transcendence" (Berger
1970:chap. 3). According to Berger, arguments from humor and play,
along with arguments from order, hope, and damnation, signal a discontent with "human finitude" and "human insignificance." They hint
at an "incompleteness" in what we are and "encourage the expectation
of a fulfillment whose ground" is "something or someone other than
we are" (Polkinghorne 1994:13). In short, the language of experience
depends on rhetoric and transcendence.

What about Malinowski's heroic celibacy in the field? After all, he
admits to being aroused at the sight of beautiful nude bodies in motion. You might joke that he did not have a rabbi with him to remind
him of the "biggest of sins." Did Malinowski remain celibate to preserve
his identity, as Wengle (1988:124) insists? Was identity preservation
even the issue? To my mind the answer is no. Malinowski was still Catholic enough to shape himself in the image of his highest goal—his
professional place in a "high culture." He was out to transcend, or to
present himself as having transcended, various human failings for the
sake of his future fulfillment in the profession.

Wengle (1988) interprets Malinowski's seeming abstinence, despite
desire, as Malinowski's way of handling his "weak and tenuous" sense
of self. What I take to be spiritual experiences Wengle (109–10, 140)
takes to be evidence of self-dissolution or "identity diffusion." For example, he sees Malinowski's descriptions that end with such phrases
as "I dissolved in the landscape" as evidence that Malinowski's bound-

aries of self were "weak and tenuous" (109–10). But what Malinowski actually said, as quoted and translated from German by Kohl (1986:47), was: "Walked on the island; moments of peace and joy; then again despair at yearning for E.R.M. and for 'life.' . . . Sat on a bench for a while; stars, the ocean, the immeasurable emptiness of the universe within which the human being can lose himself; moments in which one melts into the objective reality, when the drama of the universe ceases to be backstage and becomes performance—these are the moments of the true Nirvana."

Malinowski, like Leiris, like the authors in this volume it seems, and like myself certainly, was acutely aware of the limitations of sex as a physical desire and act. He was also acutely aware of the importance of the loss of self in order to achieve a higher union—a spiritual union. In a somewhat analogous way, do not some of these authors feel a loss of self, although it may be fear of a loss of the professional self in writing these essays? Is that why most begin with disclaimers? And yet they wrote and presented these discussions. Could it be that the participants too are willing to lose a sense of self in order to achieve something higher?

Even in these essays we become aware of an important distinction, that between data collecting, which is what anthropologists do, and experiencing, which has to do with what happens to anthropologists. Now experiencing happenings is closely related to empathy. Empathy is the faculty that allows people to experience a happening. It has to do with the power of something outside of the anthropologist—be it an event, a person, or an atmosphere—to call forth buried memories. Put broadly, empathy is the ability to share in another's emotions and feelings. It is not, however, as it tends to be defined in the dictionary and by many anthropologists (Geertz 1983; Wengle 1988), a matter of projecting one's own personality into the personality of another in order to understand that person better. More frequently, empathy has to do with the projection, in the sense of impact, of the other's personality and culture onto one's own. Particularly at moments of intimacy, the other's personality and culture create a happening that requires thoughtful exploration by an open-minded or receptive researcher (Hastrup 1987:293).

## Conclusion

When all is said and done, this collection of essays tells stories about one, often the first, fieldwork encounter. Can a fieldwork experience, one that involved tangentially or directly the ethnographer's sexuality, have the intellectual ground-breaking importance here described? Yes, said Wolff (1976). Yes also said Kulick, who observes that "erotic subjectivity in the field is a potentially useful source of insight" (1995:5). Let me answer this way. Fieldwork in Luapula, where I married not a man but my history, defined my life's work and purpose. Love unlocked not only memories of war and destruction but also of an infinite number of small acts of human kindness. The past, which my mother in her pain had sealed away from me, burst forth to inspire and still guide my intellectual activities. Africa is ever-present in my work but so, too, is the time Germans call *stunde null*—a time of bombs, rubble, and displaced persons.

# REFERENCES CITED

Abbott, Susan. 1982. "Local Politics and the Fieldworker: The Analysis of an African Case." *Anthropology and Humanism Quarterly* 7:28–34.

Abe, H., and R. Wiseman. 1983. "A Cross-Cultural Confirmation of the Dimensions of Intercultural Effectiveness." *International Journal of Intercultural Relations* 7:53–67.

Abramson, Allen. 1993. "Between Autobiography and Method: Being Male, Seeing Myth, and the Analysis of Structures of Gender and Sexuality in the Eastern Interior of Fiji." In *Gendered Fields: Women, Men, and Ethnography*, ed. Diane Bell, Pat Caplan, and Wazir Jahan Karim, 63–77. London: Routledge.

Abramson, Paul R., and Steven D. Pinkerton, eds. 1995. *Sexual Nature, Sexual Culture*. Chicago: University of Chicago Press.

Abramson, Paul. 1990. "Sexual Science: Emerging Discipline or Oxymoron?" *Journal of Sex Research* 27:147–65.

Abu-Lughod, Lila. 1991. "Writing against Culture." In *Recapturing Anthropology: Working in the Present,* ed. Richard G. Fox, 137–62. Santa Fe: School of American Research Press.

Allison, Anne. 1994. *Nightwork: Sexuality, Pleasure, and Corporate Masculinity in a Tokyo Hostess Club*. Chicago: University of Chicago Press.

Angrosino, Michael. 1986. "Son and Lover: The Anthropologist as Nonthreatening Male." In *Self, Sex, and Gender in Cross-Cultural Fieldwork*, ed. Tony Larry Whitehead and Mary Ellen Conaway, 64–83. Urbana: University of Illinois Press.

Associated Press. 1975. "Anthropologists Admit Hangup on Sex." *Los Angeles Times,* Dec. 5, p. 23.

Bachofen, Johann Jakob. 1861. *Das Mutterecht*. Basel: Schwabe.

Back, Les. 1993. "Gendered Participation: Masculinity and Fieldwork in a South London Adolescent Community." In *Gendered Fields: Women, Men, and Ethnography*, ed. Diane Bell, Pat Caplan, and Wazir Jahan Karim, 215–33. London: Routledge.

Bateson, Mary Catherine. 1984. *With a Daughter's Eye*. New York: William Morrow.

Bawer, Bruce. 1993. *A Place at the Table: The Gay Individual in American Society*. New York: Poseidon Press.

Bell, Diane. 1993. "Yes, Virginia, There Is a Feminist Ethnography." In *Gendered Fields: Women, Men, and Ethnography*, ed. Diane Bell, Pat Caplan, and Wazir Jahan Karim, 28–43. London: Routledge.

Bell, Diane, Pat Caplan, and Wazir Jahan Karim, eds. 1993. *Gendered Fields: Women, Men, and Ethnography*. London: Routledge.

Bell, Peter D. 1984. *Peasants in Socialist Transition: Life in a Collectivized Hungarian Village*. Berkeley: University of California Press.

Benveniste, Emile. 1971. *Problems in General Linguistics*. Coral Gables: University of Miami Press.

Berger, Peter. 1970. *Rumor of Angels*. Garden City: Doubleday.

Bernard, H. Russell. 1988. *Research Methods in Cultural Anthropology*. Newbury Park: Sage Publications.

Berreby, David. 1995. "Unabsolute Truths: Clifford Geertz." *New York Times Magazine*, April 9, pp. 44–47.

Blaiklock, E. M., trans. 1983. *The Confessions of Saint Augustine: A New Translation with Introductions*. Nashville: Thomas Nelson Publishers.

Bolton, Ralph. 1995. "Tricks, Friends, and Lovers: Erotic Encounters in the Field." In *Taboo: Sex, Identity, and Erotic Subjectivity in Anthropological Fieldwork*, ed. Don Kulick and Margaret Willson, 140–67. London: Routledge.

Bolton, Ralph, Michelle Lewis, and Gail Orozco. 1990. "AIDS Literature for Anthropologists: A Working Bibliography." *Journal of Sex Research* 28:307–46.

Bourdieu, Pierre. 1977. *Outline of a Theory of Practice*. New York: Cambridge University Press.

Bourke, John. 1891. *Scatalogic Rites of All Nations*. Washington, D.C.: W. H. Lowdermilk.

Bowen, Elenore Smith [Laura Bohannan]. 1954. *Return to Laughter*. New York: Harper and Row.

Broude, Gwen, and Sarah Greene. 1976. "Cross-Cultural Codes on Twenty Sexual Attitudes and Practices." *Ethnology* 4:409–30.

Buda, Béla. 1986. "Szexualitás ma Magyarországon" (Sexuality in contemporary Hungary). In *Fejezetek a szexualitás történetéből* (Chapters from the history of sexuality), ed. Tamás Oláh, 259–66. Budapest: Gondolat.

Butler, Judith. 1990. *Gender Trouble: Feminism and the Subversion of Identity*. London: Routledge.

Caffrey, Margaret. 1989. *Ruth Benedict: Stranger in This Land*. Austin: University of Texas Press.

Caplan, Pat, ed. 1987. *The Cultural Construction of Sexuality*. London: Tavistock Publishing.

———. 1993. "Learning Gender: Fieldwork in a Tanzanian Coastal Village, 1965–1985." In *Gendered Fields: Women, Men, and Ethnography*, ed. Diane Bell, Pat Caplan, and Wazir Jahan Karim, 168–81. London: Routledge.

Cesara, Manda [Karla Poewe]. 1982. *Reflections of a Woman Anthropologist*. New York: Academic Press.

Charney, Maurice. 1981. *Sexual Fiction*. London: Methuen.

Chuang, Hui-ch'iu, ed. 1993. *Chung-kuo-Jen Te T'ung-Hsing-Lien* (Homosexuality in China). Taipei: Chang Lao-Shih Yueh-Kan Ch'u-Pan-She.

Clark, Scott. 1994. *Japan: A View from the Bath*. Honolulu: University of Hawaii Press.

Clifford, James, and George E. Marcus, eds. 1986. *Writing Culture: The Poetics and Politics of Ethnography*. Berkeley: University of California Press.

Climo, Jacob. 1968. "Protestant Sectarianism in Mexico: The Case of Los Judios Espirituales." M.A. thesis, Michigan State University.

———. 1971. "El Innovador Religioso y el Cambio Social e Ideologico en una Secta Religiosa." *Revista de la Universidad de Yucatan*, March–April, pp. 72–81.

———. 1992. *Distant Parents*. New Brunswick: Rutgers University Press.

———. 1995. "Prisoners of Silence: A Vicarious Holocaust Memory." In *The Labyrinth of Memory: Ethnographic Journeys*, ed. Marea Teski and Jacob Climo, 175–84. Westport: Greenwood.

Conaway, Mary Ellen. 1986. "The Pretense of the Neutral Researcher." In *Self, Sex, and Gender in Cross-Cultural Fieldwork*, ed. Tony Larry Whitehead and Mary Ellen Conaway, 52–63. Urbana: University of Illinois Press.

Condon, J. 1985. *Good Neighbors Communicating with the Mexicans*. Yarmouth: Intercultural Press.

Crapanzano, Vincent. 1980. *Tuhami: Portrait of a Moroccan*. Chicago: University of Chicago Press.

———. 1994. "Rethinking Psychological Anthropology: A Critical View." In *The Making of Psychological Anthropology*, ed. Marcelo M. Suarez-Orozco, George Spindler, and Louise Spindler. Vol. 2, 223–43. New York: Harcourt Brace.

Cui, G., and S. Van den Berg. 1991. "Testing the Construct Validity of Intercultural Effectiveness." *International Journal of Intercultural Relations* 15:227–41.

Davis, D. L., and R. G. Whitten. 1987. "The Cross-Cultural Study of Human Sexuality." *Annual Review of Anthropology* 16:69–98.

Del Valle, Teresa, ed. 1993. *Gendered Anthropology*. London: Routledge.

D'Emilio, John, and Estelle B. Freedman. 1988. *Intimate Matters: A History of Sexuality in America*. New York: Harper and Row.

Diaz-Guerrero, R. 1961. *Studies in the Psychology of the Mexican*. Mexico City: Antigua Libreria Robredo.

Donner, Florinda. 1982. *Shabono*. New York: Delacorte.

Dubisch, Jill. 1995. "Lovers in the Field: Sex, Dominance, and the Female Anthropologist." In *Taboo: Sex, Identity, and Erotic Subjectivity in Anthropological Fieldwork*, ed. Don Kulick and Margaret Willson, 29–50. London: Routledge.

Dumont, Jean-Paul. 1978. *The Headman and I: Ambiguity and Ambivalence in the Fieldworking Experience*. Austin: University of Texas Press.

Edwards, Tim. 1994. *Erotics and Politics: Gay Male Sexuality, Masculinity, and Feminism*. London: Routledge.

Erchak, G. 1992. *The Anthropology of Self and Behavior*. New Brunswick: Rutgers University Press.

Feldman, Allen. 1991. *Formations of Violence*. Chicago: University of Chicago Press.

Fél, Edit, and Tamás Hofer. 1969. *Proper Peasants: Traditional Life in a Hungarian Village*. Chicago: Aldine.

Fischer, Ann. 1986. "Field Work in Five Cultures." In *Women in the Field: Anthropological Experiences*, 2d ed., 267–90. Ed. Peggy Golde. Berkeley: University of California Press.

Fisher, Helen. 1983. *The Sex Contract*. New York: Quill.

Fisher, Lawrence E. 1980. "Relationships and Sexuality in Contexts and Cultures: The Anthropology of Eros." In *Handbook of Human Sexuality*, ed. Benjamin Wolman and John Money, 164–89. Englewood Cliffs: Prentice-Hall.

Fitzgerald, Thomas K. 1979. "The Status of Homosexuals in Finland." *SGC [Sociologists' Gay Caucus] Newsletter* 20:7.

———. 1980. "Gay Self-Help Groups in Sweden and Finland." *International Review of Modern Sociology* 10:191–200.

———. 1981. "Suicide Prevention and Gay Self-Help Groups in Sweden and Finland." *Crisis: International Suicide and Crisis Studies* 2:58–68.

———. 1991. "Identity in Ethnography: Limits to 'Reflective Subjectivity.'" *SOLGA Newsletter*, Oct., pp. 46–48.

———. 1993. *Metaphors of Identity: A Culture-Communication Dialogue*. Albany: State University of New York Press.

Foucault, Michel. 1980. *The History of Human Sexuality: An Introduction*. Vol. 1. Trans. Robert Hurley. New York: Vintage Books.

Frayser, Suzanne. 1985. *Varieties of Sexual Experience: An Anthropological Perspective in Human Sexuality*. New Haven: HRAF Press.

Freeman, Derek. 1983. *Margaret Mead and Samoa*. Cambridge: Harvard University Press.

Freud, Sigmund. 1930. *Civilization and Its Discontents*. London: Hogarth Press.

Friedl, Ernestine. 1994. "Sex the Invisible." *American Anthropologist* 96:833–44.

Fushimi, Noriaki. 1991. *Puraibēto gei raifu: Posuto renairon* (Private gay life: Postmodern love theory). Tokyo: Gakuyō Shobō.

Gal, Susan. 1978. "'Peasant Men Can't Get Wives': Language Change and Sex Roles in a Bilingual Community." *Language in Society* 7:1–16.

Geertz, Clifford. 1967. "Under the Mosquito Net." *New York Review of Books*, Sept. 14, pp. 12–13.

———. 1973. "Thick Description: Towards an Interpretative Theory of Culture." In *The Interpretation of Culture*, 3–32. New York: Basic Books.

———. 1983. *Local Knowledge*. New York: Basic Books.

———. 1988. *Works and Lives: The Anthropologist as Author.* Oxford: Polity Press.

———. 1995. *After the Facts.* Cambridge: Harvard University Press.

Giddens, Anthony. 1984. *The Constitution of Society.* Berkeley: University of California Press.

———. 1991. *Modernity and Self-Identity: Self and Society in the Late Modern Age.* Stanford: Stanford University Press.

Giovannini, Maureen. 1986. "Female Anthropologist and Male Informant: Gender Conflict in a Sicilian Town." In *Self, Sex, and Gender in Cross-Cultural Fieldwork,* ed. Tony Larry Whitehead and Mary Ellen Conaway, 103–16. Urbana: University of Illinois Press.

Goffman, Erving. 1959. *The Presentation of Self in Everyday Life.* New York: Doubleday.

Golde, Peggy. 1986. "Introduction." In *Women in the Field: Anthropological Experiences,* 2d ed., 1–15. Ed. Peggy Golde. Berkeley: University of California Press.

———, ed. 1986. *Women in the Field: Anthropological Experiences,* 2d ed. Berkeley: University of California Press.

Goldenweiser, Alexander. 1937. *Anthropology.* New York: F. S. Crofts.

Gottfried, Barbara. 1988. "What Do Men Want, Dr. Roth?" In *A Mensch among Men: Explorations in Jewish Masculinity,* ed. Harry Brod, 37–52. Freedom, Calif.: Crossing Press.

Gregor, Thomas. 1985. *Anxious Pleasures: The Sexual Life of an Amazonian People.* Chicago: University of Chicago Press.

Gudykunst, William B. 1991. *Bridging Differences: Effective Intergroup Communication.* Newbury Park: Sage Publications.

Gudykunst, William B., and Young Yun Kim. 1984. *Communicating with Strangers: An Approach to Intercultural Communication.* New York: Random House.

Gyôri, Klára. 1975. *Kiszáradt az én örömöm zöld fája* (My delight's green tree dried out). Bucharest: Kriterion.

Hamabata, Masayuki. 1986. "Ethnographic Boundaries: Culture, Class, and Sexuality in Tokyo." *Qualitative Sociology* 9:354–71.

———. 1990. *Crested Kimono: Power and Love in the Japanese Business Family.* Ithaca: Cornell University Press.

Hammer, M. 1987. "Behavioral Dimensions of Intercultural Effectiveness: A Replication and Extension." *International Journal of Intercultural Relations* 11:65–88.

Hammer, M., W. Gudykunst, and R. Wiseman. 1978. "Dimensions of Intercultural Effectiveness: An Exploratory Study." *International Journal of Intercultural Relations* 2:382–92.

Handwerker, Penn. 1989. *Women's Power and Social Revolution: Fertility Transition in the West Indies.* Newberry Park: Sage Publications.

Hann, Chris M. 1980. *Tázlár: A Village in Hungary.* New York: Cambridge University Press.

Harding, Susan F. 1987. "Convicted by the Holy Spirit: The Rhetoric of Fundamental Baptist Conversion." *American Ethnologist* 14:167–282.

Hashiguchi, Jôji [George]. 1992. *Couple (Kappuru).* Tokyo: Bungei Shunju.

Hashimoto, Osamu. 1988. *Fūga no tora no maki* (Secrets of elegance). Tokyo: Sakuhinsha.

Hastrup, Kirsten. 1987. "The Reality of Anthropology." *Ethnos* 52:287–300.

———. 1992. "Writing Ethnography: State of the Art." In *Anthropology and Autobiography*, ed. Anne Okley and Helen Callaway, 116–33. London: Routledge.

Hayamizu, Hisako. 1994. "Dai-ikai rezubian gei parēdo to kamu-auto" (The first lesbian and gay parade and coming out). *OLP no Newsletter* 2:4–7.

Hendry, Joy. 1986. *Becoming Japanese: The World of the Pre-School Child*. Manchester: Manchester University Press.

———. 1990. "Humidity, Hygeine, or Ritual Care: Some Thoughts on Wrapping as a Social Phenomenon." In *Unwrapping Japan*, ed. Eyal Ben Ari, James Valentine, and Brian Moeran, 18–36. Manchester: Manchester University Press.

———. 1992. "The Paradox of Friendship in the Field: Analysis of a Long-Term Anglo-Japanese Relationship." In *Anthropology and Autobiography*, ed. Judith Okely and Helen Callaway, 163–74. London: Routledge.

Herdt, Gilbert E. 1994. *Guardians of the Flutes*. Vol. 1. Chicago: University of Chicago Press.

Herefeld, Michael. 1987. *Anthropology through the Looking Glass: Critical Ethnography in the Margins of Europe*. New York: Cambridge University Press.

Herskovits, Melville J. 1951. "Tender and Tough-Minded Anthropology and the Study of Values in Culture." *Southwestern Journal of Anthropology* 7:22–31.

———. 1972. *Cultural Relativism*. New York: Random House.

Hollós, Marida. 1983. "Ideology and Economics: Cooperative Organization and Attitudes toward Collectivization in Two Hungarian Communities." In *New Hungarian Peasants*, ed. Marida Hollós and Béla C. Maday, 93–122. New York: Brooklyn College Press.

Hoppál, Mihály. n.d. "Népmüvészet és etnoszemiotika" (Folk art and ethnosemiotics). *Népi Kultúra–épi Társadalom* (Folk culture–folk society) 11–12:191–217.

Hovedt, Mary. 1983. "The Cross-Cultural and Historical Context." In *Sexuality in the Later Years: Roles and Behavior*, ed. Ruth Weg, 13–35. New York: Academic Press.

Howard, Jane. 1984. *Margaret Mead: A Life*. New York: Fawcett Crest.

Hsu, Frances. 1979. "The Cultural Problem of the Cultural Anthropologist." *American Anthropologist* 79:805–9.

Huseby, Éva V. 1983a. "Lebenweise und Endogamie-Exogamie in einem Nordungarischen Dorf" (Lifeways and endogamy-exogamy in a North Hungarian village). In *Ethnographica et Folkloristica Carpathia*, ed. Zoltán Ujváry, 3205–23. Debrecen: KLTE.

———. 1983b. "*Pincézés*, the Male Domain: Drinking Activities and Social Networks of Village Men." In *Muzeumi Kurir* (Museum news), ed. Imre Dankó, 73–79. Debrecen: Dery Museum.

———. 1984. "Community Cohesion and Identity Maintenance in a Northern Hungarian Village." Ph.d. diss. University of Michigan, Ann Arbor.

Huseby-Darvas, Éva V. 1987. "Elderly Women in a Hungarian Village: Childlessness, Generativity, and Social Control." *Journal of Cross-Cultural Gerontology* 1:87–114.

———. 1988. "Migrating Inward and Out: Validating Life Course Transitions through Oral Autobiography." In *Life History as Cultural Construction/Performance,* ed. Tamás Hofer and Peter Niedermuller, 379–408. Budapest: Hungarian Academy of Sciences.

———. 1990a. "Introduction." In *Gender Contradictions/Gender Transformations: Cases from Eastern Europe.* Special issue of *East European Quarterly* 23:385–88.

———. 1990b. "Migration and Gender: Perspectives from Rural Hungary." In *Gender Contradictions/Gender Transformations: Cases from Eastern Europe.* Special issue of *East European Quarterly* 23:487–98.

Jackson, Michael. 1986. *Barawa and the Ways Birds Fly in the Sky.* Washington, D.C.: Smithsonian Institution.

Jacobs, Sue-Ellen, Wesley Thomas, and Sabine Lang. 1997. "Introduction." In *Two-Spirit People: Native American Gender Identity, Sexuality, and Spirituality,* ed. Sue-Ellen Jacobs, Wesley Thomas, and Sabine Lang, 1–18. Urbana: University of Illinois Press.

Johnson, John M., and Kathleen J. Ferraro. 1987. "The Victimized Self: The Case of Battered Women." In *The Existential Self in Society,* ed. J. A. Kotarba and A. Fontana, 119–30. Chicago: University of Chicago Press.

Jones, Rose. 1994. "Songs from the Village: An Ethnography of Gender, Reproduction, and Sexuality in St. Lucia, West Indies." Ph.D. diss., Southern Methodist University.

Kakefuda, Hiroko. 1992. *"Rezubian" de aru, to iu koto* (Being "lesbian"). Tokyo: Kawade Shobō.

Kaminsky, Marc. 1992. "Introduction." In *Remembered Lives: The Work of Ritual, Storytelling, and Growing Older,* ed. Barbara Myerhoff, 5–11. Ann Arbor: University of Michigan Press.

Kawamura, Nozomu. 1994. *Sociology and Society of Japan.* London: Kegan Paul International.

Keesing, Roger. 1976. *Cultural Anthropology: A Contemporary Perspective.* New York: Holt, Rinehart and Winston.

———. 1994. "Theories of Culture Revisited." In *Assessing Cultural Anthropology,* ed. Robert Borofsky, 301–10. New York: McGraw Hill.

Kennedy-Bergen, Raquel. 1993. "Interviewing Supporters of Marital Rape: Doing Feminist Research on Feminist Topics." In *Researching Sensitive Topics,* ed. Claire M. Renzetti and Raymond M. Lee, 197–211. Newbury Park: Sage Publications.

Killick, Andrew O. 1995. "The Penetrating Intellect: On Being Straight, White, and Male in Korea." In *Taboo: Sex, Identity, and Erotic Subjectivity in Anthropological Fieldwork,* ed. Don Kulick and Margaret Willson, 76–106. London: Routledge.

Koepping, Klaus-Peter. 1987. "Authentizität als Selbstfindung durch den anderen: Ethnologie zwischen Engagement und Reflexion, zwischen Leben und Wissenschaft" (Authenticity as self-discovery through the other: Ethnology between engagement and reflection between life and science). In *Authentizität und Betrug in der Ethnologie* (Authenticity and falsity in ethnology), ed. Hans Peter Duerr, 7–37. Frankfurt/M.: Suhrkamp.

Kohl, Karl-Heinz. 1986. *Exotik als Beruf* (Exoticism as profession). Frankfurt/M.: Campus.

———. 1987. *Abwehr und Verlangen* (Rejection and desire). Frankfurt/M.: Campus.

Kon, Igor, and James Riordan, eds. 1993. *Sex and Russian Society*. Bloomington: Indiana University Press.

Kulick, Don. 1995. "Introduction: The Sexual Life of Anthropologists: Erotic Subjectivity and Ethnographic Work." In *Taboo: Sex, Identity, and Erotic Subjectivity in Anthropological Fieldwork*, ed. Don Kulick and Margaret Willson, 1–28. London: Routledge.

Kulick, Don, and Margaret Willson, eds. 1995. *Taboo: Sex, Identity, and Erotic Subjectivity in Anthropological Fieldwork*. London: Routledge.

Kürti, László. 1991. "The Wingless Eros of Socialism: Nationalism and Sexuality in Hungary." *Anthropological Quarterly* 2:55–67.

La Fontaine, J. S. 1987. "Person and Individual: Some Anthropological Reflections." In *The Category of the Person*, ed. M. Carrithers, S. Collins, and S. Lukes, 123–40. New York: Cambridge University Press.

Lampland, Martha. 1990. "Unthinkable Subjects: Women and Labor in Socialist Hungary." *East European Quarterly* 23:381–98.

Landes, Ruth. 1970. "A Woman Anthropologist in Brazil." In *Women in the Field: Anthropological Experiences*, ed. Peggy Golde, 118–39. Chicago: Aldine.

Leach, Edmund. 1954. *Political Systems of Highland Burma*. Boston: Beacon Press.

Lebra, Takie Sugiyama. 1984. *Japanese Women: Constraint and Fulfilment*. Honolulu: University of Hawaii Press.

———. 1992. "Self in Japanese Culture." In *Japanese Sense of Self*, ed. Nancy R. Rosenberger, 105–20. New York: Cambridge University Press.

Leiris, Michel. 1934. *L'Afrique fantome: De Dakar a Djibouti, 1931–1933*. Paris: Gallimard.

———. 1980 [1934]. *Phantom Afrika: Tagebuch einer Expedition von Dakar nach Djibouti, 1931–1933*. Vols. 1–2. Trans. [French to German] Rolf Wintermeyer. Frankfurt/M: Syndikat.

Lei-szu-pien. 1994. "Lei-szu-pien hsin-hsiang" (Lesbian mailbox). *Nu-p 'eng-yu* 1:20.

Lévi-Strauss, Claude. 1975. *Tristes Tropiques*. New York: Atheneum.

Lewin, Ellen, and William L. Leap, eds. 1996. *Out in the Field: Reflections of Lesbian and Gay Anthropologists*. Urbana: University of Illinois Press.

Lieberman, Morton A., and Leonard D. Borman. 1976. "Self-Help and Social Research." *Journal of Applied Behavioral Science* 12:455–603.

Lindenbaum, S. 1991. "Anthropology Rediscovers Sex." *Social Science and Medicine* 33:865–66.

Lükô, Gábor. n.d. *A magyar lélek formái* (The configurations of the Hungarian psyche). Budapest: Hasonmás.

Lunsing, Wim. 1994. "'Homo senshinkoku' Oranda ga boku o sodateta" ("Gay frontline state" the Netherlands brought me up). *Fujin Kōron* 2:336–42.

———. 1997. "'Gay Boom' in Japan: Changing Views of Homosexuality?" In *Thamyris: Myths and Mythmaking from Past to Present* 4:267–93.

———. 1998. *Beyond Common Sense: Negotiating Constructions of Sexuality and Gender in Contemporary Japan.* London: Kegan Paul International.

Macaloon, John, and Mihaly Csikszentmihalyi. 1983. "Deep Play and the Flow Experience in Rock Climbing." In *Play, Games, and Sports in Cultural Contexts,* ed. J. Harris and R. Park, 361–84. Champaign: Human Kinetics.

Malinowski, Bronislaw. 1929. *The Sexual Lives of Savages in North-Western Melanesia.* New York: Harvest Press.

———. 1955 [1927]. *Sex and Repression in Savage Society.* New York: Meridian Books.

———. 1967. *A Diary in the Strict Sense of the Term.* New York: Harcourt, Brace and World.

Marcus, George, and Dick Cushman. 1982. "Ethnographies as Texts." *Annual Review in Anthropology* 11:25–69.

Marcus, George E., and Michael M. J. Fischer. 1986. *Anthropology as Cultural Critique.* Chicago: University of Chicago Press.

Markowitz, Fran. 1988. "Can Anthropology Be Life?" Presented at the annual meetings of the American Anthropological Association, Phoenix, Ariz.

———. 1993. *A Community in Spite of Itself.* Washington, D.C.: Smithsonian Institution Press.

———. 1995. "Striving for Femininity: (Post) Soviet Un-Feminism." *Canadian Woman Studies/Les Cahiers de la Femme* 16:38–42.

Marshall, Donald, and R. Suggs. 1971. *Human Sexual Behavior: Variations in the Ethnographic Spectrum.* New York: Basic Books.

McKeganey, Neil, and Michael Bloom. 1991. "Spotting the Invisible Man: The Influence of Male Gender on Fieldwork Relations." *British Journal of Sociology* 42:195–210.

Mead, Margaret. 1928. "Coming of Age in Samoa." In *From the South Seas: Studies of Adolescence Sex in Primitive Societies,* 1–304. New York: William Morrow.

———. 1961 [1928]. *Coming of Age in Samoa.* New York: Morrow Quill Paperbacks.

———. 1963 [1935]. *Sex and Temperament in Three Primitive Societies.* New York: Morrow Quill Paperbacks.

———. 1972. *Blackberry Winter.* New York: Touchstone.

———. 1977. *Letters from the Field: 1925–1975.* New York: Harper and Row.

Mendes-Leite, Rommel. 1993. "A Game of Appearances: The 'Ambigusexuality' in Brazilian Culture of Sexuality." In *Gay Studies from the French Cultures,* ed. Rommel Mendes-Leite and P.-O. de Busscher, 271–82. New York: Harrington Park Press.

Mies, Maria. 1983. "Towards a Methodology of Feminist Research." In *Theories of Women's Studies,* ed. Gloria Bowles and Renate Duelli Klein, 117–39. London: Routledge.

Moffatt, Michael. 1989. *Coming of Age in New Jersey: College and American Culture.* New Brunswick: Rutgers University Press.

Morgan, Lewis Henry. 1978 [1878]. "Ancient Society." In *High Points in Anthropology*, ed. Paul Bohannan and Mark Glazer, 32–60. New York: Alfred Knopf.

Morris, Brian. 1994. *Anthropology of the Self: The Individual In Cultural Perspective*. London: Pluto Press.

Morvay, Judit. 1981 [1957]. *Asszonyok a Nagycsaládban* (Women in the extended family). Budapest: Magvető.

Murray, Stephen O. 1996. "Male Homosexuality in Guatamala: Possible Insights and Certain Confusions from Sleeping with the Natives." In *Out in the Field: Reflections of Lesbian and Gay Anthropologists*, ed. Ellen Lewin and William L. Leap, 236–60. Urbana: University of Illinois Press.

Nagy, Olga. 1977. *Paraszt Dekameron* (Peasant Decameron). Budapest: Magvető.

Narayan, Kirin. 1993. "How Native Is a 'Native' Anthropologist?" *American Anthropologist* 95:671–86.

Nas, P. J. M., W. J. M. Prins, and W. A. Shadid. 1987. "A Plea for Praxeology." In *The Research Relationship: Practice and Politics in Social Policy Research*, ed. G. Clare Wenger, 18–42. London: Allen and Unwin.

Newton, Esther. 1993. "My Best Informant's Dress: The Erotic Equation in Fieldwork." *Cultural Anthropology* 8:3–23.

Oboler, Regina Smith. 1986. "For Better or Worse: Anthropologists and Husbands in the Field." In *Self, Sex, and Gender in Cross-Cultural Fieldwork*, ed. Tony Larry Whitehead and Mary Ellen Conaway, 28–51. Urbana: University of Illinois Press.

Ōhama, Hōei. 1988. *Nihon no eizu: Sekaiteki shibyō to no tatakai* (AIDS in Japan: The fight against a lethal global disease). Tokyo: Saimaru Simul Shuppan.

Okami, Paul, and Laura Pendleton. 1994. "Theorizing Sexuality: Seeds of a Transdisciplinary Paradigm Shift." *Current Anthropology* 35:85–91.

Ortner, Sherry B. 1984. "Theory in Anthropology since the Sixties." *Comparative Studies in Society and History* 26:126–66.

———. 1995. "Resistance and the Problem of Ethnographic Refusal." *Comparative Studies in Society and History* 37:173–93.

Ortutay, Gyula. 1935. *A magyar parasztság szerelmi élete* (The sexual life of the Hungarian peasantry). Budapest: Atheneum.

Parker, R., G. Herdt, and M. Carballo. 1991. "Sexual Culture and HIV Transmission and AIDS Research." *Journal of Sex Research* 6:255–70.

Paul, William. 1982. "Minority Status for Gay People: Majority Reaction and Social Context." In *Homosexuality*, ed. William Paul, J. D. Weinrich, J. C. Gonsiorek, and M. E. Hotvedt, 351–69. Newberry Park: Sage Publishers.

Paz, Octavio. 1961. *The Labyrinth of Solitude: Life and Thought in Mexico*. New York: Grove Press.

Poewe, Karla. 1996. "Writing Culture and Writing Fieldwork: The Proliferation of Experimental and Experiential Ethnographies." *Ethnos* 61:177–206.

Polkinghorne, John. 1994. *The Faith of a Physicist: Reflections of a Bottom-Up Thinker*. Princeton: Princeton University Press.

Probyn, Elspeth. 1993. *Sexing the Self: Gendered Positions In Cultural Studies*. London: Routledge.

Pym, Barbara. 1955. *Less Than Angels*. London: Jonathan Cape.

Rabinow, Paul. 1977. *Reflections on Fieldwork in Morocco.* Berkeley: University of California Press.

Rappaport, Roy A. 1994. "Disorders of Our Own." In *Diagnosing America,* ed. Shepard Forman, 234–94. Ann Arbor: University of Michigan Press.

Redfield, Robert. 1960. *The Little Community.* Chicago: University of Chicago Press.

Reinharz, Shulamit. 1983. "Experiential Analysis: A Contribution to Feminist Research." In *Theories of Women's Studies,* ed. Gloria Bowles and Renate Duelli Klein, 162–92. London: Routledge.

Rich, Adrienne. 1980. "Compulsory Heterosexuality and Lesbian Experience." *Signs: Journal of Women in Culture and Society* 5:631–60.

Róheim, Géza. 1925. *A Magyar Néphit és Népszokások* (Hungarian folk beliefs and folk customs). Budapest: Athenaeum.

Rohlen, Thomas P. 1974. *For Harmony and Strength: Japanese White-Collar Organization in Anthropological Perspective.* Berkeley: University of California Press.

Ross, Michael, and Olli Stälström. 1979. "Exorcism as Psychiatric Treatment: A Homosexual Case Study." *Archives of Sexual Behavior* 8:379–83.

Roth, Philip. 1985. *Reading Myself and Others.* New York: Penguin Books.

Rozenblum, Serge-Alain. 1982. *Etre Juif en U.R.S.S.* (To be Jewish in the U.S.S.R.). Paris: Collection de la R.P.S.

Salamone, Frank A., ed. 1974. *In the Field.* Lexington, Ky.: Xerox.

———. 1979. "Epistemolological Implications of Fieldwork and Their Consequences." *American Anthropologist* 8:146–60.

———. 1982. "Anthropologists and Missionaries: An Empirical Investigation." *Euntes Docete* 35:389–426.

———. 1983–84. "Subjectivity and Fieldwork." *Journal of Northern Luzon* 14:2–14.

———, ed. 1985. *Missionaries and Anthropologists: Case Studies.* Studies in Third World Societies. Williamsburg: College of William and Mary.

———. 1986. "Missionaries and Anthropologists: An Inquiry into Their Ambivalent Relationship." *Missiology* 14:55–70.

———. 1993. "The Reconstruction of Main Street: The American Diplomatic Corps in Nigeria." *Mosaic* 26:87–102.

———. 1995. *The Fulbright Experience in Nigeria.* Studies in Third World Societies. Williamsburg: College of William and Mary.

Scheper-Hughes, Nancy. 1995. "The Primacy of the Ethical: Propositions for a Militant Anthropology." *Current Anthropology* 36:409–20.

Schrijvers, Joke. 1985. *Mothers for Life: Motherhood and Marginalization in the North Central Province of Sri Lanka.* Delft: Eburon.

———. 1993. "Motherhood Experienced and Conceptualized: Changing Images of Sri Lanka and the Netherlands." In *Gendered Fields: Women, Men, and Ethnography,* ed. Diane Bell, Pat Caplan, and Wazir Jahan Karim, 143–67. London: Routledge.

Scupin, Raymond. 1992. *Cultural Anthropology: A Global Perspective.* Englewood Cliffs: Prentice-Hall.

Sedgwick, Eve Kosofsky. 1990. *Epistomology of the Closet.* Berkeley: University of California Press.

Shokeid, Moshe. 1992. "Committment and Contextual Study in Anthropology." *Cultural Anthropology* 7:464–77.

Shostak, Marjorie. 1983. *Nisa.* New York: Vintage.

Shweder, Richard A. 1986. "Storytelling among the Anthropologists." *New York Times Book Review,* Sept. 21, pp. 37–39.

Siebers, Joan E. 1993. "The Ethics and Politics of Sensitive Research." In *Researching Sensitive Topics,* ed. Claire M. Renzetti and Raymond M. Lee, 15–26. Newbury Park: Sage Publications.

Smith, Robert J. 1978. "Introduction." In *The Namahage,* ed. Yoshiko Yamamoto. Philadelphia: Institute for the Study of Human Issues.

Sobo, Elise J. 1993. *One Blood: The Jamaican Body.* New York: State University of New York Press.

Sorenson, E. 1993. "Sensuality and Consciousness: Psychosexual Transformation in Eastern Andaman." *Anthropology of Consciousness* 4:1–9.

Sozan, Michael. 1985. *A Határ Két Oldalán* (On two sides of the border). Paris: Irodalmi Vjság Kiadó.

Stocking, George. 1987. *Victorian Anthropology.* New York: Free Press.

Stoller, Paul, and Cheryl Olkes. 1989. *In Sorcery's Shadow: A Memoir of Apprenticeship among the Songhay of Niger.* Chicago: University of Chicago Press.

Stonequist, Everett. 1937. *The Marginal Man.* New York: Scribner.

Strasser, Sabine, and Ruth Kronsteiner. 1993. "Women in the Field: Reflections on a Never-Ending Journey." In *Gendered Anthropology,* ed. Teresa del Valle, 162–76. London: Routledge.

Suggs, Robert C., and Donald S. Marshall. 1971. "Anthropological Perspectives on Human Sexual Behavior." In *Human Sexual Behavior: Variations in the Ethnographic Spectrum,* ed. Donald S. Marshall and Robert C. Suggs, 218–43. New York: Basic Books.

Szendrey, Ákos. 1938. "A Népi Élet Társas-összejövetelei" (Special gatherings of folklife). *Ethnographia* 40:273–86.

Tax, Sol. 1975. "Action Anthropology." *Current Anthropology* 16:514–17.

Tsutamori, Tatsuru. 1993. *Otoko de mo naku, onna de mo nai: Shinjidai no andorojinasutachi e* (Neither man nor woman: To the androgynous people of the new times). Tokyo: Keisô Shobô.

Turnbull, Colin M. 1986. "Sex and Gender: The Role of Subjectivity in Field Research." In *Self, Sex, and Gender in Cross-Cultural Fieldwork,* ed. Tony Larry Whitehead and Mary Ellen Conaway, 17–27. Urbana: University of Illinois Press.

Turner, Victor. 1974. *The Ritual Process.* Harmondsworth, U.K.: Penguin.

Tuzin, D. 1991. "Sex, Culture, and the Anthropologist." *Social Science and Medicine* 33:867–74.

Ujváry, Zoltán. 1978. *A Temetés Parodiéja* (A parody of burial). Debrecen: Kossuth Lajos Tudomány Egyetem Néprajzi Tanszék.

Vajda, Mária. 1982. "Szerelmi élet Balmazujváros" (Sexual life in [the provincial city of] Balmazujváros). *Forrás* 1:58–67, 2:84–96, 3:66–74, 4:56–69.

———. 1988. *Hol a Világ Közepe? Parasztvallomások a Szerelemröl* (Where is the world's center? Peasant recollections on love). Kecskemét: Forrás.

Vance, Carole. 1991. "Anthropology Rediscovers Sexuality: A Theoretical Comment." *Social Science and Medicine* 33:875–84.

Vásáry, Ildikó. 1991. "The Sin of Transdanubia: The One-Child System." *Continuity and Change* 4:429–68.

Vayda, Andrew P. 1994. "Actions, Variations, and Change: The Emerging Anti-Essentialist View in Anthropology." In *Assessing Cultural Anthropology*, ed. Robert Borofsky, 320–30. New York: McGraw Hill.

Vöö, Gabriella. 1969. *Többet Ésszel, Mint Erővel* (Attain more with brain than with brawn). Bucharest: Kriterion.

Wade, Peter. 1993. "Sexuality and Masculinity in Fieldwork among Columbian Blacks." In *Gendered Fields: Women, Men, and Ethnography*, ed. Diane Bell, Pat Caplan, and Wazir Jahan Karim, 199–214. London: Routledge.

Wafer, James. 1996. "Out of the Closet and into Print: Sexual Identity in the Textual Field." In *Out in the Field: Reflections of Lesbian and Gay Anthropologists*, ed. Ellen Lewin and William L. Leap, 261–73. Urbana: University of Illinois Press.

Warren, Carol A. B. 1977. "Fieldwork in the Gay World: Issues in Phenomenological Research." *Journal of Social Issues* 33:93–107.

———. 1988. *Gender Issues in Field Research*. Newbury Park: Sage Publications.

Weeks, Jeffrey. 1986. *Sexuality*. New York: Tavistock and Ellis Horwood.

Weibust, Patricia Snyder. 1983. "Filipinos Were My Teachers." In *Fieldwork: The Human Experience*, ed. Robert Lawless, Vinson H. Sutlive, Jr., and Mario D. Zamora, 153–68. New York: Gordon and Breach.

Wengle, John. 1988. *Ethnographers in the Field: The Psychology of Research*. Tuscaloosa: University of Alabama Press.

Whitehead, Tony Larry. 1986. "Breakdown, Resolution, and Coherence: The Fieldwork Experiences of a Big, Brown, Pretty-Talking Man in a West Indian Community." In *Self, Sex, and Gender in Cross-Cultural Fieldwork*, ed. Tony Larry Whitehead and Mary Ellen Conaway, 213–39. Urbana: University of Illinois Press.

Whitehead, Tony Larry, and Judith Brown. 1986. "Gender-Related Issues in Carrying Out Rapid Team Fieldwork in the Cameroon." In *Self, Sex, and Gender in Cross-Cultural Fieldwork*, ed. Tony Larry Whitehead and Mary Ellen Conaway, 196–210. Urbana: University of Illinois Press.

Whitehead, Tony Larry, and Laurie Price. 1986. "Summary: Sex and the Fieldwork Experience." In *Self, Sex, and Gender in Cross-Cultural Fieldwork*, ed. Tony Larry Whitehead and Mary Ellen Conaway, 289–304. Urbana: University of Illinois Press.

Whitehead, Tony Larry, and Mary Ellen Conaway, eds. 1986. *Self, Sex, and Gender in Cross-Cultural Fieldwork*. Urbana: University of Illinois Press.

Wikan, Unni. 1982. *Behind the Veil in Arabia*. Baltimore: Johns Hopkins University Press.

Wilson, Peter. 1973. *Crab Antics: The Social Anthropology of English-Speaking Negro Societies in the Caribbean*. New Haven: Yale University Press.

Winkelman, Michael. 1982. "The Effects of Formal Education upon Extrasensory Abilities: The Ozolco Study." *Journal of Parapsychology* 45:321–36.

————. 1986. "Frequently Used Medicinal Plants in Baja California Norte." *Journal of Ethnopharmacology* 18:109–31.

————. 1989. "Ethnobotanical Treatments of Diabetes in Baja California Norte." *Medical Anthropology* 11:399–412.

————. 1993. *Ethnic Relations in the U.S.* St. Paul: West Educational Publishers.

————. 1994. "Cultural Shock and Adaptation." *Journal of Counseling and Development* 73:121–26.

Wolff, Kurt. 1976. *Surrender and Catch.* Boston: D. Reidel.

Yengoyan, Aram A. 1986. "Theory in Anthropology: On the Demise of the Concept of Culture." *Comparative Studies in Society and History* 28:368–74.

Zick, Jane, and Lydia Temoshok. 1986. "Applied Methodology: A Primer of Pitfalls and Opportunities in AIDS Research." In *The Social Dimensions of AIDS: Method and Theory,* ed. Douglas Feldman and Tom Johnson, 41–60. New York: Praeger.

CONTRIBUTORS

MICHAEL ASHKENAZI has conducted research in Japan, Korea, China, and Israel and has taught anthropology and East Asian studies in the United Kingdom, Israel, and Canada. His interests are in Japanese culture, particularly food, and in East Asian business cultures. He is a coeditor of *Ethiopian Immigrants and Israel* and the author of *Matsuri* (1993) and of articles on outer space, Ethiopian immigrants, Japanese religion, food, and business. He has also written a textbook (in Hebrew) on anthropological methodology.

Y. ANTONIA CHAO earned a Ph.D. in cultural anthropology from Cornell University in 1996. She is currently an assistant professor in the Department of Sociology at Tunghai University, Taiwan.

JACOB CLIMO is a professor of anthropology at Michigan State University. He has conducted field research and taught in Michigan, Mexico, Ethiopia, and Israel. His interests lie in local responses to national agrarian development projects, relationships and communications among generations, gerontology, and memory. His books include *Distant Parents* (1992) and (coedited with Marea Teski) *The Labyrinth of Memory* (1995).

THOMAS K. FITZGERALD, a professor of anthropology at the University of North Carolina at Greensboro, is a coauthor of *Culture, Society, and Guidance* and the author of *Education and Identity: Aspirations and Identity among Second-Generation Cook Islanders in New Zealand* and *Metaphors of Identity*. His interests lie in culture and communication.

ÉVA V. HUSEBY-DARVAS has a Ph.D. in cultural anthropology and since 1985 has been conducting research in Hungary and among American-Hungarians, along with teaching regularly at the University of Michigan's Dearborn Campus and periodically in Ann Arbor. She has published on the topics of gender relations, women's roles throughout the life-cycle, ethnicity, identity, nationalism, and the social and cultural trauma in socialist and postsocialist Hungary.

ROSE JONES is a medical anthropologist and the director of Culture Consulting and Training in Dallas. Her research interests include women's health, sex and power, cross-cultural medicine, and medical training. She is writing a book on cultural competency for health-care providers and conducting research on mammography and breast cancer.

WIM LUNSING, an associate research professor at the University of Copenhagen, earned a Ph.D. in 1995 from Oxford Brookes University in the United Kingdom. A former research fellow at the University of Tokyo, he has conducted fieldwork in Vienna, Amsterdam, and Japan.

FRAN MARKOWITZ teaches anthropology in the Department of Behavioral Sciences at Ben-Gurion Unversity of the Negev in Beersheva, Israel. She is the author of *A Community in Spite of Itself* (1993) and has published articles on identity, community, immigrants, adolescence, and the cultural construction of gender. Her current research includes a study of teenagers and culture change in Russia and of the African Hebrew Israelites in Dimona, Israel.

KARLA POEWE is a professor of anthropology at the University of Calgary and the author of several books dealing with religion, gender, economics, and fieldwork, including *Matrilineal Ideology, Reflections of a Woman Anthropologist, Religion, Kinship, and Economy in Luapala, Zambia, Understanding Cults and New Religions,* and *Charismatic Christianity as a Global Culture.*

ROBERT ROTENBERG is a professor of anthropology and director of international studies at DePaul University in Chicago. He is the author of *Time and Order in Metropolitan Vienna* and *Landscape and Power in Vienna* and the coeditor of *The Cultural Meaning of Urban Space.*

FRANK A. SALAMONE is a professor of anthropology at Iona College in New Rochelle, New York. His publications include *Bridges to Humanity: Anthropological Narratives on Friendship, The Fulbright Experience in Nigeria, The Bori and I: Reflections of a Mature Anthropologist,* and a chapter on Anne Rice as anthropologist in *The Gothic World of Anne Rice* (in press). He has published more than a hundred articles and conducted fieldwork in Nigeria, Ghana, Kenya, Venezuela, the United Kingdom, and the United States.

MICHAEL WINKELMAN is a senior lecturer in the Department of Anthropology at Arizona State University and director of the Ethnographic Field School in Ensenada, Baja California, Mexico. His interests are in ethnic relations, cross-cultural communication, and medical anthropology, especially shamanistic and herbal healing practices. He is the author of *Ethnic Relations in the U.S.: A Sociohistorical Cultural Systems Approach* and the coeditor of *Sacred Plants, Consciousness, and Healing.*